Dedicated to horror movie freaks and geeks everywhere
M000275306

 Published by IDW in association with Fantastic Press. IDW Publishing, a division of Idea and Design Works, LLC. Editorial Offices: 5080 Sante Fe Street, San Diego, CA 92109.

ISBN 978-1-60010-707-8 First printing, September 2010. Printed in Korea.

COVER COLLAGE: an original illustration by Steven Chorney celebrates the top six horror movies as ranked by this book. FIRST PAGE: Tod Browning's *Freaks* (MGM, 1932) in a endearing family portrait. ABOVE: Demon barber Johnny Depp wields a mighty razor in Tim Burton's *Sweeney Todd* (DreamWorks/Warner Bros., 2007).

FANTASTIC PRESS
presents

Written, Edited and Designed by
GARY GERANI
KEN RUBIN
Production Coordinator

POSTER/PHOTO CREDITS. Hammer Films (8, 14-15, 50-53, 108-109, 122-124, 164-165, 184-187, 189, 196), Warner Bros. (16-17, 24-25, 40-41, 45,50-53, 56, 69, 103-104,120-121, 182-183, 184-185), Paramount Pictures (62, 80-81, 133, 178-179, 180-181, 189), Universal Studios (5, 31-33, 71, 73-75, 78-79, 84, 94-95, 108-109, 118-119, 122-123,125-127, 130-131, 136-139, 146-147, 162-163, 164-165, 170, 176-179, 188, 189, 191), Lopert (128), Walter Reade Organization (74-75), RKO Pictures (46-47, 72, 100-101, 132, 151, 172-173), Teklu-Film Productions Ltd. (167), Film Arts Guild (166), Goldwyn Distributing Company (161), Buena Vista Pictures (1999), American International Pictures (7, 12, 70-71, 85-86, 142-143, 156-157, 158-159, 188, 189), F.P. Productions (18-19, 96-97, 152-153), Alfred Leone Trust (110-111, 140-141) Orion Pictures Corporation (12, 150), Ealing Studios (148-149), UFA (145), Toho Company Ltd. (144), Turner Entertainment Co. (1, 10-11, 28-30, 90-91, 92-93, 98, 114-115, 134-135, 188, 189), Hong Kong Legends (129), Columbia Pictures (4, 35), United Artists (9, 23, 83, 116-117), DreamWorks (112-113), 20th Century Fox (14-15, 63, 66-67, 105-107), Artisan Entertainment (102), General Foreign Sales Corp. (99), New Line Cinema (87-89), New World Pictures (58-59, 82), Compass International (76-77), Bryanston Distributing Company (68), Polygram Filmed Entertainment (64-65), Amicus Productions (20-21, 62), Empire Pictures (60-61), El Deseo S.A. (57), Herts-Lion Entertainment (54-55), International Classics (48), British Lion Films (45), Atlantic Releasing Corporation (44), Hallmark Releasing Corporation (43), Magnolia Pictures (42), Allied Artists (40-41), Avco Embassay Pictures (38-39), Dimension Films (27, 36-37), Fox Searchlight Pictures (34), Tigon British Lion Film Productions (12, 26), Cannon Releasing Corp. (26), Saw Productions/Lions Gate Entertainment (22), Box Office Spectaculars (13).

PHOTO SOURCES: The Gary Gerani Photo and Poster Collection, Photofest (special thanks to Buddy Weiss), Jerry Ohlinger's Movie Material Store, Hollywood Movie Posters (Ronald V. Borst), Hollywood Book and Poster (Eric Caidin), Porkepyn, Stephen Sally, other sources.

SPECIAL THANKS to a plethora of first-rate horror film historians who keep interest in the genre alive with their ongoing commentary and research: Ronald V. Borst, Bill Warren, Tom Weaver, David J. Schow, Tim Lucas, Lucy Chase Williams, David Skal, Steve Haberman, among others, with a special tip of the fedora to Mr. Carlos Clarens, who started it all. EXTRA SPECIAL THANKS to Greg Goldstein and Ted Adams of IDW, who supported and encouraged Fantastic Press, managing editor Justin Eisinger and graphic artist Robbie Robbins.

Table of Contents

LEFT: Teenage girlfriend-turned-voracious vampire, from *Fright Night* (Columbia Pictures, 1987). TOP: Three key characters from *Dracula* (Universal Studios, 1931) are colorfully presented in this rare promotional poster.

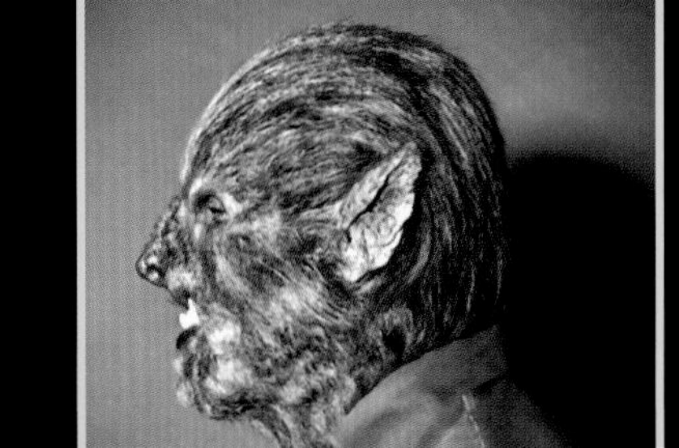

WHO'S THAT WEREWOLF?
...and what famous movie is he associated with?
For the startling answer, turn to page 191!

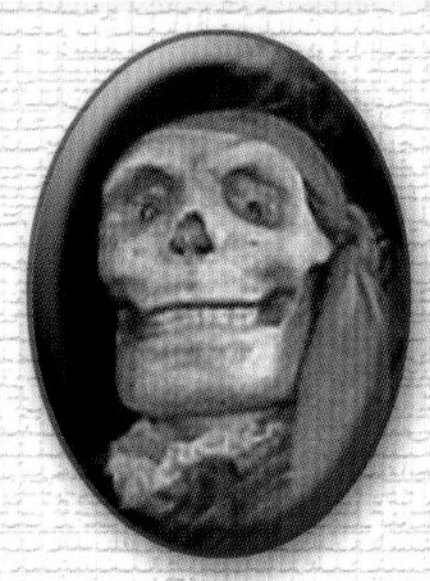

INTRODUCTION

ROGER CORMAN

Fear is an emotion everyone can relate to, from little children to the oldest among us.

Certainly Edgar Allan Poe understood its power in a way that few authors have. I tried to capture this with my various film adaptations of his work in the 1960s, combining Poe's unique artistic qualities with my own personal experience in psychoanalysis. A working knowledge of Sigmund Freud's theories also came in handy. Somehow, that combination seemed to hit a collective nerve: the Poe movies received great reviews in their day, made a great deal of money for American International Pictures, and are now considered classics. Of course, having a tremendous talent like Vincent Price as your star was nothing short of a blessing, and the same can be said for my wonderful screenwriters Richard Matheson and Chuck Beaumont, art director Daniel Haller, cinematographer Floyd Crosby, and music composer Les Baxter. Their combined efforts gave those films a special quality that I'll always be grateful for.

Of course, most artists are never content with their work, and as director of those movies I'm no different. When I watch them now, I'm always thinking about what could have been done more effectively if we had a little more time and money. That said, I've very proud of what we actually did accomplish under less-than-ideal circumstances, and it's gratifying to see new generations embracing these pictures in festivals and on DVDs.

As for today's horror offerings, I find them something of a mixed bag. They are certainly superior in terms of production value and special effects, but very often these technical gimmicks take precedence over the narrative. You don't need elaborate CGI to terrify an audience. As a matter of fact, less is generally more in this particular genre. It's your imagination that needs to do the heavy-lifting, so to speak, not some digital effects house in Hollywood.

Still, the future is bright for horror films, and young filmmakers in general. The new media, particularly the Internet, are revolutionizing this industry in ways we never dreamed possible. The competition's fiercer as a result, of course, and the creative bar's been raised significantly. My advice to young picture directors? Prepare! Don't get discouraged. And remember: The reward of seeing your vision on a movie screen is a visceral thrill like no other. You'll face the same challenges James Whale, Hitchcock and all the other legendary directors needed to confront when conveying scenes of exquisite terror and suspense. So let yourself go, embrace your darkest, most elemental fears...and get it all out of your system by scaring the rest of us silly!

--and the deep and dank tarn
closed silently over the
fragments of the House of Usher.
--POE
" . . . the agony of my soul
found vent in one loud, long,
and final scream of despair."
-- POE
"and darkness and decay and
the red death held illimitable
dominion over all."
edgar allan poe

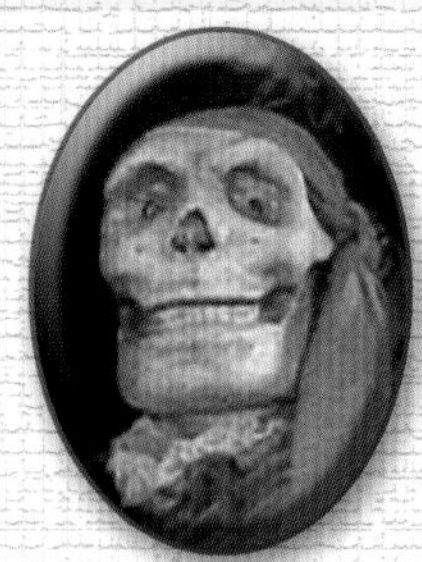

OVERVIEW

GARY GERANI

What makes a good horror movie so special, and why are we forever drawn to them? As a lifelong fan, screenwriter and professional film historian, it's a question I've asked myself many times over the years.

To begin with, let's look at the genre itself, and how our most imaginative filmmakers have approached and defined it. Whether an artist is working in color or black and white, silent or sound, widescreen or the latest version of 3D, he faces an infinite number of creative ways to involve and ultimately terrify a movie audience. Sometimes viewers are rudely jolted by visceral shocks, as with Terence Fisher or William Friedkin thrillers, other times they are gently escorted into darkly unsettling, dream-like environs that confound, intrigue and captivate (think Roman Polanski or Val Lewton). What all of these approaches have in common is that they somehow manage to replicate the fragile, visceral quality of nightmares, transcending reality and touching us intimately in a way that no other genre can.

All things considered, it's a surprisingly healthy indulgence. Like rollercoaster rides, horror movies are often defended as therapeutic releases of our pent-up tensions and frustrations. These fanciful journeys bring us to the very point of abstract, thrilling death and surreal carnage, but the awareness that we're safe enables us to sit back and relish every outrageous twist and turn. It's been proven that without this kind of emotional uncorking on a regular basis, a person will inevitably go mad. Put another way, a steady diet of horror movies is like being inoculated against the legitimate horrors (or pressures) of real life. No wonder we have such an instinctive fondness for the genre!

In revisiting all 100 films and their directors for this book, I was reminded and delighted at how each and every one of these gifted storytellers found his own unique way into the nightmare zone. It occurs to me that we often laugh at extreme moments in horror pictures not because we're incredulous or feel superior, but because something deep inside of us is actually grateful for the weird catharsis they provide. The louder we laugh, it seems, the more we know the movie's doing us some good.

Much-needed medicine for the soul, fellow freaks and geeks…

TOP: Max Schreck as ratlike, blood-lusting vampire *Nosferatu* from the 1922 German classic. RIGHT: Our elemental fear of spiders heightens this high-tension "conjuring" moment from *The Devil Rides Out/The Devil's Bride* (Hammer/ 20th Century-Fox, 1968).

ABOUT THE BOOK

Ranking the Royal 100

Why another book about the world's greatest horror movies? I suppose for the same reason we check out those "Top Ten" lists at the end of every film year. Although these groupings are bound to contain many of the same celebrated titles, it's the reviewer's unique perspective and creative priorities that generally catch our interest, often shedding light on some artistic or thematic qualities the rest of us may have missed.

Of course, there are more than just a hundred great horror movies...way more. It so happens that cinema is ideally suited to realizing imaginative, spooky scenarios, all the more effective in a darkened theater with an audience full of receptive nail-biters.

As a result, my woefully under-numbered Top 100 list kept changing even while I was preparing it. Terrific titles by brilliant filmmakers came and went, making way for arguably worthier selections. Then there's those revered science fiction movies with a high horror quotient: *Invasion of the Body Snatchers*, *The Thing*, *The Fly*, *Creature from the Black Lagoon*, et al. Simply put, if science plays an inordinate role in a "monster movie" that doesn't have gothic overtones (like *Frankenstein* or mad scientist melodramas), then it belongs in my next Fantastic Press compilation, *Top 100 Sci-Fi Movies*. And while I may be a tad partial to the groundbreakers of my Baby Boomer youth, no worthy horror offering, past or present, is being intentionally ignored. Except, perhaps, for IDW's *30 Days of Night* and my very own *Pumpkinhead*, directed by the late, great Stan Winston; both were ineligible for *Top 100* because of obvious conflict-of-interest realities.

But rules and subjective rankings aside, all of the films presented here are exceptional in their own peculiar way and should be eagerly applauded by fans of the genre. So revel now in the lasting brilliance of cinema's most accomplished scarefests...and, for the sake of both your fingernails and your eyesight, keeps the lights on while you're reading!

Gary Gerani, 2010

KEY TO UNDERSTANDING

97 | 1.85

Clock: Running time
Monitor: Aspect Ratio
Full headphone: Stereo soundtrack
Half headphone: Mono soundtrack

ABOVE: Preliminary Cover Art by Steve Chorney

ABOUT THE AUTHOR

First professional writing assignment: impersonating the *Creature from the Black Lagoon* for *The Monster Times* (1972), a monthly tabloid devoted to scary movies. Book #1: 1977's *Fantastic Television* is the very first to explore sf/horror/fantasy on the small screen. A lifelong creative relationship with the Topps Company yields books, magazines, sticker albums, and hundreds of trading card sets for over four decades, including cult fave *Dinosaurs Attack!* Finally, co-writing the screenplay for Stan Winston's *Pumpkinhead* results in a brand-new, snaggle-fanged, rubber-suited Famous Monster of Filmland...sadly ineligible for this marathon match-up. Sorry about that, Pumps!

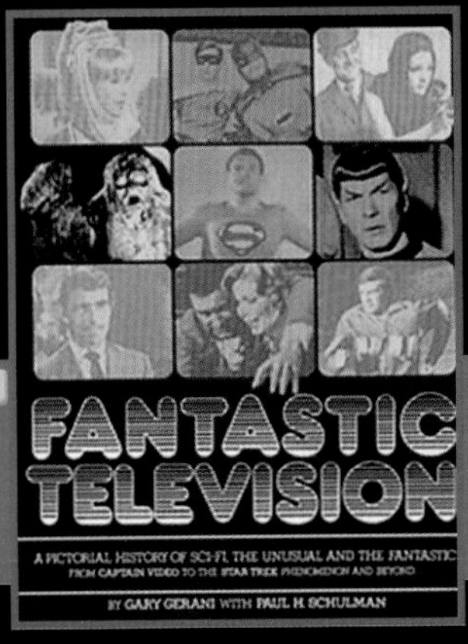

The screen's first Byronic vampire in a stylish, action-filled gorefest...

100 HOUSE OF DARK SHADOWS 1970

 97 1.85

WHO MADE IT:

MGM/Dan Curtis Productions (U.S.). Director: Dan Curtis. Producer: Dan Curtis. Writers: Sam Hall and Gordon Russell, based on episodes of the *Dark Shadows* ABC-TV series. Cinematography (Metrocolor): Arthur Ornitz. Music: Bob Cobert. Starring Jonathan Frid (Barnabas Collins), Grayson Hall (Dr. Julia Hoffman), Kathryn Lee Scott (Maggie Evans), Roger Davis (Jeff Clark), Thayer David (Prof. Stokes), Joan Bennett (Elizabeth Collins Stoddard), Nancy Barrett (Carolyn Stoddard), John Karlen (Willie Loomis), Louis Edmonds (Roger Collins).

WHAT IT'S ABOUT:

Vampire Barnabas Collins, accidentally freed from a chained coffin, returns to his ancestral home of Collinwood and falls in love with family governess Maggie Evans, the reincarnation of his beloved Josette. Efforts to cure Barnabas of vampirism are attempted by Dr. Julia Hoffman, and for a while it seems as if he and Maggie might consummate their romantic relationship. But jealous Julia sabotages their happiness, transforming Collins into his true, 175-year-old self. He's eventually restored to youthful form by drinking Maggie's blood and is relentlessly hunted by the single-minded Professor Stokes, working with a stunned New England police team. But Barnabas succeeds in killing many members of the Collins family by transforming them into vampires, ripe for the staking. He ultimately kidnaps Maggie for a mist-shrouded wedding ceremony, but is foiled by Evans' boyfriend Jeff and the Renfield-like Willie Loomis, who, tormented by a guilty conscience, turns against his vampire master at the moment of truth.

WHY IT'S IMPORTANT:

House of Dark Shadows is a surprisingly impressive and innovative film adaptation of the long-running ABC soap opera from the mid-'60s. The TV version was itself groundbreaking in that it introduced pop culture's first "romantic vampire" in the Byronic mold...a crowd-pleasing archetype that continues to this day (*Bram Stoker's Dracula, Angel, Twilight*).

But apart from this pedigree, *House of Dark Shadows* benefits from director Dan Curtis' hyper-stylish, Peckinpah/Hill-influenced gore sequences (blood kills in slow motion) and flamboyant cinematic choices. After more than a decade of Hammer's relatively stately approach to the vampire thriller, Curtis' loose, hand-hand action photography and refreshingly different New England settings added some much-needed new blood to the (at the time) tired genre. Real locations -- you can practically smell the lakeside mist -- blend with over-the-top art direction and some notably peculiar performances to create a thoroughly satisfying, if slightly loopy, fantasy landscape. Star Jonathan Frid may not have the stature of Christopher Lee's aristocratic Dracula, but he's unique and irreplaceable as the tortured vampire lover Barnabas. Thayer David is equally formidable as the Van Helsing-like Professor Stokes, especially after he "switches sides" during the suspenseful third act.

Best scenes: Caroline's capture and staking (cops with crucifixes!), ancient Barnabas restored to youthful form; Stokes' surprise attack on Jeff by the lake; the extended, oh-so-bloody slow-motion climax.

A hit at the box office, *House of Dark Shadows* spawned an equally stylish but unbearably dull sequel, *Night of Dark Shadows* (1971). It unwisely dumped the Barnabas/vampire storyline in favor of sexy witch Angelique's ghostly doings. The severely-edited possession drama, also directed by Dan Curtis, failed with critics, fans and just about everyone else.

Volatile Barnabas Collins (Jonathan Frid) will let nothing stand in the way of his wedding to Maggie Evans, the reincarnation of a former flame. *House*'s memorably spooky music score, composed by Bob Cobert, was lifted almost entirely from the TV series.

To restore his youth, decaying vampire Barnabas must drink from the we
of Maggie's pure blood. She is too weak to resist and welcomes his bite

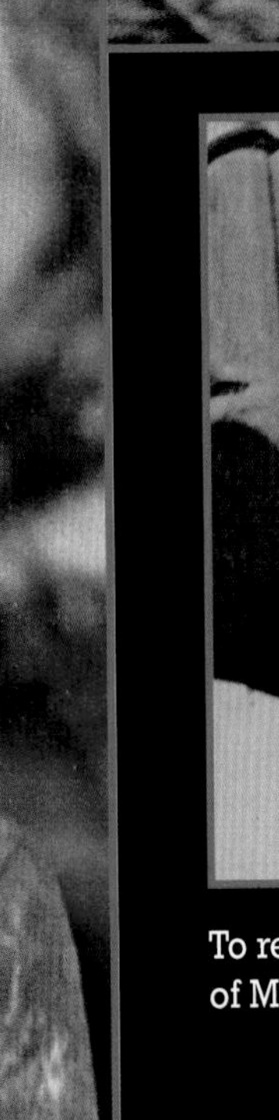

Held fast by cross-wielding cops, bitten Carolyn finds her new life as a vampire dramatically cut short by Professor Stokes' ready stake. In recent times, Johnny Depp has expressed interest in playing Barnabas Collins in what would amount to a rebooted version of the franchise.

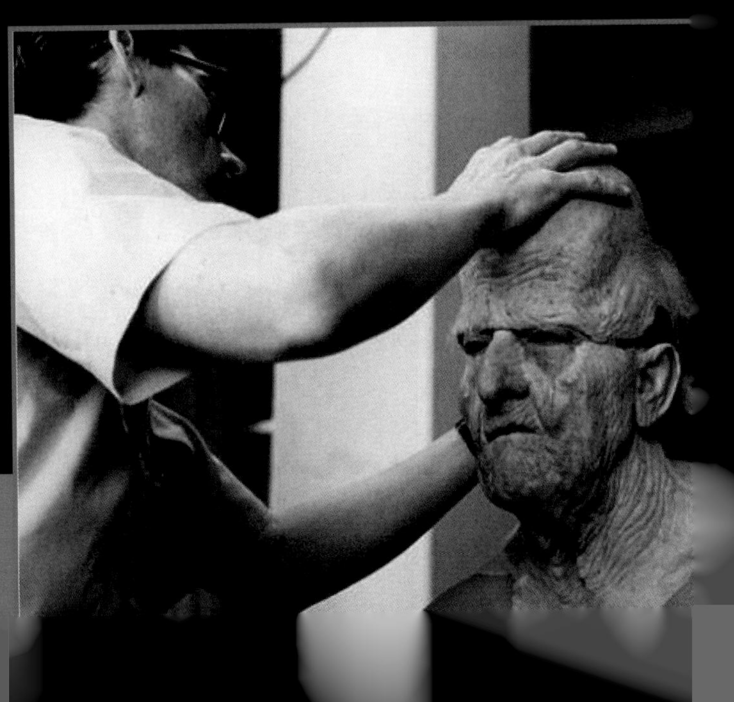

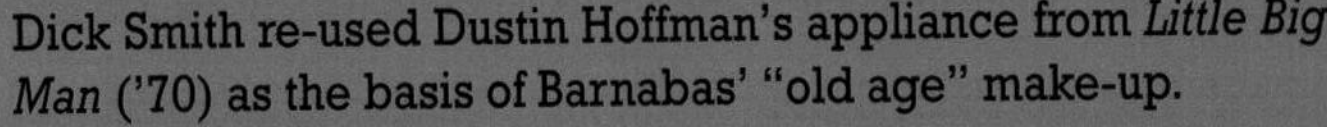

Dick Smith re-used Dustin Hoffman's appliance from *Little Big Man* ('70) as the basis of Barnabas' "old age" make-up.

Aggressively brutal, disturbingly realistic portrait of corrupt moral authority...

99 WITCHFINDER GENERAL 1968

87 1.85 

aka: The Conqueror Worm

LEAVE THE CHILDREN HOME!
...and if YOU are SQUEAMISH
STAY HOME WITH THEM!!!!!!!

A crawling shape intrude!
A blood-red thing that writhes
from out The scenic solitude!
It writhes!–it writhes!–
with mortal pangs
The mimes become its food,
And seraphs sob at vermin fangs
In human gore imbued.
EDGAR ALLAN POE

EDGAR ALLAN POE'S
THE CONQUEROR WORM
IN COLOR by PERFECT
FROM AMERICAN INTERNATIONAL

STARRING VINCENT PRICE · IAN OGILVY · RUPERT DAVIES · AND INTRODUCING HILARY DWYER
EXECUTIVE PRODUCER TONY TENSER · PRODUCED BY LOUIS M. HEYWARD · DIRECTED BY MICHAEL REEVES · SCREENPLAY BY MICHAEL REEVES & TOM BAKER

WHO MADE IT:

Tigon British Film Productions (U.K.)/American International Pictures (U.S.). Director: Michael Reeves. Producers: Arnold L. Miller, Louis M. Heyward. Writers: Michael Reeves, Tom Baker; based on the novel by Ronald Bassett and (loosely) a poem by Edgar Allan Poe. Cinematography (color): John Coquillon. Music: Paul Ferris. Starring Vincent Price (Matthew Hopkins), Ian Ogilvy (Richard Marshall), Hilary Dwyer (Sara), Rupert Davies (John Lowes), Robert Russell (John Stearne), Patrick Wymark (Oliver Cromwell).

WHAT IT'S ABOUT:

In 1645, during the English Civil War, an opportunistic witchfinder named Matthew Hopkins and his equally vile assistant John Stearne travel from one demoralized village after another, imposing their own brand of sadistic "justice" for a handsome price. After accusing local priest John Lowes of witchcraft and torturing him to death, along with other victims, Hopkins is pursued by Roundhead soldier Richard Marshall, a heroic young man who loves Lowes' daughter Sara and has now pledged himself to revenge. Anticipating his actions, Hopkins and Stearne manage to capture both the soldier and his beloved Sara long enough to accuse them of witchcraft and initiate torturer proceedings. Marshall, however, soon gains the upper hand in a final, hate-maddened confrontation that results in the sadistic witchfinder's bloody demise.

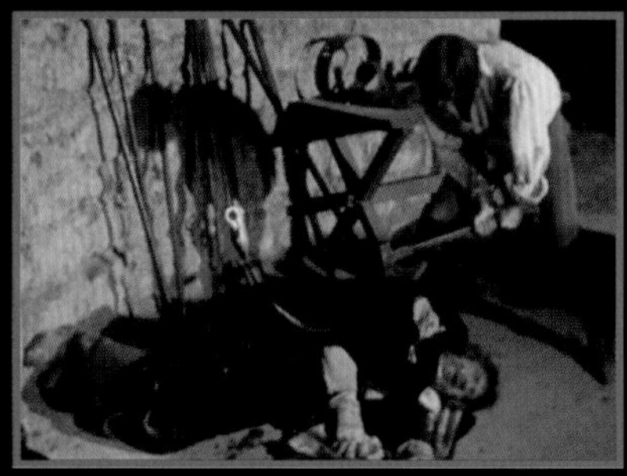

WHY IT'S IMPORTANT:

A success with both critics and audiences despite some minor controversy, Michael Reeves' *Witchfinder General* (sold to U.S. audiences as AIP's newest Poe film) rightfully belongs to a specific, difficult-to-stomach horror sub-genre from the late '60s/early '70s, perhaps best exemplified by Ken Russell's *The Devils* and *Mark of the Devil*. There is no fantasy element at all; only the preternatural sadism of seemingly soulless human beings on a rampage of county-to-county murder sanctioned by church (sort of) and state (possibly). A solid director, Reeves keeps his colorful suspense/action storyline moving, but never loses sight of the scathing moral irony that hovers over all. Strangely, the witch-dunkings are somehow more disturbing and memorable than the burnings, perhaps because they rob their victims of final dignity, and because torture/"purification" by water is less common in horror films. Pushing audience tolerance right to the edge, *Witchfinder*'s captured heroine is punctured in close-up during the bloody climax, and the General's nonstop hacking at the hands of the now-obsessed, nearly deranged hero is almost a necessary release for viewers.

Just as harrowing were events behind the screen, apparently. Price at this point considered stylish camp a necessary part of his screen persona; Reeves disagreed, demanding a dead-on straight characterization. So they continually sparred. In the end, Reeves was right. Realizing Mr. R had cajoled the legendary Vincent into delivering one of his best later-era performances, Price himself wrote a letter of apology, praising the filmmaker's artistic skills and regretting their differences. Reeves' response: "I knew you'd eventually see it my way." Cool director, creepy person. Maybe a little dunking would help...

Two Thousand Maniacs 1964

87 1.85

WHO MADE IT:

Box Office Spectaculars (U.S.) Director/Writer: Herschell Gordon Lewis. Producer: David F. Friedman, Cinematography (Eastmancolor): Herschell Gordon Lewis. Music: Larry Wellington. Starring Connie Mason (Terry Adams), William Kerwin (Tom White/Thomas Wood), Jeffrey Allen (Mayor Buckman), Shelby Livingston (Bea Miller), Ben Moore (Lester MacDonald).

WHAT IT'S ABOUT:

Six unsuspecting tourists are held captive in a literal ghost town made up of two thousand redneck citizens, all of them out for Yankee blood. It happens during the centennial celebration of the day union troops destroyed the small southern town of Pleasant Valley. Condemned as natural enemies, the tourists are tormented and forced to participate in various sadistic "death" games. Somehow, two of them manage to escape. But when they return with a local sheriff, the town itself has disappeared. It won't be seen again until the next centennial in 2065, when ghostly Pleasant Valley will once again rise to renew its vendetta against the Yankees.

WHY IT'S IMPORTANT:

It's not possible to defend director Herschell Gordon Lewis, but he can be explained. At a time when the polished pleasures of Hammer's period horror films and the Corman Poe adaptations were losing their edge, along came rural producer David F. Friedman's raw, home movie-style confections, ultra-cheapos that revel in sadism and freewheeling gore. Independent pictures of this kind rarely make an impression beyond their local venues. But *Two Thousand Maniacs*, like its companion efforts *Blood Feast* and *Color Me Blood Red*, actually broke new genre ground. Although shoddily made, Lewis' flicks are a solid ten years ahead of their time, clearly anticipating the bare-bones fright masterpieces of George Romero (*Night of the Living Dead*) and Wes Craven (*Last House on the Left*).

At least *Maniacs* has the *Brigadoon*-inspired ghost village idea working for it, a legitimate high concept before the term was even invented. Filmmaker Lewis is truly an auteur, whatever one thinks of him, directing and photographing his audacious creations. Often this results in out-of-frame actors delivering dialogue, or nervous camera set-ups that begin to tilt up or sideways, then chicken out. Is there more on Lewis' mind than gleeful, over-the-top sadism? One intriguing shot begins with victims fleeing pinpoints of light that soon reveal themselves to be flashlight-brandishing locals; but this was probably a lucky accident. As for the cast, some of the good ole boys are reasonably entertaining, with the peeved, candy-craving youngster Billy (Vincent Wood), who inadvertently rescues two of the targeted strangers, actually demonstrating some legitimate comedy timing. Also worth a few seconds of praise is the jaunty bluegrass music provided throughout, credited rather ambiguously to "The Pleasant Valley Boys."

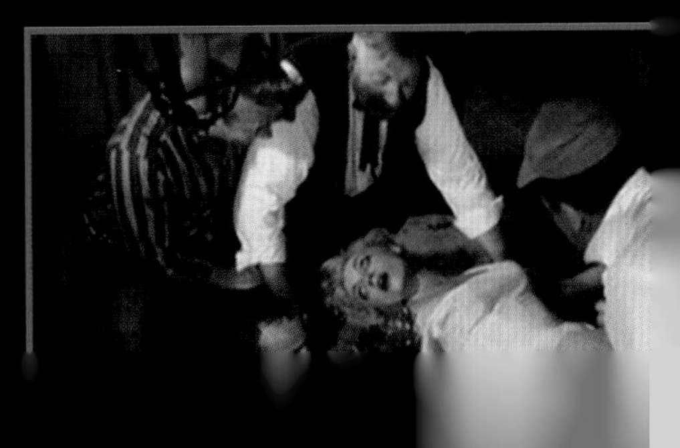

Best scene (and there really is one): the amusing epilog. After a poorly-paced resolution, we return to the vanishing ghost town long enough to witness one of its residents, who had been swallowed up by quicksand during an earlier chase, dramatically emerge from the muck and nonchalantly join his crap-kicking neighbors as they prepare for another 100-year slumber. It's an effective finale to a crudely-filmed, but nevertheless significant and

Stately duel between good and evil, with Lee as a commanding, darkly-seasoned hero...

97 THE DEVIL'S BRIDE 1968

 1.66

aka: The Devil Rides Out

Poster/photos: © 1968 Hammer Films. Released by 20th Century-Fox.

The beauty of woman– the demon of darkness– the unholy union of "The Devil's Bride"!

20th Century-Fox presents THE DEVIL'S BRIDE

COLOR by DeLUXE

starring CHRISTOPHER LEE
CHARLES GRAY
NIKE ARRIGHI · LEON GREENE
also starring PATRICK MOWER · GWEN FFRANGCON-DAVIES
SARAH LAWSON · PAUL EDDINGTON
Screenplay by RICHARD MATHESON · From the Novel "The Devil Rides Out" by DENNIS WHEATLEY
Produced by ANTHONY NELSON KEYS · Directed by TERENCE FISHER · A Seven Arts-Hammer Film Production

WHO MADE IT:

Hammer Films amd EMI (U.K.)/20th Century Fox (U.S.). Director: Terence Fisher. Producer: Anthony Nelson Keys. Writer: Richard Matheson, based on the novel by Dennis Wheatley. Cinematography (Technicolor {U.K.}/Deluxe {U.S.}): Arthur Grant. Music: James Bernard. Starring Christopher Lee (Duc de Richleau), Charles Gray (Mocata), Nike Arrighi (Tanith Carlisle), Leon Greene (Rex Van Ryn), Patrick Mower (Simon Aron), Gwen Ffrangcon Davies (Countess), Sarah Lawson (Marie Eaton), Paul Eddington (Richard Eaton), Russell Waters (Malin), Yemi Ajibade (African), Ahmed Khalil (Indian).

WHAT IT'S ABOUT:

Concerned that a young friend, Simon Aaron, is absent from their annual reunion, the Duc de Richleau and Rex Van Ryn find their worst suspicions confirmed when they visit him unexpectedly. Aaron has thrown in with a mysterious "astrological society" headed by the sinister-looking Mocata. It isn't long before Richleau realizes that Mocata's group is actually a devil cult that takes control of innocent people through demonic spells and bloody ceremonies. Through the use of the group's mentalist, Tanith Carlisle, Aaron's friends manage to challenge Mocata and disrupt his unspeakable activities, even thwarting the diabolical, supernaturally-conjured Goat of Mendes in a foul outdoor ritual. Upping the ante, Richleau's innocent relatives are drawn into this spiritual battle. Together, they take part in an elaborate ceremonial process that places them within a magic circle drawn on the floor, even as a succession of evil entities surround and threaten them. Ultimately, an innocent child is kidnapped to replace the now-dead Tanith, but Richleau and his friends arrive in time to disrupt the young girl's heinous sacrifice. With the help of a friend beyond the grave, Mocata is foiled and his evil devil-worshipping group is destroyed by fire. Time itself is reversed, Tanith returns to life, and Richleau thanks God for their victory over dark forces.

WHY IT'S IMPORTANT:

The missing link between classic-era Hammer horror and the ultra-chic satanic thrillers of the late '60s/early '70s, *The Devil's Bride* (aka *The Devil Rides Out*) is a more than respectable film adaptation of Dennis Wheatley's pulp-inspired novel. Playing a legitimate hero for a change, Christopher Lee excels as the Duc de Richleau, a kind of occult-minded Sherlock Holmes, providing his own semi-snobby spin on colleague Peter Cushing's Van Helsing characterization from Hammer's *Dracula* series. Charles Gray is equally effective as the villainous Mocata, a one-dimensional practitioner of evil who views magic as a form of science to be mastered...and exploited.

A full ten years after inaugurating Hammer horror and establishing a new direction for the genre, Terence Fisher embraces the fashionable occultism of this era with some agreeably fresh, energetic cinematic choices. A shaky camera catches everything from a roundhouse right to Aaron's supernatural seizure, and there are far more special effects on display than is usual for a Hammer scarefest. Best scenes: the initial encounter with a conjured African spirit, thwarting the Goat of Mendes, the giant spider attack on Eaton's child.

While not in the same relatable, culture-impacting league of mainstream hits like *Rosemary's Baby* or *The Exorcist*, *The Devil's Bride* stands as an important entry in the occult movie pantheon, true to its literary inspiration and stylish in all departments. It is also the best demonology-themed thriller ever produced by Hammer.

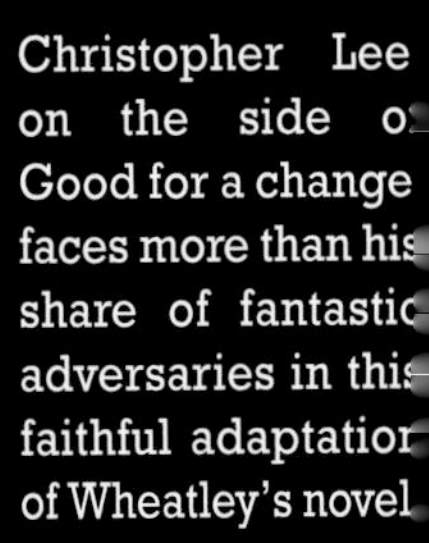

Christopher Lee on the side of Good for a change faces more than his share of fantastic adversaries in this faithful adaptation of Wheatley's novel.

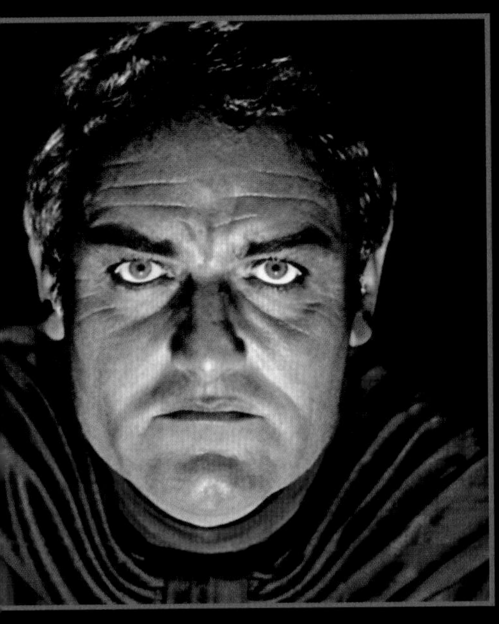

ABOVE: Various supernatural entities were designed by Eddie Knight and Roy Ashton, including the bestial Goat of Mendes (in reality, a latex mask).

RIGHT: Devil-worshipping Macata (Charles Gray) proves a formidable opposite number for Lee's self-righteous Duc de Richleau.

ABOVE: A distraught Tanith proves the enigmatic key to undoing Macata's evil. BELOW: A monster spider threatens Richleau and his allies as they try to maintain their position within the magic circle.

Macata's final act of dark vengeance is the attempted sacrifice of an innocent little girl, daughter of Richleau's niece.

Another Dennis Wheatley novel, *Uncharted Seas*, was filmed a year later by Hammer/20th Century-Fox as *The Lost Continent*.

96 IT'S ALIVE 1974

91 1.85 

THERE'S ONLY ONE THING WRONG WITH THE DAVIS BABY...
IT'S ALIVE
THE ONE FILM YOU SHOULD NOT SEE ALONE
A LARRY COHEN FILM · "IT'S ALIVE" · A LARCO PRODUCTION
starring JOHN RYAN · SHARON FARRELL · ANDREW DUGGAN · GUY STOCKWELL
JAMES DIXON · MICHAEL ANSARA · music by BERNARD HERRMANN
TECHNICOLOR® · written, produced and directed by LARRY COHEN
from Warner Bros. A Warner Communications Company.

WHO MADE IT:

Warner Bros./Larco Productions (U.S.). Director, Producer, Writer: Larry Cohen. Cinematography (Technicolor): Fenton Hamilton. Music: Bernard Herrmann. Special monster make-up effects: Rick Baker. Starring John Ryan (Frank Davis), Sharon Farrell (Lenore Davis), James Dixon (Lieutenant Perkins), William Wellman Jr. (Charley), Shamus Locke (The Doctor), Andrew Duggan (The Professor), Guy Stockwell (Bob Clayton), Daniel Holzman (Chris Davis), Michael Ansara (The Captain), Robert Emhardt (The Executive), Nancy Burnett (Nurse).

WHAT IT'S ABOUT:

Middle-class family man Frank Davis suffers the tortures of the damned when his wife gives birth to a monstrous mutant, a killing creature that tears everyone in the maternity operating theater to shreds. The infant beast remains at large, attacking unsuspecting victims for sustenance, even as Frank becomes a social pariah. Obsessed with destroying this monstrosity he somehow fathered, Frank nearly succeeds when the infant finds its way into the Davis home. With his wife and young son feeling sympathy for the creature, Frank begins to confront his elemental responsibilities as a parent, even under the bizarre circumstances. He rescues his infant "son" from a police hunt in the city sewers before federal authorities close in.

WHY IT'S IMPORTANT:

Is nothing sacred? Not in the perverse, darkly satiric universe of filmmaker Larry Cohen. The more hallowed the societal institution, the juicier the target. Much of horror cinema's appeal to begin with is the "naughty wink" factor: we're allowed to indulge in the wildest and bloodiest nightmare fantasies because everything depicted is so over-the-top and audacious. *Rosemary's Baby* and *The Exorcist* took the notion of demonic children to new unsavory heights; *It's Alive* pushes this premise even further, turning the twin fears of pregnancy and parenthood into potent horror movie fodder. Along the way, the dehumanization of institutionalized civilization is laid bare, with the unconscious need to conform to a generally accepted view of normalcy compelling tortured protagonist Frank Davis (John Ryan) to reject his own flesh-and-blood. And while Davis' child is unquestionably a monster, it is also a primal innocent without sin...unlike the corporate geniuses who callously polluted our environment and caused this life-threatening mutation to begin with. Self-pitying Frank is part of this denial process for most of the story, comparing himself to Dr. Frankenstein (hence the film's title, based on the most famous line of dialogue in horror pictures) and obsessed with destroying the marauding "thing" he somehow fathered. Only when his rattled but ultimately protective wife (Sharon Farrell) and sympathetic son (Daniel Holzman) open his eyes to a higher priority, the profound biological/moral obligation that automatically accompanies parenthood, does Davis see the light. This is an average, relatable man finding his inherent humanity in the most grotesque of situations.

Cohen effectively depicts his murdering mini-monster through quick cuts, fish-eye lenses and gross ultra-close-ups of its befanged, munching mouth. Also notable is Bernard Herrmann's often sad, sometimes enraged musical score, perfectly reflecting *Alive*'s emotional sensibilities. Best scenes: the birthing bloodbath, death in a milk truck (white liquid spilling against the red vehicle provides an almost poetic reversal of expectations), Frank's Frankenstein observation, the surreal sewer hunt, Davis' final confrontation with authorities.

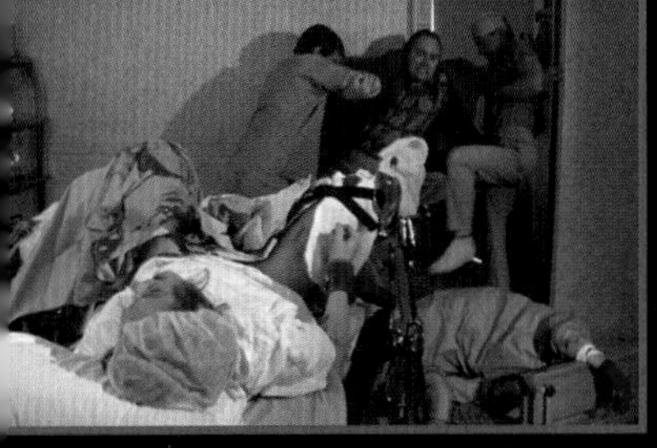

Birthing a beast child: New father Frank Davis (John Ryan) is dragged away from sudden carnage in the operating room.

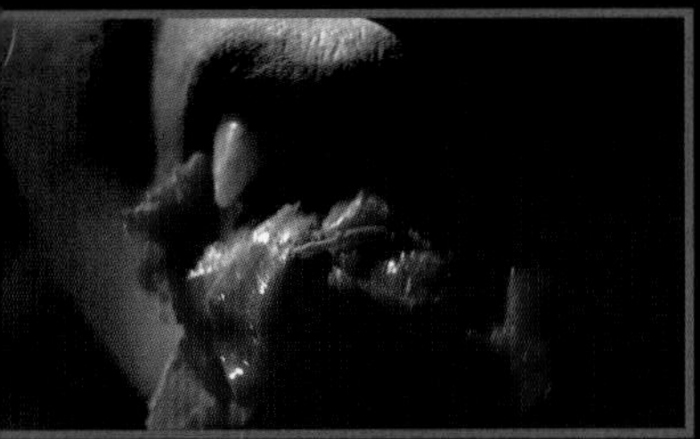

Alive's infant monster is depicted in brief glimpses and extreme close-ups. BELOW: Davis takes a shot at his marauding infant.

Director Larry Cohen is careful to keep his horrible little mutation well-hidden throughout the film. Re-released wide in 1977, *It's Alive* performed well enough at the box office to spawn two reasonably effective sequels, *It Lives Again* and *Island of the Alive*, both helmed by Cohen. He also directed the equally off-beat flying monster melodrama, *Q – the Winged Serpent.*

Surrounded by police, Frank Davis finds his humanity in the compelling final scenes.

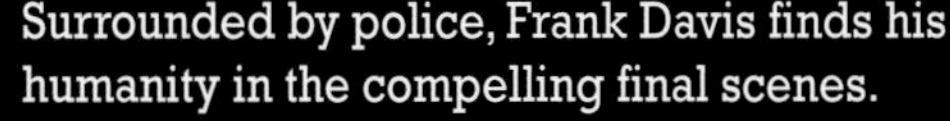

Oscar-winning make-up artist Rick Baker shows off the full-size *It's Alive* prop, built to move, change expression…and chew.

Cheeky horror romp juiced by exotic, gleefully sadistic revenge gags...

95 The Abominable Dr. Phibes 1971

95 | 1.85

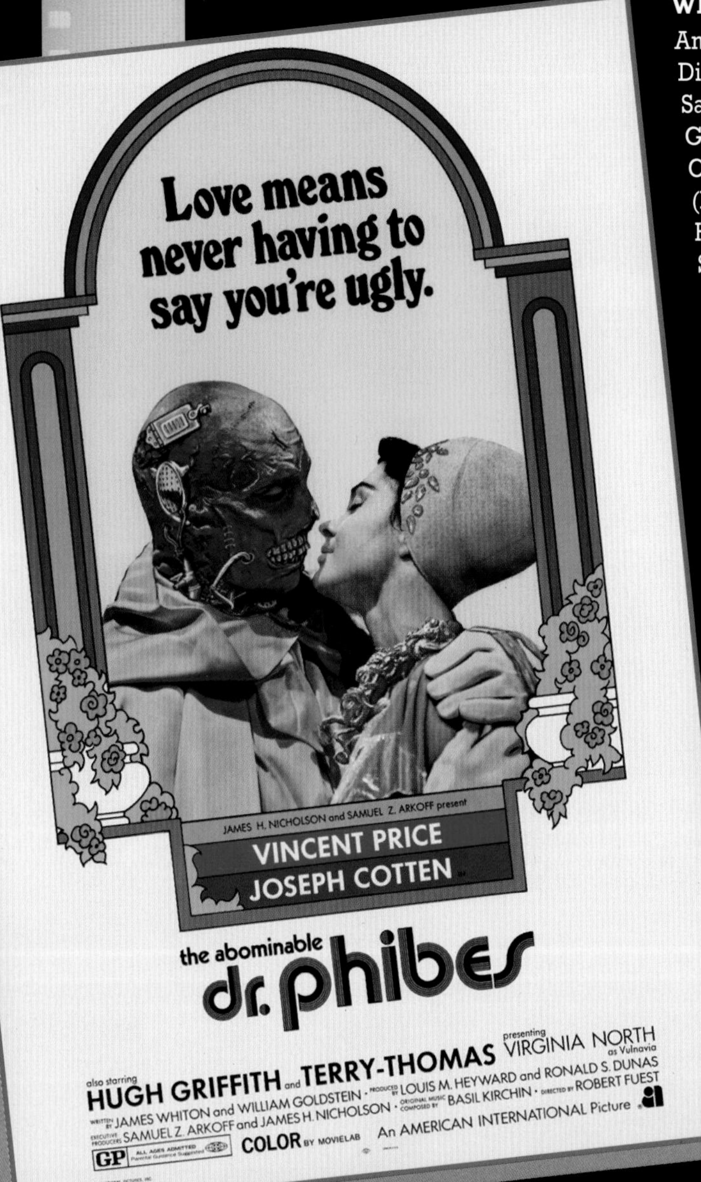

Love means never having to say you're ugly.
JAMES H. NICHOLSON and SAMUEL Z. ARKOFF present
VINCENT PRICE
JOSEPH COTTEN
the abominable dr. phibes
also starring HUGH GRIFFITH and TERRY-THOMAS presenting VIRGINIA NORTH as Vulnavia
written by JAMES WHITON and WILLIAM GOLDSTEIN · produced by LOUIS M. HEYWARD and RONALD S. DUNAS
executive producers SAMUEL Z. ARKOFF and JAMES H. NICHOLSON · original music composed by BASIL KIRCHIN · directed by ROBERT FUEST
An AMERICAN INTERNATIONAL Picture
GP ALL AGES ADMITTED Parental Guidance Suggested
COLOR BY MOVIELAB
71/172

WHO MADE IT:

Anglo-EMI/MGM-EMI (U.K.)/American International Pictures (U.S.). Director: Robert Fuest. Producers: Ronald S. Dunas, Louis M. Heyward, Samuel Z. Arkoff, James H. Nicholson. Writers: James Whiton and William Goldstein; Robert Fuest (uncredited). Cinematography (Movielab Color): Norman Warwick. Music: Basil Kirchin. Starring Vincent Price (Dr. Anton Phibes), Joseph Cotton (Dr. Vesalius), Peter Jeffrey (Inspector Harry Trout), Virginia North (Vulnavia), Terry-Thomas (Dr. Longstreet), Sean Bury (Lem Vesalius), Susan Travers (Nurse Allen).

WHAT IT'S ABOUT:

Thought to have been killed in a car crash, horribly disfigured organist Anton Phibes resurrects himself for a dark and sinister purpose: to exact revenge on the doctors and nurses who failed to save his beloved wife on the operating table. Flesh-masked and thoroughly mad, Phibes uses the Biblical Ten Plagues of Egypt as inspiration for his various audacious, extremely offbeat killings, confounding the authorities. Phibes saves the best for last: first born to Dr. Vesalius, head of the original team, is set to die from released acid unless his father can operate and retrieve a key embedded within the unconscious boy in time. Although the final phase of his plan is thwarted, Phibes manages to "escape" his captors via a stone sarcophagus and some handy embalming fluid.

WHY IT'S IMPORTANT:

Vincent Price's 100th movie slyly ushers in a new decade, and with it, a somewhat different sensibility for mainstream chillers. While independent filmmakers were just beginning to register on the pop cultural landscape, mainstream distributors like American International were still calling the shots in 1970, now seeking newer, slicker ways to make their fright product relevant. By turning former Poe superstar Price into a wickedly foxy self-parody, but within the context of a stylish and aggressively gross revenge melodrama, AIP threw the creative dice and scored with one of their most self-assured and best-received releases.

Director Robert Fuest (a veteran of TV's equally arch *The Avengers*) helms this offbeat tale of a zombified band leader who re-creates Bibical plagues to punish the surgical team that failed to save his beloved wife. It's an ingenious idea for a tongue-in-cheek chiller, with one murderous set-piece after another eliciting both gasps and laughs from viewers. Fuest earns our respect instantly by using real bats in the first killing – horror movie fans are so used to enduring obvious models on all-too-visible wires. The bizarre, self-contracting Frog headpiece provides another sadistically original method of murder. But by far the most outlandish and memorable of Phibes' various revenges is the grisly dispatching of a dozing nurse who had assisted in the original operation; carefully deposited locusts eagerly feast on her unprotected face, leaving a ravaged skull behind.

Price himself has never been better, trading on his famous screen persona but in a perversely different, completely satisfying way. Unable to use his flamboyant facial expressions (living-dead Phibes is grim-faced throughout), the actor conveys his character's elemental pain with intense, agonized looks, and ultimately a halting synthesized voice that mixes despair with mad purpose. Co-star Joseph Cotton is equally game as a decent surgeon caught up in all the colorful mayhem, desperately fighting against time to save his imperiled son from Phibes' meticulous murder scenario.

He does it all for love: the diabolical Dr. Phibes is romantic at heart. Fantasy film favorite Carolin Munro plays his beautiful, tragically dead young wi seen here as a photo in the doctor's private shrine.

A desperate Dr. Vesalius (Joseph Cotto fights the clock to save his imperiled son fro madman Phibes' gruesome revenge. That bad girl Vulnavia (Virginia North) looking o

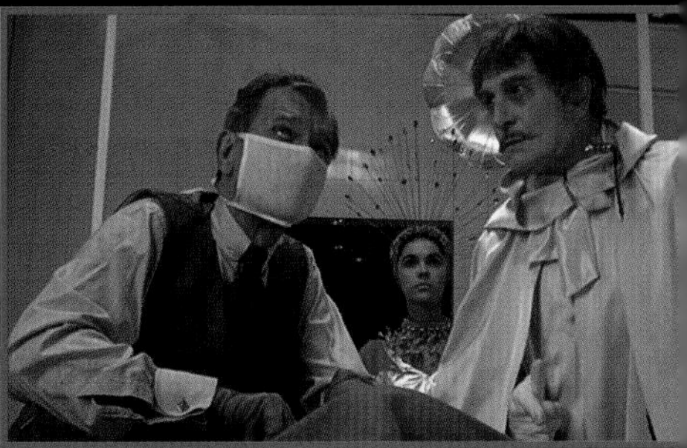

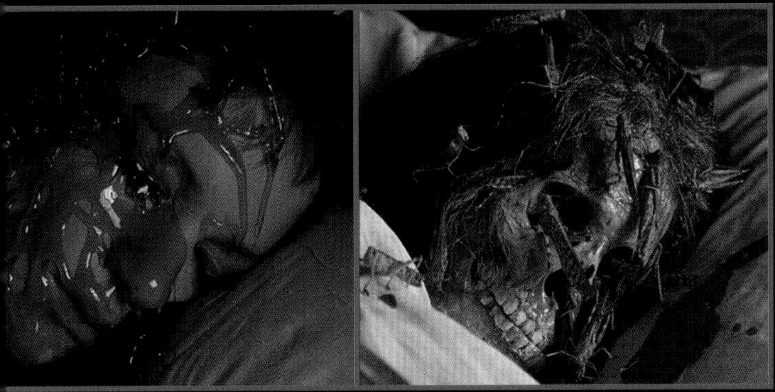

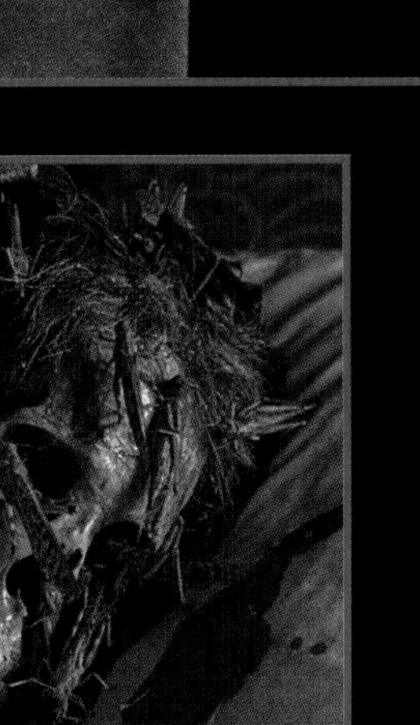

Nurse Allen (Susan Travers) dozes through her own demise as hungry locusts, courtesy of the always resourceful Dr. Phibes, make a meal of her unprotected face.

A surprise success for AIP, *The Abominable Dr. Phibes* spawned a less-satisfying sequel in 1972, *Dr. Phibes Rises Again*.

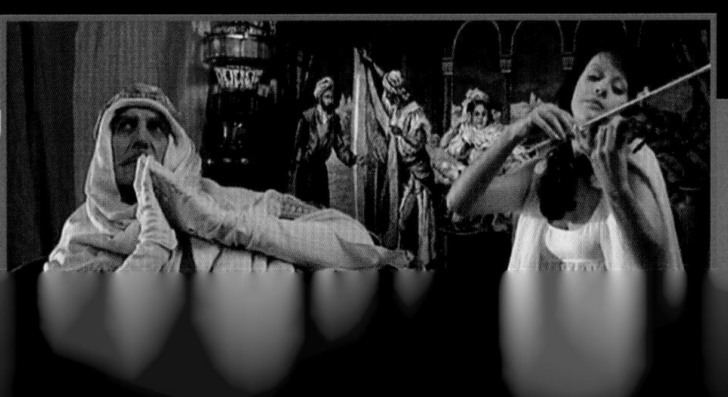

Amicus debuts with a with a tidy, ultra-atmospheric Halloween greeting card...

94 HORROR HOTEL 1960

76 1.66

aka: The City of the Dead

300 years old! Human blood keeps them alive forever!
HORROR HOTEL
Just ring for doom service!
DENNIS LOTIS · CHRISTOPHER LEE · BETTA ST. JOHN · PATRICIA JESSEL · VENETIA STEVENSON

WHO MADE IT:

Vulcan/Britannia Films (U.K.)/Trans Lux (U.S.). Director: John Llewellyn Moxey. Producers: Max Rosenberg, Milton Subotsky, Donald Taylor. Writers: George Baxt, Desmond Dickinson. Cinematography (b/w): Desmond Dickinson. Music: Douglas Gamley, Kenneth V. Jones. Starring Dennis Lotis (Richard Barlow), Christopher Lee (Prof. Alan Driscoll), Patricia Jessel (Elizabeth Selwyn/Mrs. Newless), Tom Naylor (Bill Maitland), Betta St. John (Patricia Russell), Venetia Stephenson (Nan Barlow), Valentine Dyall (Jethrow Keane), Ann Beach (Lottie), Norman Macowan (Reverend Russell), Red Johnson (The Elder),

WHAT IT'S ABOUT:

Seeking first-hand research for her paper on witchcraft, college student Nan Barlow is sent to the little New England community of Whitewood by her professor, Alan Driscoll, an expert on the occult. In this moody, fog-shrouded hamlet, Nan encounters innkeeper Mrs. Newless and befriends Patricia Russell, granddaughter of the local priest and a relative newcomer to Whitewood herself. One evening in her room, Nan hears strange, religious chanting. Summoning her courage, she enters a hidden doorway leading to a subterranean lair where a black mass is being performed by Newless and other town residents, witches all. The young girl is sacrificed in a monstrous satanic ritual, even as visiting coven member Alan Driscoll looks on. Soon after, both Nan's brother Richard and boyfriend Tom investigate her disappearance and encounter more violence at Whitewood. With Patricia next to be sacrificed, a wounded Tom manages to carry a tombstone cross into the black mass ceremony just at the hour of sacrifice. Instantly the witches are set aflame by the shadow of the cross, and Barlow and Patricia manage to escape with their lives. Mrs. Newless, in reality the witch Elizabeth Selywn burned at the stake 300 years earlier, is reduced to a charred corpse.

WHY IT'S IMPORTANT:

Impressed by the success of Hammer Films in the late '50s, producers Max Rosenberg and Milton Subotsky partnered up to create low-budget, relatively high-quality horror thrillers of their own. The company they formed came to be called Amicus, and *Horror Hotel* (aka *The City of the Dead*) was their first serious entry in the genre.

Instead of following Hammer's luminous Technicolor lead, Rosenberg and Subotsky embraced classic, cobwebbed-filled black-and-white for this stylish little foray into supernatural suspense, pretty much paralleling the same creative techniques Alfred Hitchcock was employing simultaneously with his groundbreaking *Psycho*. As a matter of fact, *City of the Dead* offers up a leading lady (Venetia Stephenson) who is unexpectedly murdered a third of the way into the story a la Janet Leigh in Hitchcock's film, turning viewers' preconceived plot notions on their heads...and *Dead* may have stumbled upon this gimmick a few months earlier. No wonder the U.S. distributor insisted on a title change to *Horror Hotel*, making the entire experience seem even more *Psycho*-like.

Cushing's frequent co-star, Christopher Lee, was at the height of his early success in horror movies when he made *City of the Dead*. His Alan Driscoll character, erudite college professor by day, murdering devil worshipper by night, is effectively realized, and Lee handles an American accent quite well (mispronouncing "clientele" briefly gives him away). Also doing memorable work are Patricia Jessel as the reincarnated witch/Whitewood innkeeper, and Valentine Dyall (who would turn up next in Robert Wise's *The Haunting*) as her grim-faced, semi-salacious warlock lover.

ABOVE: *Horror Hotel*'s opening sequence sets up the accursed town of Whitewood, as vengeful witch Elizabeth Selwyn (Patricia Jessel) is apprehended by hate-crazed villagers and burned at the stake.

The shadow of a tombstone cross proves to be the witches' undoing, setting each of them ablaze as it draws nearer.

Playing an American college professor, Christopher Lee sends a pretty young student (Venetia Stephenson) on a trip to Whitewood, an eerie, New England village famed for witch-burnings.

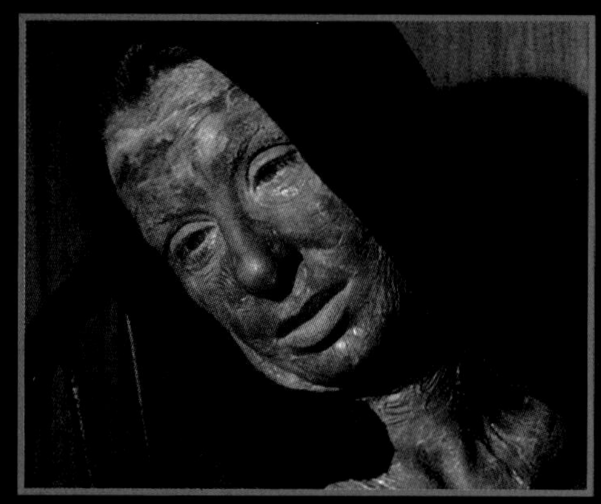

The ultimate fate of witch Elizabeth Selwyn (aka Mrs. Newless): she is burned to a crisp by the wrath of God, just as she originally was at the stake nearly three centuries earlier.

Director John Moxey discusses the film's fiery climax with his coven of "witches," Christopher Lee among them.

93

SAW 2004

103 1.85

OW MUCH BLOOD WOULD YOU SHED TO STAY ALIVE?

CARY ELWES DANNY GLOVER MONICA POTTER

SAW

WHO MADE IT:

Evolution Entertainment/Saw Productions/Twisted Pictures (Australia) Lions Gate (U.S.). Director: James Wan. Producers: Gregg Hoffman, Oren Koules, Mark Burg. Writers: Leigh Whanell, James Wan. Cinematography: David A. Armstrong. Music: Charlie Clouser. Starring Leigh Whannell (Adam Faulkner Stanheight), Cary Elwes (Dr. Lawrence Gordon), Danny Glover (Detective David Tapp), Ken Leung (Detective Steven Sing), Dina Meyer (Detective Allison Kerry), Mike Butters (Paul Leahy), Paul Gutrecht (Mark), Michael Emerson (Zep Hindle), Shawnee Smith (Amanda Young), Makenzie Vega (Diana Gordon), Monica Potter (Alison Gordon), Ned Bellamy (Jeff Ridenhour), Alexandra Bokyun Chun (Carla), Tobin Bell (John Kramer/Jigsaw), Oren Koules (Unnamed Man).

WHAT IT'S ABOUT:

Two men, Dr. Lawrence Gordon and Adam Faulkner Stanheight, find themselves chained to pipes in a derelict basement, and between them is a corpse clutching a hand-held tape player. After managing to play prepared tapes, they discover they are part of serial killer Jigsaw's sick but ingenious plan: one must slaughter the other within an allotted time, or their respective families will die. This madman doesn't murder his victims, but forces them to eventually kill themselves...or become better people as a result of his sadistic games. Gordon's only hope is a hacksaw, which he finally uses to cut his leg off and escape. But just when it seems that Jigsaw has been foiled, the dead man lying in the bathroom rises and reveals his true identity.

WHY IT'S IMPORTANT:

Along with Eli Roth's *Hostel*, *Saw* is credited (or blamed) for inaugurating "torture porn," an edgy sub-division of horror cinema that could only exist in the smugly ironic 21st Century, at least in mainstream offerings. Confounding would-be critics, *Saw* happens to be an ingeniously conceived and executed psycho-thriller that never lets up, teasing and taunting viewers by consistently crossing the endurance line and getting away with it. Working hand-in-glove with this rollercoaster approach is a most welcome, possibly accidental subtext. The fact that victims are often made "better people" after winning their bizarre duels with death, appreciating the sheer joy of being alive as they never did before, adds some unexpected intellectual depth to an already well-crafted suspense scenario.

Still, is *Saw* a horror film proper? As with *Silence of the Lambs*, *Psycho* and *Repulsion*, the lines are somewhat blurred; I suppose a case could be made that all serial killers have a sick flavor of fantasy about them, given their extreme, often jaw-dropping behavior and colorful mental aberrations. Then there's the imaginative face of a monster, no better indicator of a traditional horror flick. Almost for the sheer fun of it, and to certify its solid place in the bogeyman movie pantheon, Wan and company provide not one, but two nonhuman visages to contend with. The mocking, cycle-riding clown-thingie makes for a serviceable icon, while the barely-glimpsed pig mask has a weirdness all its own. In the final analysis, however, it's the sick ultimatum of the film's title that gives *Saw* its brutal frisson, a reminder that real horror is a uniquely persona

Offbeat, well-played and visually inventive suspenser boasts a nifty gimmick...

92 I BURY THE LIVING 1958

1.85

Poster/photos: © 1958 United Artists

WHO MADE IT:

United Artists/Maxim Productions (U.S.). Director: Albert Band. Writer: Louis Garfinkle. Cinematography (b/w): Frederick Gately. Music: Gerald Fried. Starring Richard Boone (Robert Kraft), Theodore Bikel (Andy McKee), Peggy Maurer (Ann Craig), Howard Smith (George Kraft), Herbert Anderson (Jess Jessup), Robert Osterloh (Lt. Clayborne).

WHAT IT'S ABOUT:

Newly-appointed chairman of a committee that oversees a huge cemetery, Robert Kraft accidentally places a pair of black pins into a map kept in the cemetery office. This map covers the entire grounds, with white pins representing unoccupied but sold graves, black indicating graves that are filled. When the young couple Kraft has "pinned" happen to die in an automobile accident, he gradually becomes obsessed with the idea that whenever he "black pins" someone on the cemetery map, they are doomed. He tries this repeatedly, supervised by friends and even business partners, with the same tragic results each time. Ultimately, the murders are revealed as the handiwork of cemetery caretaker Andy McKee, who, when confronting Kraft, has a mental breakdown under the strain of the elaborately macabre scheme he himself set in motion.

WHY IT'S IMPORTANT:

Producer Charles Band became something of a cottage industry in the 1980s, producing an ungodly number of modestly-budgeted horror films under the banner of Empire Pictures (later Full Moon). But long before these agreeably kitschy efforts, Band's father Albert impressed the horror film community with a small-scale, highly stylized psychological thriller that put two solid performances front-and-center, showing mainstream doubters that he was a force to be reckoned with.

I Bury the Living offers a central gimmick that is so satisfying in its simplicity that the movie earns points right out of the gate. If you get black-pinned on this weird-looking cemetery map that shows your pre-designated grave, you wind up dead...it's that simple. One wonders at what point did screenwriter Band realize that he could flip his central gimmick with even juicier results: if black pins cause death, white ones can restore buried corpses to life. This inevitable reversal is saved for the third-act breakdown of the story's true mass murderer, vengeful caretaker Andy. He's played with fearless theatricality by Theodore Bikel, very effectively counterpointing star Richard Boone's dry and laconic Robert.

Anticipating even weirder independent efforts like *Carnival of Souls*, *I Bury the Living* is an interesting example of psychological terror pushed to the stylistic max, the kind of movie some fans classify as "really great until the last act, and then everything falls apart." Once the supernatural is ruled out and we realize we're watching an offbeat whodunit, it doesn't take a genius to peg shambling Andy McKee as the only possible culprit, and his final "death by the map" seems a tad contrived, a convenient all-purpose wrap-up. Still, it's cinematically satisfying like the rest of the movie, with innovative Band demonstrating real chops as a visual director of suspense. Also worth mentioning are cinematographer Frederick Gately's surreal compositions and Gerald Fried's high-strung jazz fusion score, which comes complete with a dirge sung periodically by the always-game Bikel.

91

INTERVIEW WITH THE VAMPIRE 1994

 1.85

aka: Interview With the Vampire: The Vampire Chronicles

Poster/photos: © 1994 Warner Bros./Geffin Films

WHO MADE IT:

Warner Brothers/Geffen Films (U.S.). Director: Neil Jordan. Producers: David Geffen, Stephen Woolley. Writer: Anne Rice, based on her novel. Cinematography (Technicolor): Philippe Rousselot. Music: Elio Goldenthal. Starring Tom Cruise (Lestat de Lioncourt), Brad Pitt (Louis de Pointe du Lac), Christian Slater (Daniel Malloy—The Interviewer), Antonio Banderas (Armand), Kirsten Dunst (Claudia).

WHAT IT'S ABOUT:

Journalist Daniel Malloy is granted an unexpected interview with Louis de Pointe du Lac, the mysterious, elusive man he has been pursuing. Louis explains that he is a vampire and has been one since 1791, retaining his youthful 24-year-old appearance throughout the centuries. It was a seasoned blood-drinker named Lestat who "turned him," following the soul-shattering death of Louis' pregnant wife, a loss which left him morally vulnerable. Still, Louis despises killing human beings for sustenance, while Lestat revels in it. When the plague eventually hits New Orleans, the duo chance upon a young girl named Claudia, who has lost both of her parents. Hoping to give this child a merciful death, Louis drinks her blood...but Lestat transforms her into one of their own, and the three soon comprise an offbeat family unit. In time, however, the voracious Claudia becomes enraged that she cannot grow beyond her youthful state, and without Louis' knowledge savagely slays the unsympathetic Lestat. The two immortals escape to Europe, and eventually encounter fellow blood-drinker Armand, 400 years old and the leader of a vampire theatrical troupe. It isn't long before both are captured and condemned for taking Lestat's life...Claudia and her new vampire "mother" are locked in a deep tunnel and reduced to ashes by the rays of the morning sun. Louis is rescued from eternal confinement by Armand, but there's no consoling him; he soon vents his mighty rage against Claudia's killers by annihilating the entire vampire troupe. Finally, after years of aimless wandering, Louis returns to New Orleans in 1988 for a reunion with his sickly, maimed, but still alive (or "undead") vampire father. Journalist Malloy seems to have learned the wrong lesson from Louis' tale, and ultimately finds his darkest wish granted by none other than the fully-restored Lestat himself.

WHY IT'S IMPORTANT:

Anne Rice's novel, begun in 1969, became the most successful vampire story of its generation, with decadent, unapologetic Lestat rivaling Count Dracula as popular culture's most significant undead hero. The movie version honors this legacy with a first-class treatment in all creative departments. And while Tom Cruise may not be ideal casting – Rice herself had problems with this choice, at first – he wins over most doubters with a smart, committed performance. Equally good is Brad Pitt as his guilt-plagued companion Louis, sadly enduring the lonely centuries in his preternatural condition. Even Christian Slater is agreeably snarky as the reporter who ultimately bites off more than he can chew. But it's little Kirsten Dunst who truly steals this horror show, much as her character had fully captured our interest in Rice's novel. Dunst isn't the first screen vampire to be eternally trapped in the body of a child (*Near Dark* delved into the issue six years earlier as a kind of sidebar), but Claudia's frustrating plight is center-stage and affects protagonists Louis and Lestat profoundly. At age twelve, Dunst gives the most striking performance of her career, evolving (or devolving) from petulant youngster to murderous she-monster with total believability. Her death by incineration is the most remarkable scene in the film, a horrific blend of gut-wrenching pathos and extreme sadism, brought to vivid life by Stan Winston's state-of-the-art special effects.

ABOVE: The unique bond between Lestat (Tom Cruise) and Louis (Brad Pitt) fuels the drama of this globe-trotting, centuries-spanning "horror of immortality" epic, written for the screen by Anne Rice herself.

ABOVE: Restless young Claudia (Kirsten Dunst) adds a forlorn spin to the vampire's celebrated gift of immortality.

Although not a perfect film (at least an hour of footage was cut from pre-release), *Interview* succeeds in capturing the thematic essence of what made Anne Rice's new take on vampirism so irresistible. Somewhere between the formal period pieces of European horror and the teen angst/romantic scenarios of the 21st Century lies her unique, compelling and picturesque vision of melancholy immortals.

Enraged after Armand's vampire troupe reduces his beloved Claudia to ashes, Louis sets the entire coven ablaze.

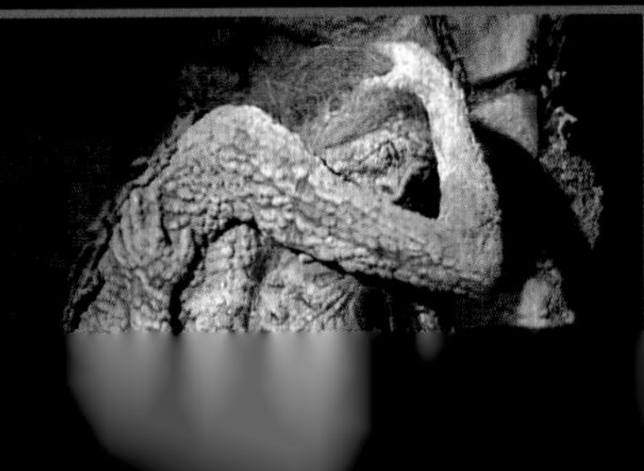

The huddled, incinerated figures of Claudia and her vampire "mother" resulted in one of Stan Winston's most elegant sculptures.

Rural peasants versus a reconstituting demon in this solid, stylish possession fable...

90 The Blood On Satan's Claw 1971

97 1.85 

Poster/photos: © 1971 Tigon British Film Productions

CHILL-FILLED Festival of HORROR!
THE BLOOD ON SATAN'S CLAW
DENNIS FRIEDLAND AND CHRISTOPHER C. DEWEY PRESENT "THE BLOOD ON SATAN'S CLAW"
STARRING PATRICK WYMARK AND LINDA HAYDEN • EXECUTIVE PRODUCER TONY TENSER
PRODUCED BY PETER L. ANDREWS & MALCOLM B. HEYWORTH • DIRECTED BY PIERS HAGGARD
A TIGON BRITISH / CHILTON FILM PRODUCTION • COLOR • A CANNON RELEASE
R

WHO MADE IT:

Tigon British Film Productions (U.K.)/Cannon Releasing Corporation (U.S.) Director: Piers Haggard. Writers: Robert Wynne-Simmons, Piers Haggard. Cinematography (Eastmancolor): Dick Bush. Music: Mark Wilkinson. Starring Patrick Wymark (The Judge), Linda Hayden (Angel Blake), Barry Andrews (Ralph Gower), Michele Dotrice (Margaret), James Hayter (Squire Middleton), Anthony Ainley (Reverend Fallowfield).

WHAT IT'S ABOUT:

In rural England, a young farmer uncovers the remains of a demon-like creature while plowing his field. Soon, local youngsters, led by a beautiful teenage girl named Angel Blake, become possessed agents of this evil entity; it intends to become a whole figure again through the sacrifice of human limbs, and uses the children to procure them. As killings increase, help is sought from nearby authorities who ultimately recognize the true nature of this threat. Finally, with the demon fully formed, a fierce commanding figure known as the Judge leads a violent community counterattack, defying a ritualistic ceremony and slaying Angel Blake. The monster is itself impaled and roasted alive in purifying flames.

WHY IT'S IMPORTANT:

As the Hammer horror product became slicker in the late '60s/early '70s, alternate creative approaches were explored by other British film companies still looking to mine the period chiller genre. Following the success of *Witchfinder General*, Tigon embarked on a similarly-themed project about rural witchcraft and the religious establishment's need to vanquish all things "demonic."

In the case of *The Blood on Satan's Claw*, however, there really is a demon at large, initially discovered in fossil form by a young farmer (Barry Andrews). Using the local children as "henchmen," the creature gradually becomes whole by making use of their sacrificed body parts. Leader of this deadly clan of feral youngsters is the demon's chosen lover, a wanton teen played by pouty, Lolita-like Linda Hayden. Her full-frontal nude scenes were rather startling for movie audiences in '71 (once seen, Angel Blake's seduction of Reverend Fallowfield is never forgotten), and the film's full-out, ritualistic climax also pushed the permissive envelope for genre offerings of this sort.

But *The Blood on Satan's Claw* is clearly no exploitation film. With cleverly designed and photographed scare scenes and naturalistic acting as assets, it takes on the flavor of a dark fable, honest, poetic and surprisingly involving. We feel the loss of innocent children through the pain of their parents and shudder at the monstrous scheme that's been set in motion. Even "bad girl" Angel is not acting entirely of her own free will...though that doesn't stop no-nonsense Judge Patrick Wymark from having her impaled on a pitchfork. Director Piers Haggard wisely keeps his mysterious demon in the shadows for most of the film, using slow-motion and other filmmaker tricks to disguise its rubber-suited tangibility.

An impressive example of what can be achieved with limited financial means and a surfeit of creative talent, *The Blood on Satan's Claw* remains one of the best demon-

89

SCREAM 1996

111 1.85

one has taken their love of scary movies one step too far. Solving this mystery is going to be murder.

SCREAM

David Arquette Neve Campbell Courteney Cox Matthew Lillard Rose McGowan Skeet Ulrich and Drew Barrymore

Dimension

The highly acclaimed new thriller from Wes Craven

WHO MADE IT:

Dimension Films (U.S.). Director: Wes Craven. Writer: Kevin Williamson. Cinematography (color): Mark Irwin. Music: Marco Beltrami. Starring Neve Campbell (Sidney Prescott), Courtney Cox (Gale Weathers), David Arquette (Deputy Dewey Riley), Rose McGowan (Tatum Riley), Drew Barrymore (Casey), Skeet Ulrich (Billy Loomis), Matthew Lillard (Stuart "Stu" Macher), Jamie Kennedy (Randy Meeks), Liev Schreiber (Cotton Weary), Francis Lee McCain (Mrs. Riley), Linda Blair (Obnoxious Reporter - uncredited), Henry Winkler (Principal Arthur Himbry - uncredited).

WHAT IT'S ABOUT:

Two high school students are brutally slain, reminding young Sidney Prescott of her own mother's killing one year ago. The following night, Sidney is attacked by the same psychotic killer, who wears a Ghostface mask, and boyfriend Billy Loomis seems the likely suspect. Adding to the girl's anxiety is TV newswoman Gale Weathers, who believes the man Sidney previously identified as her mom's killer is actually innocent. Ghostface claims additional victims, including the school principal, before a curfew party reveals the true culprits: Billy and wacky friend Stu, who also murdered Sidney's mother the previous year and framed the man Sidney identified. Now they intend to do the same to Sidney's captured father. But unexpected help from Gale enables the much-abused Ms. Prescott to turn the tables on her movie-obsessed assailants.

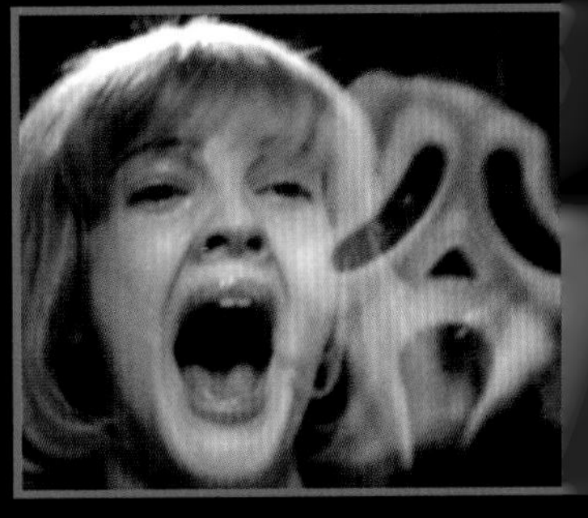

WHY IT'S IMPORTANT:

Scream did more than just revive the teen-slasher thriller; it gave director Wes Craven a whole new slant on the generally played-out genre. By turning inward and having the film's sadistic killer(s) use these movies as inspiration and reference points for real acts of horrific mayhem, screenwriter Kevin Williamson achieves something brilliant: our obsession with fright flicks has come full circle, with real life (more or less) plausibly imitating art. Craven seizes on the potential of this irresistible premise from frame one and never lets his audience forget it.

Right away, we know we're in for an interesting ride with Drew Barrymore's ultra-sadistic demise in the prologue. This attack is so sudden and seemingly ahead-of-time that we are momentarily disoriented; is this high-intensity killing for real? A nightmare? Part of the film's "game"? It's wickedly real, all right, and a great way to set up this self-aware wink of a flick. Beautiful but mature Neve Campbell as troubled teen Sidney leads an engaging cast of young performers who clearly relish their colorful, career-making roles. Johnny Depp-lookalike Skeet Ulrich is pegged early on as the culprit by his own movie-obsessed pals, but it's doubtful that anyone watching *Scream* could have guessed this wacko's masterful, generation-spanning killing-and-framing scheme. Redeeming selfish reporter Gale Weathers (Courtney Cox) is a smart move as well, given that she was deceptively set up as inevitable creep-kill. And that spooky Ghostface mask, a pre-existing commercial confection, makes for a memorable icon.

Best scenes (among many): Casey's opening murder, Sidney's first attack, the "rules" of horror movies, delayed video viewing and slaying of Gale's assistant, Tatum's garage door capture, Billy's revelation and ensuing mayhem.

88 MARK OF THE VAMPIRE 1935

1.37

WHO MADE IT:

Metro-Goldwyn-Mayer (U.S.). Director: Tod Browning. Writers: Guy Endore, Bernard Schubert. Cinematography (b/w): James Wong Howe Music: Stock. Starring Lionel Barrymore (Professor Zelen), Elizabeth Allen (Irena Borotyn), Bela Lugosi (Count Mora), Lionel Atwill (Inspector Neumann), Jean Hersholt (Baron Otto Von Zinden), Donald Meek (Dr Doskil), Carroll Borland (Luna Mora).

WHAT IT'S ABOUT:

When Sir Karell Borotyn is found murdered in his own house, with two tiny pinpoint wounds on his neck, curious suspicions are aroused The attending physician Dr. Doskil and Sir Karell's friend Baron Otto have come to the conclusion that the murderer is a blood-drinking vampire. Suspect #1 is the cadaverous, bullet-wounded Count Mora who haunts the nearby cemetery area with his equally ghoulish daughter, Luna. Initially, Prague police inspector Neumann has tremendous difficulty accepting the existence of these supernatural predators. But his stubborn views change when Bortyn's daughter, Irena, becomes the vampire Count's next target. Enlightening all to the ways of such nether-world creatures is the learned Professor Zelen, a vampire expert, who winds up shedding some unexpected light on Sir Karell's very-earthbound murder The true culprit is dramatically exposed, and the entire vampire scenario is revealed as an elaborate hoax to trap a killer. Part o the con job involved actors playing the vampiric Mora and Luna Job now finished, these two divas happily take their make-up of and prepare for their next melodramatic gig.

WHY IT'S IMPORTANT:

MGM's answer to Universal's *Dracula* was Dracula himself, Bela Lugosi, as just about the same character, distinguished only by an enigmatic gunshot wound at his temple. The movie is *Mark of the Vampire*, helmed by *Dracula* director Tod Browning and reworked from a lost Lon Chaney classic, *London After Midnight*. Unsure of whether to be a legitimate chiller or a mystery-comedy, Browning opts for both approaches; the spooky vampires are supposed to be paid actors playing these bizarre roles in order to catch a crook. But the objective film viewer observes them magically walking through cobwebs (a *Dracula* gag in the privacy of their bug-infested castle...which is hardly normal behavior for actors, even if one of them does happen to be Bela Lugosi.

Since the movie (or at least most of it) is a con game in action, it's hard to judge the exaggerated, unreal performances; Barrymore is actually required to be over-the-top, so realism fans should be forewarned. It certainly is interesting to see MGM's most respected and distinguished thespian doing his spirited take on the Van Helsing archetype. As for Lugosi, he is the essence of classic-era vampirism presented adoringly in arty close-ups and disturbing "moonglow" lighting. Relatively cute Carroll Borland as his companion Luna sometimes mistaken for *Dracula's Daughter* (a Universal film Lugosi was supposed to appear in), is unique in her generation as Dr. Pretorius might put it, especially when gliding about in outsized batwings.

Enriched or burdened by the MGM A-look (the more sumptuous sets play a tad contrived), *Mark of the Vampire* is often panned by horror buffs because of the abrupt "cop-out" ending; other critics find it a cheeky, atmospheric one-of-a-kind delight and revel in tha very twist. In terms of vintage Lugosi, it's the closest we ever came to a sequel to *Dracula*, and with no less than Tod Browning in charge

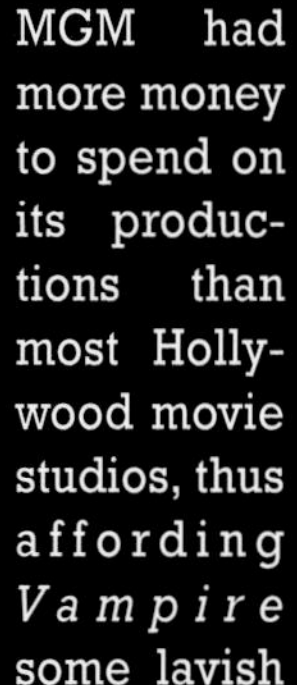

MGM had more money to spend on its productions than most Hollywood movie studios, thus affording *Vampire* some lavish sets and a truly eye-opening special effect: Luna descending on batwings, something never attempted by Universal. BELOW: Bela Lugosi was everybody's idea of a vampire in the mid-1930s.

A first-rate cast distinguishes Browning's film from less prestigious horror offerings of the day.

LEFT: the scary yet sexy Luna Mora, as portrayed by Carroll Borland.

BELOW: Jean Hersholt turns out to be *Mark of the Vampire*'s real villain.

Lon Chaney played a toothsome terror in the original silent version of *Mark of the Vampire*, the sadly lost *London After Midnight*.

FACES IN THE DARK

LEFT: Most of the *Mark of the Vampire* cast played suspicious types, under the scrutiny of "vampire-hunting" detective Lionel Barrymore. ABOVE: Also pursued, but this time by a legitimate supernatural sleuth, is deformed, demon-invoking Professor Malaki (Werner Klemperer, a year before he became immortalized as Colonel Klink on TV's *Hogan's Heroes*).

Sharp, vest-pocket gaslight chiller boasts the screen's first supernatural sleuth...

87

Dark Intruder 1965

59

1.37

WHO MADE IT:

Universal Pictures (Shamley Productions). Director: Harvey Hart. Producer: Jack Laird. Writer: Barre Lyndon. Cinematography (b/w): John F. Warren. Music: Lalo Schifrin. Make-up: Bud Westmore. Starring Leslie Nielsen (Brett Kingsford), Mark Richman (Robert Vandenburg), Judi Meredith (Evelyn Lang), Gilbert Green (Harvey Misbach), Werner Klemperer (Prof. Malaki), Vaughn Taylor (Dr. Kevin Burdett), Charles Bolender (Nicola), Peter Brocco (Chi Zang).

WHAT IT'S ABOUT:

In the late 1890s, San Francisco is bedeviled by a savage, Jack the Ripper-like serial killer who leaves arcane stone gargoyle statuettes after each murder. But instead of using a knife on victims, this mass-slayer appears to have razor-sharp claws. Stumped, Police Inspector Misbach seeks the help of his offbeat ally, playboy Brett Kingsford, who is in truth a master detective and expert on the occult. By coincidence, it is Kingsford's good friend from high society, Robert Vandenberg, who is being targeted by this unearthly force. Probing into the past, Kingsford discovers that Vandenberg had a deformed twin brother that the family kept secret. Envious, this mysterious brother – who grew up to be famous prognosticator Professor Malaki – sought the aid of Sumerian demons in order to switch places with his perfectly-formed sibling. The recent string of ritual killings committed by Malaki now enables him to complete his heinous mission, but Kingsford ultimately learns the truth and finally confronts his possessed "friend" in a cemetery. The two men struggle as Vandenberg's horrified, disbelieving fiancée Evelyn looks on, until a gunshot from Inspector Misbach saves the grateful detective from being throttled. In death, Vandenberg's handsome facial features revert to the monstrous contours of his deformed, demon-bargaining brother Malaki.

WHY IT'S IMPORTANT:

Produced as a TV pilot called *Black Cloak* but released theatrically, *Dark Intruder* broke new ground with its original hero (a handsome playboy detective specializing in supernatural crimes) and offbeat villain (a weird, wizened, serial killer demonoid). Leslie Nielsen's Brett Kingsford represents Universal's first attempt to develop a phantom chaser for prime time television in the dashing leading man tradition. He'd soon be followed by elegant demon-obsessed psychiatrist Louis Jourdan (the TV-movie pilots *Fear No Evil* and *Ritual of Evil*), stalwart parapsychologist Gary Collins (*The Sixth Sense* series) and ultimately rumpled reporter Darren McGaven (*Kolchak: the Night Stalker*), who brought the genre full circle with an energetic semi-parody. As a character intended for weekly adventures, Kingsford is crafted along Sherlock Holmes lines, but actually has more in common with Bruce Wayne: he uses his charming playboy persona as a smokescreen for serious crime-sleuthing (and demon slaying).

Anticipating greater violence to come, *Dark Intruder*'s "monster attack" sequences have a frenzied, hand-held, Dan Curtis-like physicality about them that is a tad startling for 1965. It's also interesting to note that less than a year after Roger Corman introduced H.P. Lovecraft's demonic "elder gods" in *The Haunted Palace*, Universal was rather bravely embracing similar notions for a network television series.

Predictably, and unfortunately, NBC got cold feet at the eleventh hour and Jack Laird's *Black Cloak* was nixed as an ongoing property. Judging from this first storyline, a wonderful potpourri of arcane metaphysics, Siamese twins and demonic possession, the resulting series would have been a pip.

Dark Intruder began life as the pilot for a TV series entitled *Black Cloak*. NBC planned on broadcasting *Cloak*'s first story, "Something with Claws," as an installment of *The Alfred Hitchcock Hour* during its '64-'65 season. This explains why famous Hitchcock actor/producer Norman Lloyd wound up providing the distinctively creaky, Maude Frickert-like voice of Professor Malaki (Werner Klemperer, right, menacing Mark Richman).

Leslie Nielsen plays a sleuth obsessed with the occult in 1890s San Francisco.

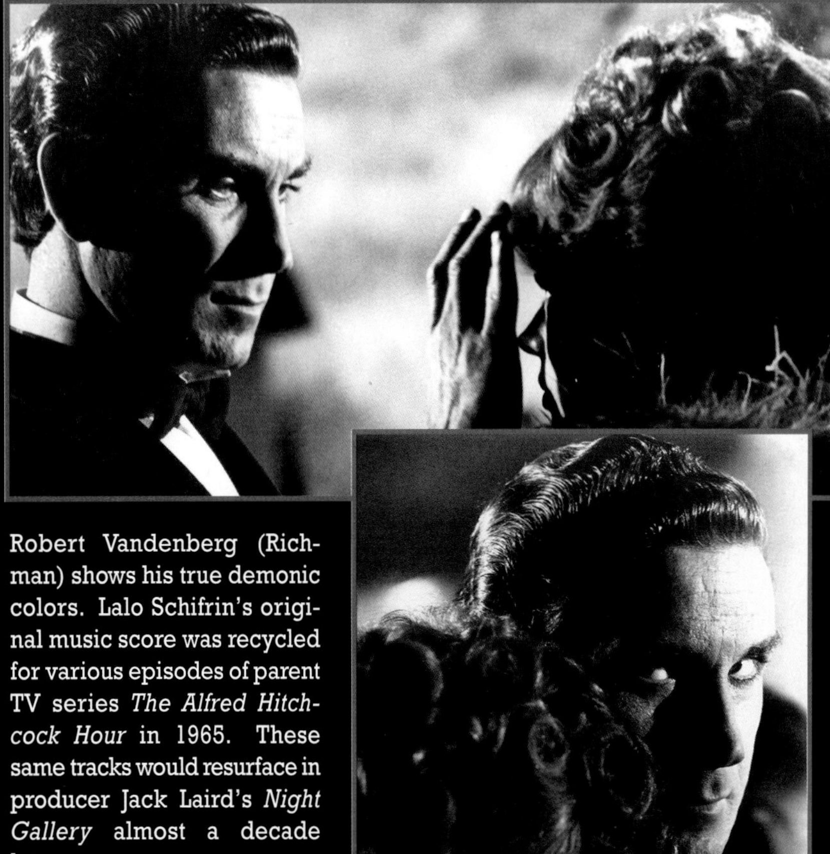

Robert Vandenberg (Richman) shows his true demonic colors. Lalo Schifrin's original music score was recycled for various episodes of parent TV series *The Alfred Hitchcock Hour* in 1965. These same tracks would resurface in producer Jack Laird's *Night Gallery* almost a decade later.

Humanoid demon Werner Klemperer makes a phone call in this studio-generated publicity shot.

Pseudo-zombies run amok in this horrific, exciting contamination thriller...

86

28 Days Later 2002

113

1.85

WHO MADE IT:

Fox Searchlight Pictures (U.K.). Director: Danny Boyle. Producer: Andrew Macdonald. Writer: Alex Garland. Cinematography (Technicolor): Anthony Dod Mantle. Music: John Murphy. Starring Cillian Murphy (Jim), Naomie Harris (Selena), Brendan Gleeson (Frank), Megan Burns (Hannah), Christopher Eccleston (Major Henry West), Noah Huntley (Mark), Stuart McQuarrie (Sergeant Farrell).

WHAT IT'S ABOUT:

Trying to free chimpanzees from medical research testing, British animal rights activists invade a Cambridge facility and inadvertently unleash a devastating infection that drives victims mad with rage. Twenty-eight days later, a bicycle courier named Jim awakens from a coma, then discovers, much to his horror, that a devastated London has been evacuated. Jim is rescued from murderous, quasi-human "rage" survivors by uninfected Selena, who feels that sympathy for victims is a weakness in the new, bleak environment. They eventually connect with a man named Frank and his young daughter Hannah. After Frank is contaminated by a drop of infected blood, Jim, Selena and Hannah are "rescued" by a rag-tag military unit run by Major Henry West. These soldiers, hoping to use both women for breeding stock, become a heinous new threat. After much bloodshed (and with a little help from a formerly captured Infected), the threesome manage to escape, and are eventually spotted and retrieved by true, airborne authorities.

WHY IT'S IMPORTANT:

Sci-fi as much as horror, Danny Boyle's unapologetic *28 Days Later* raises the zombie sub-genre up several notches, Alex Garland's screenplay openly inspired by the seminal works of Matheson, Wyndham and Romero. In this case the ghoulish monsters are pathetic human beings infected by an experimental "rage" virus, which drives them murderously mad and turns their eyes a pupiless red. They also seem to move at warp speed (Boyle loses a few frames when depicting these crazies in action), establishing a new, 21st Century horror flick cliché: the Olympian-level wretched mutant. We'll see him again in an official adaptation of *I Am Legend* a few years down the line, giving Will Smith a run for his money.

But Boyle got there first, at least in terms of modern fright cinema. As usual with scenarios of this sort, some of the best scenes are early on, with everyman hero Jim (Cillian Murphy) wandering from his hospital bed into the silent streets of a weirdly deserted London. The brutality of this monstrous new world swiftly established (heroine Selena starts out especially no-nonsense), humanity's grim survivors must look deeply into their hearts and find a legitimate reason to go on living. Picking up good-natured Frank and his loving daughter Hannah along the way certainly helps; humanity's rotten side is succinctly represented by the faux-military unit that promises our heroes salvation, but offers murder and "justifiable" rape instead.

Brutal but sharp and ultimately optimistic, *28 Days Later* reminds us that killing is part of our human heritage but not all of it, and sometimes the most dangerous monsters we face have very human faces.

Teen takes on the dashing vampire-next-door in this effective semi-parody...

Fright Night 1985

2.35

Poster/photos: © 1987 Columbia Pictures

WHO MADE IT:

Columbia Pictures (U.S.). Director: Tom Holland. Producer: Herb Jaffe. Writer: Tom Holland. Cinematography (Metrocolor): Jan Kiesser. Music: Brad Fiedel. Starring Chris Sarandon (Jerry Dandridge), William Ragsdale (Charley Brewster), Amanda Bearse (Amy Peterson), Roddy McDowall (Peter Vincent), Stephen Geoffreys ('Evil' Ed Thompson), Jonathan Stark (Billy Cole), Dorothy Fielding (Judy Brewster), Art Evans (Detective Lennox), Stewart Stern (Cook), Nick Savage (Bouncer #1), Heidi Sorenson (Hooker).

WHAT IT'S ABOUT:

Teenager Charley Brewster, a horror movie fan, begins to suspect that his new next door neighbor is a vampire. Spying on handsome Jerry Dandridge with binoculars, he discovers that he's right...but no one will believe him. The police, his mom, girlfriend Amy, weirdie pal "Evil" Ed, even local horror movie TV host/washed-up actor Peter Vincent think he's hallucinating. Only Dandridge and his equally wicked young bodyguard take Charley's threat seriously. Escalating events manage to convince Vincent, however, and soon both the teenage boy and aging actor must put aside their fears and take on both of these monsters. Ed is turned into a vampire himself and even Amy is stricken; but Charley and a guilt-plagued Vincent, who has regained his spiritual faith during the ordeal, eventually manage to destroy their bloodsucking adversary. Or have they?

WHY IT'S IMPORTANT:

Fright Night probably would've been a hit just by virtue of its multiple high concepts (my next door neighbor is a vampire, aging horror movie star is forced to take on the real thing, etc.). But director Tom Holland's colorful little excursion into suburban blood-sucking (and a good deal of blood-letting) manages to work on audiences in ways that are a tad unexpected, even for an agreeably humorous chiller.

Chris Sarandon's disco devil-style vampire is typical of this era's Frank Langella/George Hamilton approach to the undead: dark, smartly-coiffed and irresistibly sexy. Top-billed Chris Sarandon is clearly enjoying his tasty role, whether seducing an enemy's girlfriend or seething like an animal in grotesque horror make-up (one of the film's several strengths). Just as much fun to watch is veteran character actor Roddy McDowall as down-on-his-luck horror actor Peter (Cushing) Vincent (Price), whose initial lack of faith dooms his first crucifix-brandishing assault on Sarandon. And while both the male and female teenage leads are serviceable, it's Stephen Geoffreys as weirdo/monster expert "Evil" Ed who nearly steals the show, evolving from wacky comedy relief to an almost unbearably tragic figure – his protracted, fx-driven death sequence elicits tears not only from a horrified and semi-regretful Vincent, but surprised viewers as well. Best scenes: elongated fingers lowering the window shade, Dandridge's Anne Rice-like seduction of Evil Ed, Ed's grotesque demise before Vincent, dancing with Amy, Dandridge's bat metamorphosis, the "blinking red eyes from next-door" coda.

Wiseguys take on vampires in a genre-bashing killfest…

84 FROM DUSK TIIL DAWN 1996

108 | 1.85

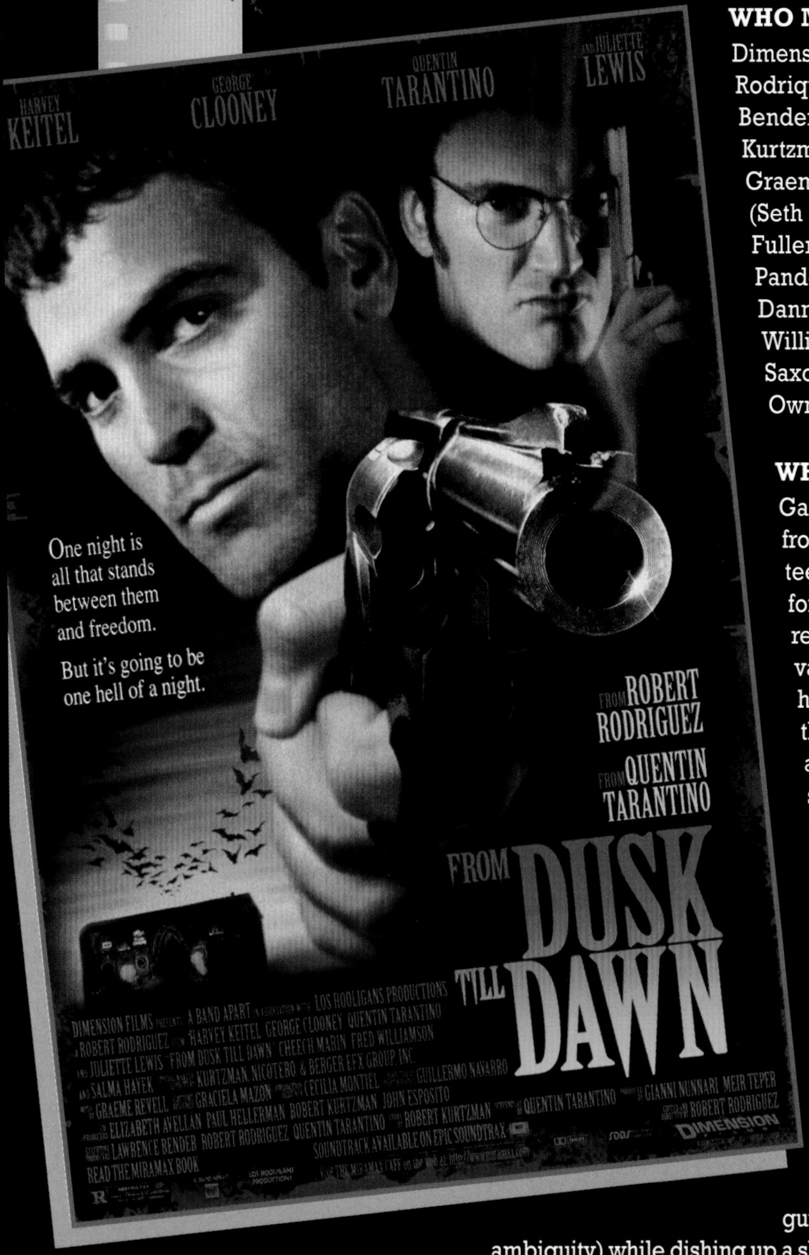

WHO MADE IT:

Dimension Films/A Band Apart/Los Hooligans (U.S.). Director: Robert Rodriquez. Producers: Robert Rodriquez, Quentin Tarantino, Lawrence Bender. Writers: Quentin Tarantino, based on a story by Robert Kurtzman. Cinematography (Technicolor): Guillermo Navarro. Music: Graeme Revell. Starring Harvey Keitel (Jacob Fuller), George Clooney (Seth Gecko), Quentin Tarantino (Richie Gecko), Juliette Lewis (Kate Fuller), Ernest Liu (Scott Fuller), Salma Hayek (Santanico Pandemonium), Cheech Marin (Border Guard/Chet Pussy/Carlos), Danny Trejo (Razor Charlie), Tom Savini (Sex Machine), Fred Williamson (Frost), Michael Parks (Texas Ranger Earl McGraw), John Saxon (FBI Agent Stanley Chase), Marc Lawrence (Old Timer Motel Owner), Kelly Preston (Newscaster Kelly Houge).

WHAT IT'S ABOUT:

Gangsters Seth Gecko and his younger brother Richard, fugitives from a bloody bank robbery, kidnap Pastor Jake Fuller and his two teenage children, Kate and Scott. They use the Fuller family's R.V. for a daring escape across the border. But when they arrive at their rendezvous point in Mexico, the group runs afoul of some hungry vampires that operate a local strip joint/private bar. Calling upon his dark skills as a professional killer, Seth manages to ward off the colorful monsters, but Richard and eventually both Scott and a self-sacrificing Jake are killed in the fracas. Young Kate survives, hardened and matured by the experience, and even Seth discovers that's he's not the totally heartless character he always believed himself to be.

WHY IT'S IMPORTANT:

Writer-director Quentin Tarantino, of *Pulp Fiction* fame, shook up the movie-going world in the '90s with his super-sharp command of language, offbeat characterization and raw, unrelenting violence. Given this brazen artist's love for exploitation films, it's not surprising that he (along with fellow genre-buster Robert Rodriquez) would someday tackle a mainstream horror scenario with all the bloody trimmings. *From Dusk till Dawn* provides the ideal opportunity for these guys to indulge their guiltiest pleasures (murder, mayhem and moral ambiguity) while dishing up a shit-kicking action piece that redefines vampire movie conventions.

The "trick" of spending half a story in one genre (crime and kidnapping) only to wind up in another (the thirsty undead on a rampage) has been attempted before in fantasy films, John McTiernan's sci-fi bloodbath *Predator* coming to mind. And while some reviewers were turned off by this sudden shift, most were amused by the sheer audacity of it, which fits right in with *Dusk*'s overall wiseass tone.

At the heart of this hyper-violent adrenaline rush of a movie is the serviceable "disillusioned priest has lost his Faith, but finds it again when confronting supernatural Evil" plot premise, utilized most memorably in Friedkin's *The Exorcist*. As weathered family man/former minister Jacob Fuller, top-billed Harvey Keitel is so good he should have been nominated for an Oscar. His humility, stability and warmth serve as the ideal counterpoint to Clooney's amoral aggressiveness. Typically for a Tarantino-scripted movie, the characters all have discernable arcs; Clooney's partial reformation is believable and satisfying, given the fantastic circumstances. Chaste Juliette Lewis evolves from petulant Gidget-type to blood-splattered terminator, and even Gecko's sicko brother (played by Tarantino himself) seems to grow a semi-conscience before becoming vampire stew in the first major attack.

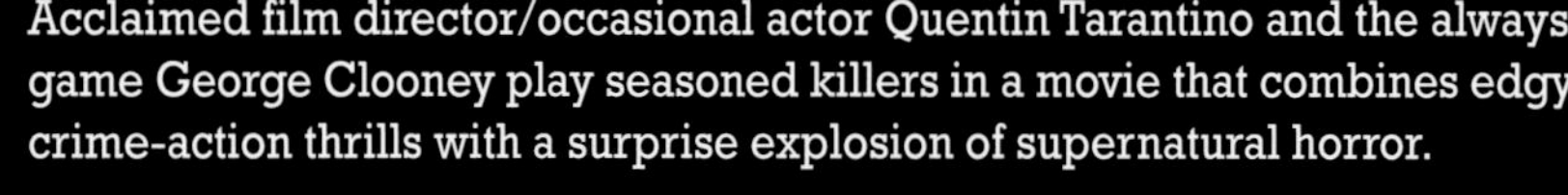

Acclaimed film director/occasional actor Quentin Tarantino and the always game George Clooney play seasoned killers in a movie that combines edgy crime-action thrills with a surprise explosion of supernatural horror.

Director Robert Rodriquez, a movie guru like his partner/pal Quentin Tarantino, populates *Dusk* with some colorful personalities in small roles: veteran actors Marc Lawrence and Fred Williamson are joined by Cheech Marin and make-up wizard Tom Savini.

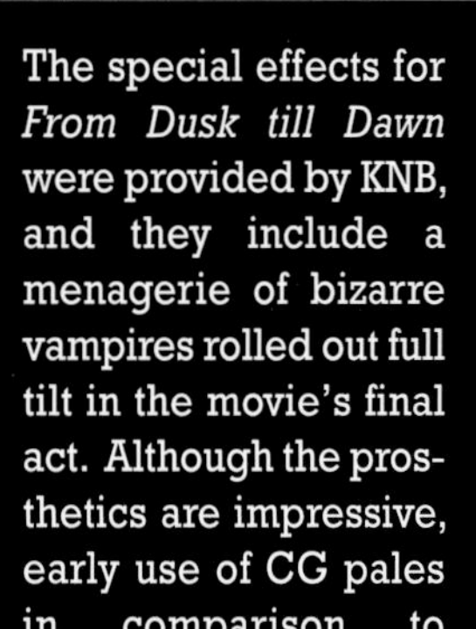

The special effects for *From Dusk till Dawn* were provided by KNB, and they include a menagerie of bizarre vampires rolled out full tilt in the movie's final act. Although the prosthetics are impressive, early use of CG pales in comparison to today's state-of-the-art techniques. RIGHT: The beautiful, always seductive Salma Hayek (best known for her Oscar-nominated lead performance in *Frida*) enjoys what amounts to a sexy cameo in the film.

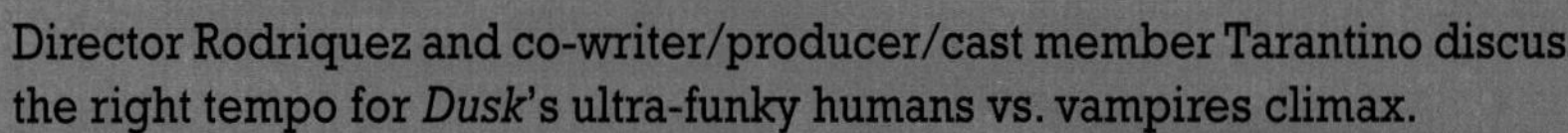

Director Rodriquez and co-writer/producer/cast member Tarantino discuss the right tempo for *Dusk*'s ultra-funky humans vs. vampires climax.

Glib and sleek take on modern lycanthropy, from health resorts to TV newsrooms...

83 THE HOWLING 1981

91

1.85

WHO MADE IT:

Sony Pictures Entertainment (U.S.) Director: Joe Dante. Producers: Jack Conrad, Michael Finnell. Writers: John Sayles and Terence H. Winkless, from the novel by Gary Brandner. Cinematography: John Hora. Music: Pino Donaggio. Make-up: Rob Bottin. Starring Dee Wallace (Karen White), Patrick Macnee (Dr. George Waggner), Dennis Dugan (Chris), Christopher Stone (R. William "Bill" Neill), Belinda Balaski (Terry Fisher), Kevin McCarthy (Fred Francis), John Carradine (Erie Kenton), Slim Pickens (Sam Newfield), Elisabeth Brooks (Marsha Quist), Robert Picardo (Eddie Qiuist), Jim McKrell (Lew Landers), Kenneth Tobey (Older Cop), Dick Miller (Walter Paisley).

WHAT IT'S ABOUT:

Los Angeles TV reporter Karen White has a harrowing experience working with the police in a scheme to trap a serial killer, Eddie Quist. To help her recover, Karen's therapist sends White and her husband Bill to The Colony, a secluded resort in the countryside. But the colony is filled with bizarre characters, including a sultry nymphomaniac with eyes for Bill. Before long it becomes clear that this is a gathering of actual werewolves, and that Eddie Quist was (and still is) one of these murderous shape-shifters. After trapping the creatures in a barn and setting it on fire, Karen and ally Chris barely manage to escape with their lives. But Karen, like her husband, has been bitten, and in a prearranged, televised LA appearance, she transforms into a werewolf to convince viewers that the threat is all too real. As TV viewers look on skeptically, she is shot to death on camera by silver bullets fired by Chris.

WHY IT'S IMPORTANT:

A horror movie buff from the wilds of New Jersey, director Joe Dante became part of Steven Spielberg's fantasy entourage during those magical boon years of the 1980s, bringing his lifelong love for dark fantasy and wiseacre cartoons to the big screen. *The Howling*, smartly scripted by John Sayles (his creative partner for the cult hit *Piranha*), is a colorful, semi-satiric werewolf thriller that certified Dante's reputation as a significant pop fantasist. It is also, at least by my lights, his finest hour as a mainstream filmmaker.

An enjoyable ensemble cast (John Carradine is especially effective as an aging 'thrope) helps sell the fanciful notion of "trendy" werewolf colonies in our midst. Dante handles big-city indifference (the TV studio and seedy street clubs) and country cousin shudders equally well, his glib and self-aware style nicely complimenting the movie without pulling viewers out of it. And like its kindred spirit of the same year, *An American Werewolf in London*, the film calls upon groundbreaking make-up techniques to realize its showcase transformation sequences. The best of these, building on a creepy act one set-up, is the dramatic step-by-step metamorphosis of psychotic bad boy Eddie Quist (Robert Picardo) into a towering, devil-eared lupine monstrosity. Lovingly paying homage to the fx approaches of his youth, director Dante even manages to work a few moments of stop motion animation into the frenzied climax.

By combining savvy social satire with flamboyantly elegant photography and musical scoring, *The Howling* emerges as a glossy entertainment that occasionally threatens to transcend the shock'n'scare genre it was designed for. Rob Bottin's remarkable make-up work alone is worth checking out. And if all that isn't enough, the movie boasts mega-hot lycanthrope Elisabeth Brooks in a steamy sex scene...lots of howling going down, to be sure, and more than a few wolf whistles.

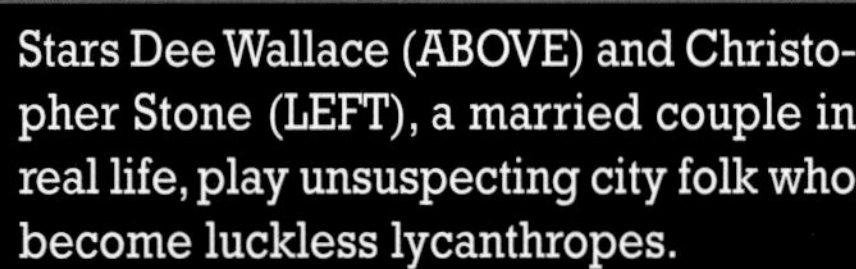

Stars Dee Wallace (ABOVE) and Christopher Stone (LEFT), a married couple in real life, play unsuspecting city folk who become luckless lycanthropes.

BELOW: File under fear... Belinda Balaski shares her folder with an unexpected friend. Joe Dante, a Saturday matinee kid from the 1950s, hoped to honor his favorite actors from this period (Kenneth Tobey, Kevin McCarthy, etc.) while moving the horror genre forward with knowing humor.

ABOVE, INSET: the only stop-motion animation shot approved by director Dante. ABOVE: Eddie Quist's grisly transformation is a *Howling* highlight. RIGHT: John Carradine as a venerable were-geezer menaces Dee Wallace.

The final result of Quist's memorable metamorphosis: a full-size Jack Buehler werewolf outfit, bathed in evocative shadows.

Scary, over-the-top Vincent Price haunted house party, skeleton included...

82

HOUSE ON HAUNTED HILL 1959

WHO MADE IT:

Allied Artists (U.S.). Director: William Castle. Producers: William Castle, Robb White. Writer: Robb White. Cinematography (b/w): Carl E. Guthrie. Music: Von Dexter. Starring Vincent Price (Frederick Loren), Carol Ohmhart (Anabelle Loren), Richard Long (Lance Schroeder), Elisha Cook Jr. (Watson Pritchard), Alan Marshal (Dr. David Trent), Carolyn Craig (Nora Manning), Julie Mitchem (Ruth Bridges), Leona Anderson (Mrs. Slydes), Howard Hoffman (Jonas Slydes).

WHAT IT'S ABOUT:

Millionaire Frederick Loren and his wife Anabelle host a mysterious party at a reputedly haunted house. Five strangers are invited: a test pilot, psychiatrist, society woman, a young girl who works for his company, and the original owner, a drunk who warns everyone about the house's ghostly (and ghastly) history. After various unexpected scares and a number of mishaps, it appears that Anabelle has committed suicide…or was murdered. It's eventually revealed that she's very much alive, and in cahoots with the invited psychiatrist, who has cooked up an elaborate scheme to kill Frederick for his fortune. But a vengeful Loren turns the tables, murdering the doctor and terrifying Annabelle with a skeleton rigged to emerge from a vat of acid…into which she eventually plunges. The remaining guests are left wondering if Loren is truly guilty of killing two people. But one thing's for certain…the ghosts of this haunted mansion seem to have added a treacherous couple to their number, and may be coming for you next!

WHY IT'S IMPORTANT:

Kitchy and campy long before those terms were invented, *House on Haunted Hill* may well be the quintessential William Castle movie from his early, gimmick-laden period. Unlike Robert Wise's *The Haunting* or even *The Uninvited*, this is a superficial romp through an imposing haunted mansion, every corridor crammed with B-movie shock devices and improbable plot twists. Still, director Castle seems to be having great fun, and this is for the most part transmitted to his viewing audience. An agreeable cast helps. Conniving wife Carol Ohmhart is a wonderful match for silky-smooth Price, and screenwriter Robb White excels at bitchy, sing-song dialogue ("Darling, the only ghoul in the house is you."). Veteran character actor Elisha Cook Jr. is also an asset, ending the movie with a memorable closing line.

Of course, the line between genuine supernatural events and the murder plot blurs constantly, with some of the dastardly duo's scare routines simply impossible to achieve in any realistic sense. But it's that kind of movie, so we don't ask questions. Best scenes: the first appearance of the blind housekeeper in the basement, Annabelle at the window, and the final skeleton dance – "Emergo," according to producer Castle.

In 1999, an elaborate remake of *House on Haunted Hill* was produced by Dark Castle Entertainment (a company formed to make horror movies in Castle's classic tradition) and starred Geoffrey Rush as the Price-like lead. But the computer-generated effects and Lovecraftian story elements only seemed to distance this new version from the goofy but fondly-remembered original.

Exteriors of the film were shot at The Ennis House, designed by stylist Frank Lloyd Wright and located in the Hollywood Hills.

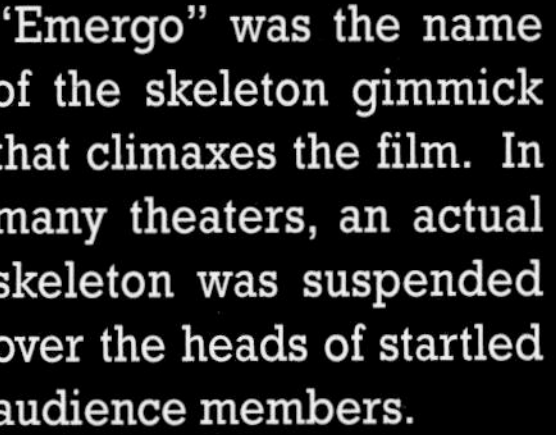

"Emergo" was the name of the skeleton gimmick that climaxes the film. In many theaters, an actual skeleton was suspended over the heads of startled audience members.

ABOVE: Sly, sarcastic Carol Ohmhart was a perfect match for Price. BELOW: The blind housekeeper (Leona Anderson) terrifies poor Carolyn Craig.

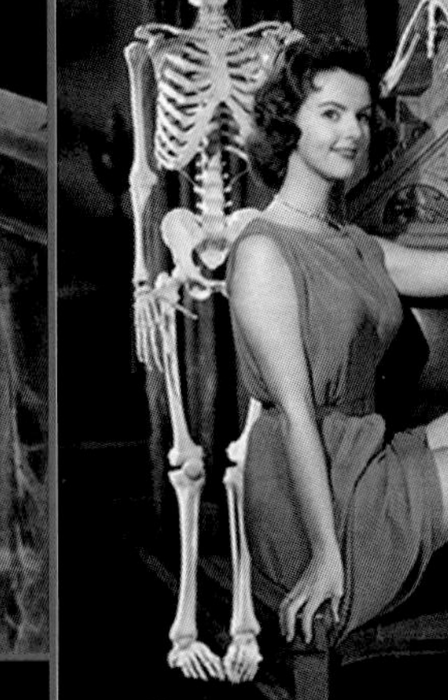

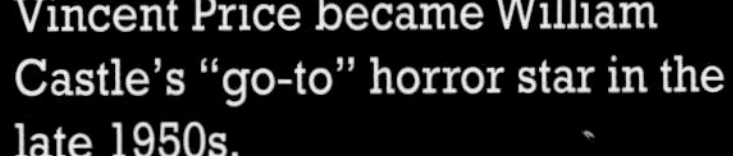

Vincent Price became William Castle's "go-to" horror star in the late 1950s.

Screenwriter/producer Robb White discusses some tasty dialogue with star Price.

Pre-teen angst mixes with bloodlusting terror in this unexpected and heartfelt gem...

81 LET THE RIGHT ONE IN 2008

2.35

Poster/photos: © 2009 Magnolia Pictures

WHO MADE IT:

Sandrew Metronome (Scandinavia)/Magnolia Pictures (U.S.). Director Tomas Alfredson. Producers: Carl Molinder, John Nordling. Writer: John Ajvide Lindqvist, based on his novel. Cinematography (color): Hoyte van Hoytema. Music: Johan Soderqvist. Starring Kare Hedebrant (Oskar), Lina Leandersson (Eli), Per Ragnar (Hakan), Henrik Dahl (Erik, Oskar's father), Karin Bergquist (Yvonne, Oskar's mother), Peter Carlberg (Lacke), Ika Nord (Virginia), Mikael Rahm (Jocke), Karl Robert Lindgren (Gosta), Anders T Peedu (Morgan), Pale Olofsson (Larry), Patrick Rydmark (Conny), Mikael Erhardsson (Martin), Rasmus Luthander (Jimmy).

WHAT IT'S ABOUT:

In Blackeberg, Stockholm, a twelve-year-old boy named Oskar is continually harassed by bullying students. Things change when he meets a mysterious young girl and gradually befriends her. But this waifish child, Eli, is in truth a bloodthirsty vampire, and some local murders can be attributed both to her and the elderly man who looks after her. Soon Eli is on her own, and she must kill to survive. Oskar becomes her devoted companion and new protector, even distracting the vengeful husband of one of her victims when he invades her apartment and nearly destroys her while she's asleep. Eli returns the favor by helping Oskar deal with the bullies, and soon both of them are off together for a new life...with Eli packed away in a trunk.

WHY IT'S IMPORTANT:

At its heart a coming-of-age romance, *Let the Right One In* quietly smashes genre conventions, standing apart from and above the avalanche of commercial vampire thrillers spawned in the new century. With a languid flavor befitting its poetic aspirations, the film won over fans and critics alike, showcasing a central relationship that might be described as *A Little Romance* with fangs. Certainly there have been vampire children in films before, most notably Kirsten Dunst's tragic character in *Interview with the Vampire*. But this special bond between two inherently decent, lonely kids is achingly honest and heartfelt without being sentimental. Making the whole thing work is the casting of the oh-so-sad twelve-year-old protagonists. In keeping with *Right One*'s gender-bending subtext young Oskar (Kare Hedebrant) looks more like a girl than his new "steady," waifish, large-eyed Eli (Lina Leandersson). Eli claims she isn't female to begin with, let alone conventionally human. Adult relationships of varying kinds are established to put the special Oskar-Eli union in perspective, suggesting that "letting the right one in" has as much to do with following your heart as the traditional vampire requirement of a stated invitation. Much is made of this rule in one of the movie's best scenes, as Eli begins to self-destruct after entering Oskar's room without his permission. Equally disturbing is the self-immolation of a recently turned, self-loathing 'pire, one of the most shocking assisted suicides ever depicted on film.

Abandoning some of the darker aspects of Lindqvist's novel (Eli's adult protector has an unsavory past), director Tomas Alfredson fashions a unique and endearing fairy tale set in a realistic but elegiac landscape of stylized jungle gyms, frozen ponds and snowdrifts. From this bleak yet strangely soothing environment comes a fable of first love that challenges our notions

Seminal sado-shocker launches Craven's career and a new direction for movie horror...

80 THE LAST HOUSE ON THE LEFT 1972

1.85

WHO MADE IT:

Hallmark Releasing Corp. (U.S.). Director: Wes Craven. Producer: Sean Cunningham. Writer: Wes Craven. Cinematography (color): Victor Hurwitz. Music: David Alexander Hess. Starring Sandra Casel (Mari Collingwood), Lucy Grantham (Phyllis Stone), David Hess (Krug Stillo), Fred J. Lincoln (Fred "Weasel" Podowski), Jeramie Rain (Sadie), Marc Sheffler (Junior), Gaylord St. James (Dr. Collingwood), Cynthia Carr (Estelle Collingwood), Ada Washington (Ada).

WHAT IT'S ABOUT:

The night before turning 17, Mari Collinwood says goodbye to her loving parents and embarks on an evening out with her friend, Phyllis Stone. But both girls are soon taken captive by a quartet of sadistic killers, led by prison escapees Krug Stillo and Fred "Weasel" Podowski. Raped and humiliated, the young women are eventually transported to the woods in the gang's convertible; there, after further abuse, they are savagely slain. The cruel killers take refuge in a nearby house, unaware that they have stumbled upon the home of now-dead Mari. Her parents finally figure out the truth, and plan an equally cruel revenge against these unsuspecting "guests." All of the gang members are murdered, with Mari's father finally tearing into Stillo with a chainsaw before the arriving police can stop him.

WHY IT'S IMPORTANT:

Often described as an American version of Ingmar Bergman's *The Virgin Spring*, *The Last House on the Left* is based on a true incident, an event so bizarre and ironic that it cried out for some kind of movie dramatization. The robust creative combination of Wes Craven and Sean Cunningham is more than up to the task, somehow transforming a ghastly bloodbath into the darkest of comedies without ever losing respect or empathy for the unfortunate victims.

Following the lead of Bergman's film, Craven is careful to set up his two female protagonists as real, relatable young people out for a fun evening. Innocent Mari's moments with her loving parents are so genuine and matter-of-fact that the dark fate hovering over her seems especially heartbreaking. It's the same thing with best friend Phyllis; the girls have an easy, charming chemistry, whether chatting about a rock concert or happily ordering ice cream. As a result, the horrors and humiliations they are subjected to seem that much crueler – "Piss your pants" being one of the most sadistic lines of dialogue ever written for a motion picture.

Shocking as these killings are, the real meat of this story is the equally sadistic revenge Mari's parents exact on Stillo's gang after the crazies accidentally find themselves in their victim's home...they actually sleep in slaughtered Mari's bed. Throughout the ordeal, authority figures (a sheriff and his comic book-reading deputy) are portrayed as laughable bumblers, whether absent-mindedly driving past the killers' parked car or ignominiously hitching a ride on a chicken truck gunned by an amused, toothless old black woman.

Ultimately, Craven and Cunningham seem to be suggesting that some of us are decent, some of us are animals, and some of us become animals when pushed to the extreme. As law enforcement is a useless, pathetic joke, we're all on our own...for better or worse. Now *that's* a horrific statement.

Capturing the disturbingly tranquil, glass-boned horror of simply ceasing to be...

79 Picnic At Hanging Rock 1975

115  1.66

WHO MADE IT:

Greater Union Organisation (Australia)/Altlantic Releasing Corporation (U.S.). Director: Peter Weir. Producers: A. John Graves, Patricia Lovell, Hal McElroy, Jim McElroy. Writer: Cliff Green, based on the novel by Joan Lindsay. Cinematography (Eastmancolor): Russell Boyd. Music (non-original): Bach, Mozart, Beethoven. Starring Rachel Roberts (Mrs. Appleyard), Vivean Gray (Miss McCraw), Helen Morse (Mlle. De Poitiers), Kirsty Child (Miss Lumley), Tony Llewellyn-Jones (Tom), Jacki Weaver (Minnie), Frank Gunnell (Mr. Whitehead), Anne-Louise Lambert (Miranda), Karen Robson (Irma), Christine Schuler (Edith), Margaret Nelson (Sara), Ingrid Mason (Rosamund), Jenny Lovell (Blanche).

WHAT IT'S ABOUT:

In 1900, on Valentine's Day, a party of schoolgirls and their teachers from Mrs. Appleyard's College visit mysterious, ancient Hanging Rock for a picnic. Three of them inexplicably disappear, along with a schoolmistress, and local authorities are baffled. Eventually, one of the girls is discovered within the geological outcropping; slightly injured, she has no memory of her ordeal. Spooked students begin withdrawing from Mrs. Appleyard's, which never recovers socially or financially. The mystery of this strange "vanishing" continues to confound one and all.

WHY IT'S IMPORTANT:

Picnic at Hanging Rock embraces the mystery of oblivion with a fragile, soft-spoken beauty that matches its protagonists, innocent virgin schoolgirls fantasizing about fulfillment in a repressed society. Their mysterious disappearance is literally the stuff of legend, at least by the film's lights. And it's impossible not to fall in love with fair, ethereal Miranda, focal point of the enigma, just as many characters in the story do.

Given *Rock*'s unique situation and set-up, it's easy to find symbolism behind every gesture and revelation. Does this bizarre disappearance in some way signify an unconscious defiance of sexual repression? What's with the vanishing of the girls' portentous governess, apparently also stricken with a strange abandonment of traditional moral values? Then there are the reports of a peculiar red cloud hovering over the rock, and later an inexplicable light near a local farm. Were the unsuspecting young ladies abducted by UFOs? Director Peter Weir keeps viewers guessing at every turn, with the investigation (taking up the second half of the film) allowing characters to fully embrace their feelings, one way or another. But by approaching the material with a kind of numbed euphoria, Weir makes us feel what these ill-fated schoolgirls must have felt at the moment of their envelopment...a slow, seductive descent into the cosmic unknown, primal fear temporarily anesthetized by a strange sense of serenity. Apparently some "pure" force of nature from the center of the earth, impassive and inexplicable, has been waiting a million years for this particular picnic and these chosen, chaste souls. Based on what is learned from the one retrieved survivor (found with a head wound but no broken bones, negating the possibility of a fall), their experience may have been a violent one. When all the theories, spiritual and otherwise, have been exhausted, we are left with a final flashback image of Miranda as she leaves for her legendary picnic, eternally beautiful and otherworldly, waving goodbye with a sweet-sad goodness that breaks the heart. It is horror at its most poetic...and potent.

Clashing social and religious dogma fuels this intense, erotic "no way out" thriller...

78 THE WICKER MAN 1973

88 1.85

Poster/photos: © 1973 British Lion Films. Distributed by Warner Bros

Flesh to touch...
Flesh to burn!
on't keep the Wicker Man waiting!
ANTHONY SHAFFER'S
THE WICKER MAN
Starring
"THE WICKER MAN" · EDWARD WOODWARD · BRITT EKLAND · DIANE CILENTO · INGRID PITT
and CHRISTOPHER LEE as Lord Summerisle
Produced by PETER SNELL · Directed by ROBIN HARDY · Screenplay by ANTHONY SHAFFER
From Warner Bros A Warner Communications Company

WHO MADE IT:

British Lion Films (U.K.)/Warner Bros. (U.S.). Director: Robin Hardy. Producer: Peter Snell. Writer: Anthony Shaffer. Cinematography (Eastmancolor): Harry Waxman. Music: Paul Giovanni. Starring Edward Woodward (Sergeant Howie), Christopher Lee (Lord Summerisle), Diane Cilento (Miss Rose), Britt Ekland (Willow), Ingrid Pitt (Librarian), Linsay Kemp (Alder MacGreagor).

WHAT IT'S ABOUT:

No-nonsense Police Sergeant Howie arrives at the isolated community of Summerisle to investigate the anonymous report of a missing child. At first the locals deny such a girl ever existed, then they claim she was recently killed. The opening of her coffin reveals a dead hare, frustrating Howie and convincing him that the residents of Summerisle are fully depraved and potentially dangerous. Being a Christian, he is horrified by the island's bizarre return to Celtic paganism, although island leader Lord Summerisle defends this development with cheery pragmatism. Convinced that the child he seeks is still alive and will be sacrificed on May Day, Howie uses his policeman's skills to eventually locate her. But Summerisle ultimately reveals the entire "missing child" scenario to be a hoax; it was the virginal Howie (who doesn't believe in premarital sex) who was always their intended sacrifice, lured to the island for a ritualistic event. Placed in a large, hollow wicker statue, which is then set on fire, the sergeant curses his murderers and defies their Pagan chanting by shouting out Psalm 23, beseeching God to accept his soul into heaven as he perishes.

WHY IT'S IMPORTANT:

In the early '70s, new directions for horror movies were being pursued by restless, imaginative filmmakers who had grown bored with the conventional fantasy scenarios. Robin Hardy's *The Wicker Man*, written by Anthony (*Sleuth*) Shaffer, is a curious combination of thriller, social commentary and existential musical, twisting these unrelated genres into a satisfying whole. The result is one of the most acclaimed horror films in cinema history.

The "no way out" formula has served many a nail-biter, but the unique circumstances of *The Wicker Man* offer a multitude of unexpected pleasures: the tranquil island of Summerisle, alive with a bizarre and deadly form of reconstructed Celtic paganism, is a self-contained universe utterly dedicated to its contorted religious dogma. Presented first as an intolerant martinet (his arrogant erasing of a school blackboard elicits gasps), Sergeant Howie eventually wins us over not only with his fervent dedication to duty, but a genuine concern for the imperiled little girl he is seeking. As opposite number Christopher Lee points out, Howie has fully earned the role of Christ-like martyr at film's end. Some have deemed his final damnation of the burners, the only salvo he can fire at his oppressors, as more than justified under the circumstances, while others view it as a defeat for his Christian faith. Whatever one's point of view, it's certainly a powerful way to end the story.

With freshness, smart players, a simple but thoughtful plot and an effective twist ending as assets, *The Wicker Man* stands as a unique experience in horror filmdom. It continues to intrigue fans of the genre, reminding us that faith in its purest form can be deadly, and that perspective is everything in life.

77 THE DEVIL AND DANIEL WEBSTER 1941

106 1.33

aka: All That Money Can Buy

WHO MADE IT:

RKO Radio Pictures (U.S.). Director: William Dieterle. Producer: William Dieterle. Writers: Dan Totheroh, Stephen Vincent Benet, based on a short story by Benet. Cinematography (b/w): Joseph August. Music: Bernard Herrmann. Starring Edward Arnold (Daniel Webster), Walter Huston (Mr. Scratch), Jane Darwell (Ma Stone), Anne Shirley (Mary Stone), James Craig (Jabez Stone), Simone Simon (Belle), Gene Lockhart (Squire Slossum), John Qualen (Miser Stevens).

WHAT IT'S ABOUT:

In New Hampshire, down-on-his-luck farmer Jabez Stone makes a deal with Mr. Scratch, aka the Devil: seven years of money, and all that money can buy…for his soul. Led into a life of selfishness and indifference to his neighbors, Jabez ignores his loving wife and mother, preferring the company of Scratch's female accomplice Belle. Eventually, statesman/friend Daniel Webster himself confronts Jabez, who finally repents, renounces his wicked pact and begs for forgiveness. Webster defends Stone in a bizarre midnight court containing a ghostly jury of tarnished Americans. Speaking eloquently, he convinces them all not to let the country "go to the Devil!" Jabez is freed, and Mr. Scratch looks for victims elsewhere.

WHY IT'S IMPORTANT:

Known under a few titles, RKO's *The Devil and Daniel Webster* succeeds as both an accurate, artistically-satisfying rendering of an American classic and as a first-rate scary movie from Hollywood's heyday, with enough Satanic iconography to justify its classification as a pseudo-horror film. It's certainly a Faustian fable of the highest rank, with director William Dieterle (just two years after *Hunchback of Notre Dame*) seizing every opportunity for weird, expressionistic cinematic staging.

Newcomer James Craig plays protagonist Jabez Stone, the misguided but decent young farmer who foolishly sells his soul for seven years of financial prosperity. But the tale's real dramatic heavyweights are actually Walter Huston as the wily Devil (or "Mr. Scratch") and Edward Arnold as his earthly opposite number, statesman Daniel Webster. Between these moral poles of wickedness and righteousness a colorful twist on the Faust scenario plays out, with rags-to-riches Jabez inevitably succumbing to greed's allure (he gets a little push from Scratch's accomplice, hellish belle Simone Simon) before realizing the tragic error of his ways, and repenting.

The film builds to Stone's trial before a ghostly "jury of the damned," reprobate Americans all. Here is where Webster demonstrates his preternatural lawyer skills, legendary in political folklore, emphatically convincing these wretched knaves to turn their backs on the Devil and give fellow sinner Stone a second chance. Using fogged lenses, cocked angles and jarring close-ups to reflect both the scene's unearthliness and Webster's semi-tipsy condition (he downs a little Medford rum before the big trial), Dieterle transforms this courtroom climax into one of fantasy cinema's darkest and most memorable set-pieces.

Cut severely over the years, *The Devil and Daniel Webster* has recently been restored to its original running time and picture quality. The striking music by Bernard Herrmann adds much to the film's spooky atmosphere, combining actual regional compositions with muffled soundscapes "from the pit" whenever necessary, as in the climax or Stone's sumptuous party for unexpected ghoul-guests.

"Such a beautiful sunset!": one created completely within a motion picture studio. Matte painted backgrounds blend seamlessly with physical sets to complete a deliciously unreal landscape for Mr. Scratch to inhabit.

The Devil (Walter Huston) challenges Daniel Webster (Edward Arnold) for the soul of Jabez Stone (James Craig).

Another brilliant scene: the dancing death of Miser Stevens (John Qualen), followed by the capture of his insect-like soul ("Help me, Jabez Stone! Help me!").

Daniel Webster's stirring speech to the "jury of the damned" is the high point of William Dieterle's splendidly staged climax. Alternate titles for the film include *Daniel and the Devil* and *Here Is a Man*.

Mr. Scratch himself, Walter Huston, lights up between shots as director Bill Dieterle and young co-star James Craig take a breather.

76 SUSPIRIA 1976

98

2.35

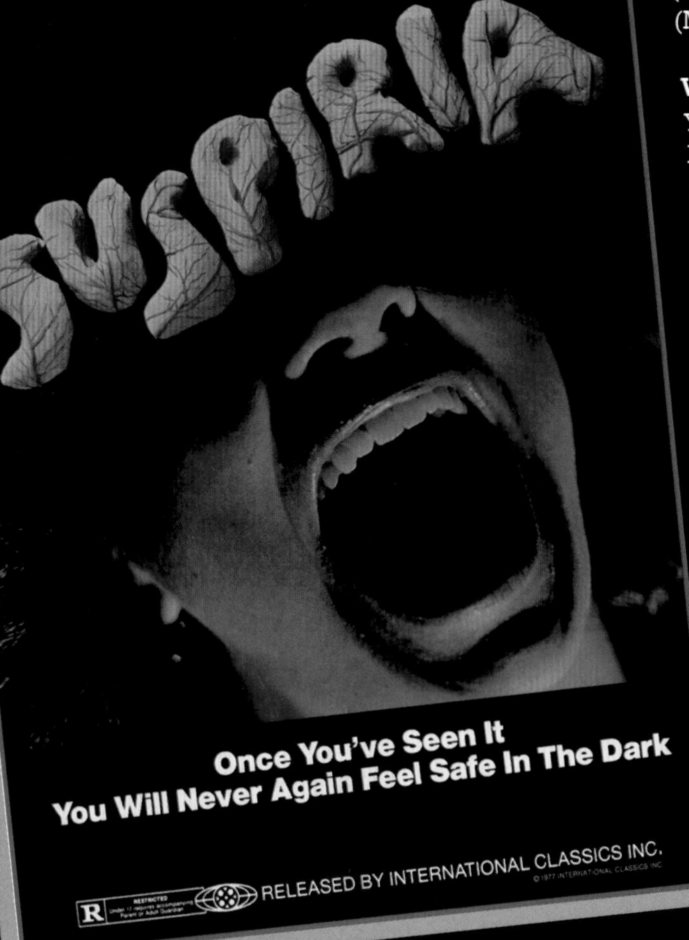

The Only Thing More Terrifying
Than The Last 12 Minutes Of This Film
Are The First 92.
SUSPIRIA
Once You've Seen It
You Will Never Again Feel Safe In The Dark
RELEASED BY INTERNATIONAL CLASSICS INC.
R

WHO MADE IT:

Seda Spettacoli (Italy)/EMI (U.K.)/International Classics (U.S.). Director: Dario Argento. Producer: Claudio Argento. Writers: Dario Argento, Daria Nicolodi. Cinematography (Technicolor): Luciano Tovoli. Music: Dario Argento, the Goblins. Starring Jessica Harper (Suzy Bannion), Stefania Casini (Sara), Flavio Bucci (Daniel), Miguel Bose (Mark), Barbara Magnolfi (Olga), Susanna Javicoli (Sonia), Udo Kier (Dr. Frank Mandel), Alida Valli (Miss Tanner), Joan Bennett (Madame Blanc).

WHAT IT'S ABOUT:

Young American dancer Suzy Bannion travels to Europe to join a famous ballet school. But the very night she arrives, another student is seen fleeing from the place; this girl is soon sadistically murdered by some mysterious, apparently nonhuman creature. As Suzy tries to fit in and develop her skills as a dancer, she is distracted by strange noises and other bizarre events that suggest malevolent motives on the part of her instructors. Eventually she learns that a sinister organization exists on behalf of an ancient witch, a creature of supreme evil that winds up directly threatening Suzy's life. A fiery conflagration that engulfs the dance school and its foul inhabitants seems to end this supernatural threat.

WHY IT'S IMPORTANT:

Mamma Mia! Imagine Mario Bava mixed with Federico Fellini and you've got a pretty good idea of director Dario Argento's eye-popping approach to fantastic cinema. The man is a genuine surrealist; like Bava, he uses "all the colors of the dark" (with a special fondness for blue and violet red) to tell his picturesque horror story, a bloody little thriller with echoes of Hammer Films (a posh girls' school under siege) and *Rosemary's Baby* (a conspiracy of modern-day witches).

Jessica Harper, not long after De Palma's *Phantom of the Paradise*, plays a wide-eyed American dance student plunged into the rainswept mystery of an imposing German academy. Although Madame Blanc (Joan Bennett) and headmistress Miss Tanner (Alida Valli) are formidable opponents, the real villain of the piece turns out to be an ancient, revenge-seeking witch with a distinctive whistle-snore. Harper's character ultimately survives a plethora of bizarre perils before literally bringing the house down in an apocalyptic finale.

Not surprisingly, Argento's horrific set-pieces often cross the line. Ultra-close-ups of sliced flesh are commonplace, and the mutilation of a still-beating heart within a human chest is Italian "giallo" at its most repulsive. It's bad enough to watch a blind man mauled to death by his own seeing-eye wolfhound; observing the beast pulling away at his dead master's flesh elicits groans of disgust from viewers. Still, there is an operatic quality to these killings in general that somehow justifies the extreme levels of violence, gore and rampant sadism. It's a dicey formula that worked quite well for Argento; the critical/commercial success of *Suspiria* inspired two sequels and a fervent cult following.

Anarchic, inventive and wildly fantastic revision of teen body count movies ...

75 THE EVIL DEAD 1983

85

1.85

Poster/photos: © 1981 New Line Cinema

WHO MADE IT:

New Line Cinema (U.S.). Director: Sam Raimi. Producers: Sam Raimi, Bruce Campbell, Robert Tapert. Writer: Sam Raimi. Cinematography (color): Tim Philo. Music: Joseph LoDuca. Make-up: Tom Sullivan. Starring Bruce Campbell (Ashley 'Ash' J. Williams), Ellen Sandweiss (Cheryl), Richard DeManincor aka Hal Delrich (Scott), Betsy Baker (Linda), Theresa Tilly aka Sarah York (Shelly), Philip A. Gillis (Fake Shemp), Dorothy Tapert (Fake Shemp), Cheryl Guttridge (Fake Shemp), Ted Raimi (Fake Shemp), Ivan Raimi (Fake Shemp), Stu Smith (Fake Shemp), Scott Spiegel (Fake Shemp).

WHAT IT'S ABOUT:

Five friends drive up to a cabin in the woods for a vacation. While there, they stumble upon a tape recorder belonging to the professor who owns the remote cabin, along with a mysterious Necronomicon – an ancient Book of the Dead. Unaware of what they are doing, the young people happen to play one of the professor's tapes of ancient spells and inadvertently unleash demonic forces from the surrounding woods. Each of the unsuspecting friends becomes possessed by evil entities, known as Deadites, and the only way to destroy one of these craven souls is by total body dismemberment. Summoning his courage, blood-splattered Ash must ward off his former companions in a grotesque battle for survival.

WHY IT'S IMPORTANT:

The self-proclaimed "ultimate experience in grueling horror," Sam Raimi's *The Evil Dead* more than lives up to its mega-gross ambitions. The movie inspired something of a cottage industry built around Bruce Campbell's Ash character, transformed into a glib sword-and-sorcery superhero as this minor film franchise progressed. But at ground zero things are squarely in the '80s horror tradition, actually more like the low-budget '70s in some ways, with an irony-free group of partying teens under siege by supernatural forces in an isolated country cabin. For a while, it seems Raimi and company are embarking on a remake of Jack Harris' 1970 potboiler *Equinox*, even down to the ill-fated discovery of a Necronomicon (spell book) and a tape of potent incantations. Inevitably a gaggle of especially sadistic demons are unleashed possessing the hapless kids one-by-one a la *The Exorcist* and Romero's first *Living Dead* flick. But by the time *Evil* enters its final act, it's pretty clear that no horror movie has ever attempted this level of fantastic violence and horror effects overkill, and all with a straight face. Mission accomplished, Sam.

At the time of release, Raimi's hyper-charged POV tracking shots (which literally plunge the viewer into frightening terrain, something Stanley Kubrick uses to similar effect in *The Shining*) and the unexpected tree attack/rape gave fright film buffs something to talk about. Raimi and cohort producer Rob Tapert smartly introduced elements of Asian cinema into the American horror genre mainstream before many viewers became familiar with *A Chinese Ghost Story* and its ilk, where evil forests coming to life and ultra-fast camera moves are commonplace.

By showcasing some of the most disgusting monster make-ups ever conceived and pushing the good taste envelope to the max and beyond, *The Evil Dead* was a colorful reminder that old restrictions no longer applied to modern horror films, paving the way for equally audacious thrillers like Clive Barker's *Hellraiser* and Stuart Gordon's

Hammer redefines classical horror with a canny blend of elegance and gore...

74 The Curse of Frankenstein 1957

1.66

THE CREATURE CREATED BY MAN AND FORGOTTEN BY NATURE

"THE CURSE OF FRANKENSTEIN" will haunt you forever!

ALL NEW AND NEVER DARED BEFORE!

PLEASE TRY NOT TO FAINT.

Presented in WARNERCOLOR by WARNER BROS.

STARRING PETER CUSHING · HAZEL COURT · ROBERT URQUHART AND CHRISTOPHER LEE

SCREEN PLAY BY JIMMY SANGSTER DIRECTED BY TERENCE FISHER EXECUTIVE PRODUCER MICHAEL CARRERAS

WHO MADE IT:

Hammer Films (U.K.)/Warner Brothers (U.S.). Director: Terence Fish Writer: Jimmy Sangster. Cinematography (Eastmancolor): Jack Ash Music: James Bernard. Starring Peter Cushing (Baron Victor Frankenste Christopher Lee (Creature), Hazel Court (Elizabeth), Robert Urquh (Dr. Paul Krempe), Valerie Gaunt (Justine), Paul Hardtmuth (Profes Bernstein), Noel Hood (Aunt Sophia), Melvyn Hayes (Young Victor).

WHAT IT'S ABOUT:

A brilliant young scientific mind, fatherless Victor Frankenstein enlists aid of teacher Paul Krempe to realize his ultimate ambition: restoring to dead tissue. The boy matures, his experiments continue, and fina Victor and Paul actually succeed in bringing a dog back to l Determined Victor then embarks on his lifelong dream, assemblin human body from scratch and imbuing it with the spark of life. Bu Frankenstein's work becomes more unorthodox, unethical and ille Paul begins to have serious doubts, and the arrival of Victor's childho sweetheart/fiancée Elizabeth only complicates matters. A murdering a visiting professor and stealing his brain, Frankenst struggles with his horrified mentor, and the professor's brain damaged. This eventually results in a murderous, psychotic human creation, a monster that Victor and Paul somehow manage to overta Resolved to correct all previous mistakes, Frankenstein works alo and restores the gruesome Creature to life. But it escapes the l nearly kills Elizabeth, and is finally dissolved after falling into a va acid, which leaves no trace of its wretched existence. Vic disbelieved by everyone and now even denied by Paul, is perha rightfully blamed for his creation's killings and led to the gallow

WHY IT'S IMPORTANT:

Although it was almost instantly eclipsed by the far superior *Horror of Dracula*, Hammer's *The Curse of Frankenstein* must be credited with introducing the official Hammer style to horror movie goers, a startling combination of class (polished performers, cinematography and art direction) and crass (blood, sex, and more blood).

Today's fans think of Frankenstein in terms of the original book or any number of adaptations, including plays and graphic novels. But in the early '50s, that name meant only one thing to most people: Boris Karloff with a square head. Remaking the Universal classic (unofficially) without embracing this iconic look was a bold gamble for Hammer, but it paid off beyond anyone's expectations. The style of every horror-action movie made today can be dated back to what Hammer first accomplished with *The Curse of Frankenstein*. Like post-war films of every genre, it offered a relatively sophisticated, slightly jaded view of reality that translated into far greater screen excitement. Horror movies simply needed to grow out of their pre-war innocence, just like westerns, crime films and other genres dealing with life-and-death issues.

Storywise, Hammer turned the Universal equation on its head, making Dr. Frankenstein (Peter Cushing) the true monster of the piece, with the pathetic Creature he animates (Christopher Lee, doing his best in patchy but interesting make-up) little more than a misshapen experiment gone awry. It's really a rather nasty study of a great man's driven nature overtaking his moral sensibilities and plunging him into wanton wickedness. Hammer was extremely fortunate to have Cushing at their disposal; no other actor could so effortlessly combine snobbery with empathy, a special talent he also tapped into for his Sherlock Holmes and Van Helsing characterizations.

Not a perfect film by any means, *The Curse of Frankenstein* works best when screened with its immediate sequel, *The Revenge of Frankenstein*. Together, these polished and colorful thrillers provide a satisfying introduction to Hammer's aggressive, audacious take on the Mary Shelley classic.

Reflecting Universal's approach, Hammer kept making sequels to their monster moneymakers. Seven additional Frankenstein films were produced, all but one featuring Cushing in his signature Hammer role.

Christopher Lee played Frankenstein's Monster (or "Creature") for the first and last time in *Curse*. His make-up, designed by Phil Leakey, was a deliberate departure from the square-headed Jack Pierce approach copyrighted by Universal Studios.

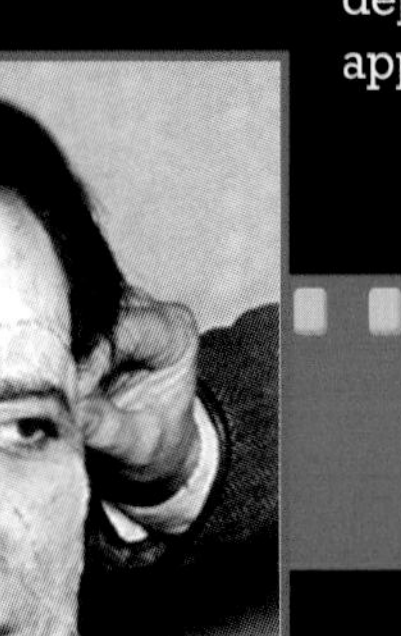

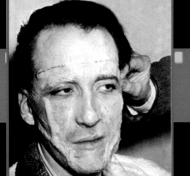

A patient Lee in the make-up chair, midway into becoming Mary Shelley's immortal monstrosity, in innovative make-up by Phil Leakey.

THIS MAN, THIS MONSTER

ABOVE/INSERT: A man of breeding, culture and consummate intelligence, Baron Victor Von Frankenstein (Peter Cushing) is ruthlessly devoted to his scientific research, but also manages to find time for the voluptuous ladies in his life, such as bride-to-be Elizabeth (Hazel Court) and family maid Justine. RIGHT: Christopher Lee as the ungodly result of Victor's life-generating experiment, grotesque centerpiece of *The Curse of Frankenstein*.

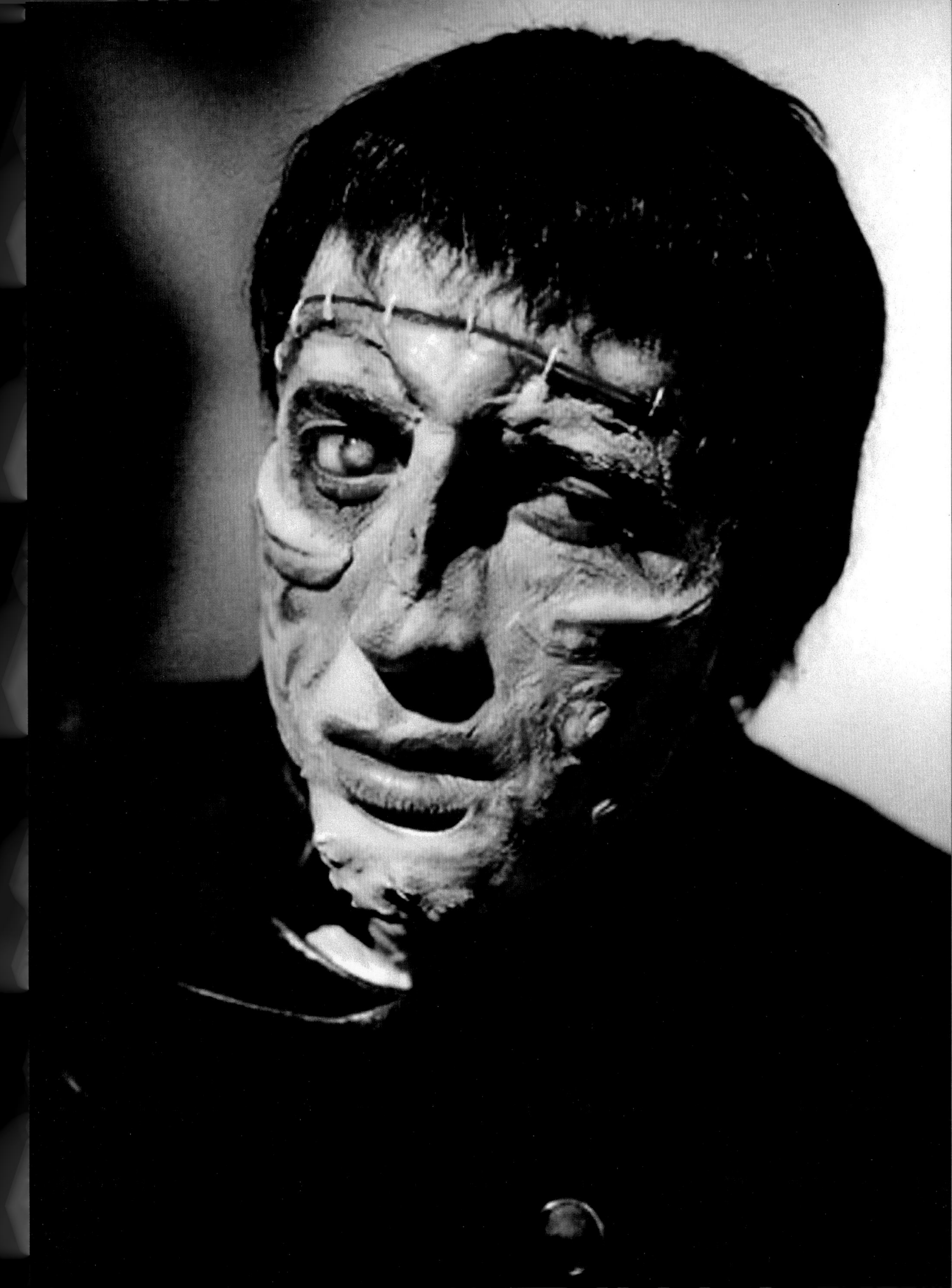

Haunting, artful and impossible-to-imitate low-budget feverdream...

73

Carnival of Souls 1962

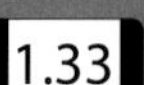

WHO MADE IT:

Herts-Lion International Corp. (U.S.). Director: Herk Harvey. Producer: Herk Harvey. Writer: John Clifford. Cinematography: Maurice Prather. Music: Gene Moore. Starring Candace Hilligoss (Mary Henry), Frances Feist (Mrs. Thomas), Sidney Berger (John Linden), Art Ellison (Minister), Stan Levitt (Dr. Samuels), Herk Harvey (The Man).

WHAT IT'S ABOUT:

A young woman named Mary survives an auto accident, and soon begins experiencing weird hallucinations. On a drive to Salt Lake City, she appears to be stalked by a spectral figure. She also passes a large, abandoned pavilion that seems to beckon to her. A talented organist, Mary manages to secure work and ward off an admirer, but soon becomes engulfed in a bizarre twilight world between reality and some living, threatening dream-state. All the while she is observed by the mysterious wraith-like figure, simply known as the Man. Eventually, a frenzied Mary finds herself within the haunted pavilion, as zombie-like Souls dance madly; it's clear she's been invited to this macabre party. She is finally chased to the beach, and vanishes. Soon after, Mary's drowned body is discovered in the car that plunged off a bridge in the original car accident...she's been dead all along.

WHY IT'S IMPORTANT:

Shot quickly and cheaply ($30,000) by independent filmmakers far removed from the Hollywood mainstream, *Carnival of Souls* achieved cult movie status after endless TV showings in the 1960s. Part art house experiment, part imitation *Twilight Zone*, this odd little gem exudes an especially haunting quality that has never really been duplicated on screen, although Romero's *Night of the Living Dead* and David Lynch's *Eraserhead* manage to catch a piece of it.

The plot borrows shamelessly from *Twilight Zone*'s popular episode "The Hitch-Hiker," filmed in 1961. Here, it's Candace Hilligoss, rather than Inger Stevens, who "survives" a nasty traffic accident, only to be plagued by portentous omens and mysterious figures before the reality of her own death is finally acknowledged. In keeping with "Hiker's" automotive motif, *Souls* follows the initial car accident with a particularly frightening set-piece on the road at dusk, as a cadaverous ghost (the Man, played by producer/director Herk Harvey) glares back at driver Hilligoss from the passenger window. This eyes-blackened, zombie-like sentinel appears throughout the story unexpectedly, occasionally in broad daylight, providing some very real jolts.

But the key location of the film and the element most people remember is the deserted pavilion (in truth, the Saltair amusement park in Salt Lake City), a magnificent "standing set" which haunts and ultimately engulfs the already half-mad heroine during the final third of the story. It also becomes the focal point for all the ghoulish Souls – this is where they literally carnival. Director Harvey demonstrates an eerie command of sight and sound in these climactic dreamlike sequences, speeding up motion and distorting the soundtrack with filtered zombie laughter as Hilligoss tries to out-run her grotesque dancing partners.

From the stylized compositional credits to its memorable use of an organ score, *Carnival* humbly stakes out new territory for the low-budget horror genre, earning its reputation as an offbeat visionary work. Never was the dreamlike nether-world between life and death more creatively conveyed.

Carnival of Souls provides a plethora of nightmare images. The Man (Herk Harvey, also the film's director) materializes unexpectedly throughout.

Souls offers a showcase for star Candace Hilligoss, one of the few professional actors in the film.

The film's well-remembered finale is an amazing, weirdly-stylized recreation of unconscious terror.

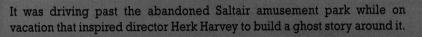

It was driving past the abandoned Saltair amusement park while on vacation that inspired director Herk Harvey to build a ghost story around it.

Kubrick's only horror film is an oblique, methodical portrait of mental disintegration...

72 THE SHINING 1980

Poster/photos: © 1980 Warner Bros.

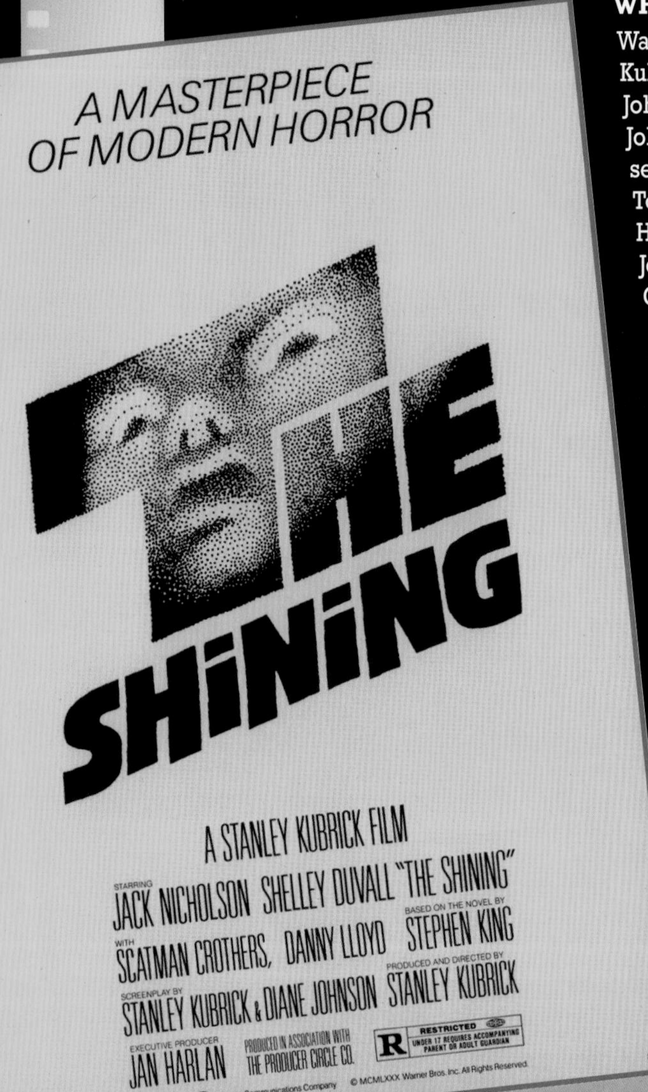

WHO MADE IT:

Warner Brothers (U.S.). Director: Stanley Kubrick. Producers: Stanley Kubrick, Jan Harlan, Martin Richards. Writers: Stanley Kubrick and Diane Johnson, based on the novel by Stephen King. Cinematography (color): John Alcott. Music: Wendy Carlos, Rachel Elkind, other pop/classic selections. Starring Jack Nicholson (Jack Torrance), Shelley Duvall (Wendy Torrance), Danny Lloyd (Danny Torrance), Scatman Crothers (Dick Hallorann), Barry Nelson (Stuart Ullman), Philip Stone (Delbert Grady), Joe Turkel (Lloyd the Bartender), Lia Beldam (Young Woman in Bath), Billie Gibson (Old Woman in Bath), Lisa Burns (Grady Twin Daughters).

WHAT IT'S ABOUT:

Schoolteacher Jack Torrance, wife Wendy and psychically-gifted son Danny become winter caretakers of a famous, isolated Midwestern hotel, which is closed for several months out of the year. A dark history taints the place (an earlier caretaker went mad and axed his family), and soon Danny begins experiencing strange and frightening visions. Although the boy is briefly comforted by hotel cook Dick Hallorann, who is equally gifted with what he calls "Shining," terrible psychic glimpses of murder and mayhem continue, and things get worse when a storm traps all three family members in the hotel. Jack becomes increasingly hostile; he is finally influenced by the ghost of Delbert Grady, the hotel's previous mass murderer, and compelled to terrorize his own loved ones. An unsuspecting Dick Hallorann is murdered, Wendy and Danny barely manage to escape with their lives, and bloodthirsty, thoroughly mad Jack is finally frozen to death in the hotel's snow-shrouded maze.

WHY IT'S IMPORTANT:

When *The Shining* was first released in 1980, critics and horror fans were split. Did Kubrick's front-and-center "vision" get in the way of Stephen King's popular terror tale, or did it penetrate the essence of this concept with a perception and style unlike anything previously seen on the screen? Here we are some thirty years later, and the jury's still out...although no one would deny *The Shining* its due as a unique, one-of-a-kind screen experience. Today the movie is generally considered a classic, mostly because of Jack Nicholson's iconic performance (viewers who forget everything else remember his signature line, "Here's Johnny!"). Indeed, schoolteacher/recovering alcoholic Jack Torrance is the centerpiece of this grim study of isolation, enveloping madness, and a hotel full of sadistic, vengeful ghosts. *The Shining* itself refers to a magical/psychic power young Danny Torrance possesses, enabling him to experience dark premonitions and just about everything else the place wants him to see. It also makes him something of a threat to his own father and the murky agenda of local phantoms, motivating Jack's murderous rage. As for oddly-cast housewife Shelley Duvall, she's appropriately open-mouthed and rattled throughout the ordeal, gamely wielding both a carving knife and formidable baseball bat for protection.

Best scenes: opening aerial tracking shots, the bathtub crone, heartfelt father-and-son chat, Grady's first talk with Torrance; Wendy's discovery of her husband's amazingly redundant work-in-progress; Jack's door-smashing rampage.

Del Toro sheds light on the dark side of childhood with this grim, ghostly fable...

71

THE DEVIL'S BACKBONE 2001

1.85

WHO MADE IT:

Anhelo Producciones (Spain). Director: Guillermo del Toro. Producers: Pedro Almodovar, Agustin Almodovar, Bertha Navarro, Rosa Bosch, Guillermo del Toro. Writers: Guillermo del Toro, Antonio Trashorras, David Munoz. Cinematography (color): Guillermo Navarro. Music: Javier Navarete. Starring Eduardo Noriega (Jacinto), Marisa Paredes (Carmen), Federico Luppi (Dr. Casares), Fernando Tielve (Carlos), Inigo Carces (Jaime), Irene Visedo (Conchita), Jose Manuel Lorenzo (Marcelo), Junio Valverde (Santi), Berta Ojea (Alma).

WHAT IT'S ABOUT:

In 1939 Spain, a ten-year-old boy named Carlos, son of a fallen Republican war hero, faces a bleak and potentially dangerous life in an isolated orphanage threatened by an unexploded bomb, which is still ticking. The cruel caretaker, Jacinto, becomes increasingly volatile as the mystery of a certain storage room with a well begins to intrigue Carlos. It isn't long before the boy is visited by ghostly Santi, a murdered occupant of the orphanage, who predicts doom and gloom for the defenseless children. He isn't far wrong, as selfish and fortune-hungry Jacinto shows his true colors and soon becomes a threat to everyone.

WHY IT'S IMPORTANT:

In the wake of *Sixth Sense*'s unexpected success, a number of ghost-themed films with child protagonists were put into production, both in the U.S. and in Europe. The best of these is *The Devil's Backbone*, Guillermo del Toro's decidedly offbeat and unpredictable thriller that offers more than just a scary story; it's a brutal view of dark human behavior in general, from the unexploded bomb that drops from the sky to the savage, remorseless behavior of a character, Jacinto, we expected better things of. The avenging spirit of a murdered youngster who "saw too much" is only part of the troubled mosaic del Toro provides.

Backbone impresses viewers in ways generally alien to horror movie buffs. While all of young Carlos' ghostly encounters with murdered little Santi are riveting and well-staged, it is the character of poetic, sentimental Dr. Casares (Federico Luppi), patriarch of the ill-fated orphanage, who resonates most strongly; his efforts to woo a younger woman are poignant and memorable. And while the final reveal of his true condition (he narrates the tale) may not have the emotional impact of *Sixth Sense*'s finale, it is more elegant and less illogical. Other oddities in this refreshingly peculiar chiller include bloodthirsty mercenaries and the facility's dutiful headmistress Carmen, who sports an artificial leg (eventually filled with gold she is trying to save from Jacinto's greedy grasp).

Not as good as some of del Toro's later fantasy films, *The Devil's Backbone* gets high marks for originality and raw courage, presenting a challenging landscape for children as bleak as anything on display in *Slumdog Millionaire*. Once again, the greatest horror is not the rotted, fly-infested manifestation of a murdered innocent, but what happens to the soul of a living person who has lost all touch with humanity.

Clive Barker's grisly, unrestrained homage to H.P. Lovecraft and sado-masochism...

70

HELLRAISER 1987

94  1.85 

Demon to some.
Angel to others.
HELLRAISER
He'll tear your soul apart.
NEW WORLD PICTURES IN ASSOCIATION WITH CINEMARQUE ENTERTAINMENT B.V. PRESENTS A FILM FUTURES PRODUCTION
A FILM BY CLIVE BARKER HELLRAISER STARRING ANDREW ROBINSON CLARE HIGGINS AND INTRODUCING ASHLEY LAURENCE
MUSIC BY CHRISTOPHER YOUNG EXECUTIVE PRODUCERS DAVID SAUNDERS CHRISTOPHER WEBSTER AND MARK ARMSTRONG
PRODUCER CHRISTOPHER FIGG WRITTEN AND DIRECTED BY CLIVE BARKER
NEW WORLD PICTURES
CINEDISC
R

WHO MADE IT:

Cinemarque Entertainment BV (U.K.)/New World Pictures (U.S.). Director: Clive Barker. Producer: Christopher Figg. Writer: Clive Barker, based on his novella "The Hellbound Heart." Cinematography (Technicolor): Robin Vidgeon. Music: Christopher Young. Starring Andrew Robinson (Larry Cotton/Frank in Larry's skin), Clare Higgins (Julia Cotton), Ashley Laurence (Kirsty Cotton), Oliver Smith (Skinless Frank/Frank the Monster), Robert Hines (Steve), Sean Chapman (Frank Cotton), Anthony Allen (Victim #1), Leon Davis (Victim #2), Frank Baker (Derelict – the Puzzle Guardian), Kenneth Nelson (Bill), Gay Baynes (Evelyn), Doug Bradley (Pinhead), Grace Kirby (Female Cenobite), Nicholas Vince (Chatterer), Simon Bamford (Butterball).

WHAT IT'S ABOUT:

Larry Cotton, his wife Clare and daughter Kirsti move into an old house. It isn't long before Larry's blood, accidentally spilled during the move, revives a repulsive entity hiding upstairs – Clare's former lover, Larry's half-brother Frank. An explorer of the unknown who discovered the secret of a magical box, Frank ran afoul of jealous Cenobites, grotesque demon-like creatures from another dimension who worship the pleasures of pain. Now Frank Cotton hopes to reconstitute his body with fresh victims, lured into the house by seductive Clare. Ultimately Kirsti discovers what's happening, alhough it's too late to save her father from possession by "Uncle Frank." Ultimately, he is vanquished by the grim-faced Cenobites, who try to claim a resourceful Kristi as well.

WHY IT'S IMPORTANT:

Most horror scenarios deal with human pain as a byproduct of the monstrous terrors they invariably unleash. A few dare to explore the perverse relationship between sadistic, torturous agony and sensual pleasure; some early examples, like *Mad Love,* present this obsession in relatively conventional terms. Clive Barker's *Hellraiser* brazenly offers an entire alien civilization dedicated to these extreme pursuits, "explorers in the further regions of experience...demons to some, angels to others." There's certainly nothing angelic about the physical appearance of Barker's extra-dimensional Cenobites, and their on-screen behavior rivals the most diabolical of demons proper. Still, it's an intriguing thought in a consistently compelling supernatural thriller that combines far-out imagination with domestic melodrama...all with a straight (if decomposed) face.

That alone differentiates *Hellraiser* from most American horror films of the period (think Landis and Dante), which were busy experimenting with hip, self-aware humor. In many ways, Barker's grim screenplay parallels the French horror classic *Eyes Without a Face*; here, a temptress entraps unsuspecting victims to reconstitute an entire human body, not just a face. The injection of a nubile stepdaughter (Ashley Laurence) into this weirdest of adult triangles allows for an fx-laden climax where a pair of stalwart teens use black magic to hold off a gaggle of bizarre, rubbery monsters. Grown-up thematic elements aside, this is still a commercial fright flick with a target demographic to satisfy. But Clive Barker's most enduring and successful contribution to the horror-fantasy genre (*Hellraiser* spawned various sequels) is finally a unique, stylish extravaganza for folks who take their soul rippers seriously.

Best scenes: the bloody rebirth of Frank, Claire's first hammer assault on an amorous guest, the pet shop munchies, carving a rat to kill a sexual climax, and, most memorable of all, "Jesus wept."

Where no madman has gone before: daring explorer of the unknown Frank Cotton (Sean Chapman) uses a magical box to trespass on the dark dimensional domain of merciless Cenobites, "angels to some, devils to others."

"Jesus wept!" exclaims a dying Frank Cotton while inhabiting the Cenobite-ravaged body of his unfortunate brother Larry (star Andrew Robinson).

Absorbing healthy young bodies to reconstitute a determined monster is an always-welcome horror movie concept.

Kirsty Cotton (Ashley Laurence) is yet another '80s heroine who spits in the eye (or whatever) of a supernatural tormentor.

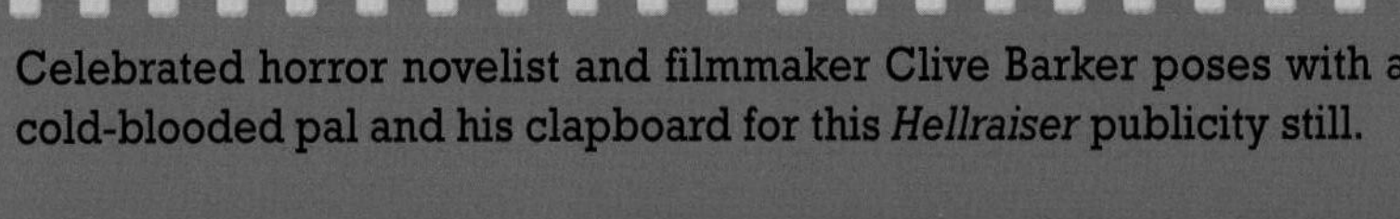

Celebrated horror novelist and filmmaker Clive Barker poses with a cold-blooded pal and his clapboard for this *Hellraiser* publicity still.

Perverse, insanely audacious "head in a tray" flick, a funky Frankenstein for the '80s...

69 RE-ANIMATOR 1985

86 1.85

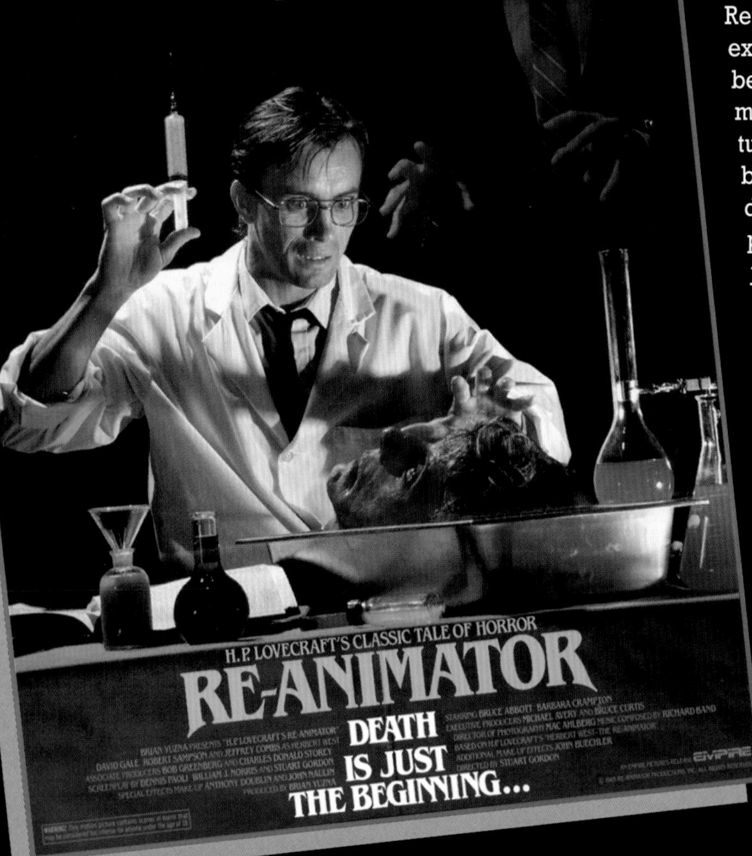

HERBERT WEST HAS A
VERY GOOD HEAD ON
HIS SHOULDERS –
AND ANOTHER
ONE IN A DISH
ON HIS
DESK
H.P. LOVECRAFT'S CLASSIC TALE OF HORROR
RE-ANIMATOR
DEATH
IS JUST
THE BEGINNING...
EMPIRE

WHO MADE IT:

Empire Pictures/Re-Animator Productions (U.S.). Director: Stuart Gordon. Producer: Brian Yuzna. Writers: Stuart Gordon, William Norris, Dennis Paoli, based on the story "Herbert West – Re-Animator" by H.P. Lovecraft. Cinematography (color): Mac Ahlberg. Music: Richard Band. Starring Jeffrey Combs (Herbert West), Bruce Abbott (Dan Cain), Barbara Crampton (Megan Halsey), David Gale (Dr. Carl Hill), Robert Sampson (Dean Alan Halsey), Al Berry (Dr. Hans Gruber), Gerry Black (Miskatonic Security Guard), Carolyn Purdy-Gordon (Dr. Harrod), Peter Kent (Re-Animated Melvin), Ian Patrick Williams (Swiss Professor).

WHAT IT'S ABOUT:

Returning from Austria after some controversial medical experiments, Dr. Herbert West enrolls at Miskatonic University and begins his life-reanimating work anew. Securing the help of a young medical student, West first brings a slaughtered cat back to life, then turns to the corpses at the university; one of these reanimated bodies savagely attacks and slays Dean Halsey, whose beautiful daughter Megan is engaged to West's increasingly apprehensive partner. Now a zombie, Halsey is experimented on by West's jealous rival, Dr. Carl Hill, who makes a habit of stealing other scientists' work. He tries this with the Re-animator, setting off a chain reaction of bloody events that result in Hill's decapitation, grotesque rebirth and a living dead free-for-all that ultimately claims West, Hill and even Megan. But will she remain dead for long?

WHY IT'S IMPORTANT:

Lord only knows what H.P. Lovecraft would have made of this hyper, outrageously over-the-top take on one of his lesser-known horror yarns. In many ways, it's the most spirited horror flick in this prestigious line-up, pushing the grotesquely bizarre to such an extreme that it cannot help but be hilarious. But Stuart Gordon's astonishing creation is no send-up. Its "laughs" stem directly from the madness of *Re-Animator*'s central premise and the alternately mild-mannered/explosive charms of its remarkable star, Jeffrey Combs.

Among other things, the movie is a modern version of the Frankenstein scenario. "I gave him life!" exclaims amoral science student Herbert West in the opening set-piece as he fathoms an experiment gone awry (the first of many). His acquiring of an assistant has echoes of Hammer's early forays and *Bride of Frankenstein*; the murdering ghoul monsters themselves are into body-raising strangulation a la Christopher Lee. But Gordon uses these influences merely as a starting point. What follows is a gleefully insane, amazingly clever, forever-escalating tale of mad scientists, killer cats, a murdered college dean instantly resurrected as a slobbering zombie, and one of the genre's least respected sub-terrors – the headless corpse carrying around its own severed head. Simply put, there's never been anything quite like this; not even Sam Raimi's colorful excesses in *The Evil Dead* can compete with Gordon's nutsy sensibilities.

Special credit and eternal thanks should also be extended to imperiled heroine Barbara Crampton. Stripped naked by her own father, strapped to a table and facing oral sex from a disembodied head...what can one say? The girl's a trooper. And this extremely popular (big surprise) climactic sequence sums up everything that makes auteur Stuart Gordon's *Re-Animator* an endearingly deranged, one-of-a-kind horror classic.

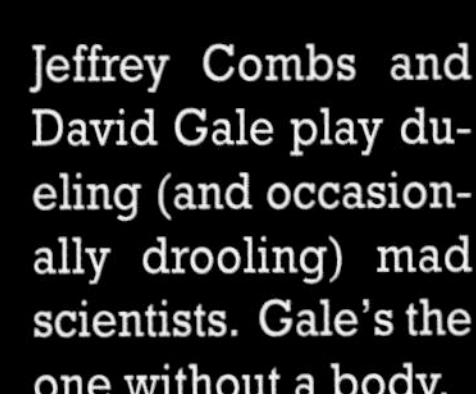

Jeffrey Combs and David Gale play dueling (and occasionally drooling) mad scientists. Gale's the one without a body.

The come-from-behind first appearance of Dr. Hill's re-animated body never fails to get a rise out of audiences.

Thank you, Miss Barbara Crampton, for one of the most memorable sequences in horror cinema.

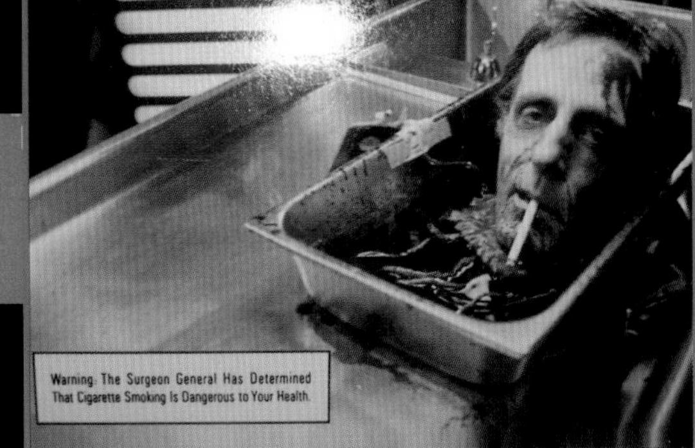

Warning: The Surgeon General Has Determined That Cigarette Smoking Is Dangerous to Your Health.

This wacky publicity shot of disembodied Carl Hill (David Gale) is almost as funny as the movie itself.

Amicus hammers Hammer with a sophisticated and stylish horror anthology...

68 DR. TERROR'S HOUSE OF HORRORS 1964 (98) 2.35 

Poster/photos: © 1964 Amicus Productions

WHO MADE IT:

Amicus Productions (U.K.)/Paramount Pictures (U.S.). Director: Freddie Francis. Producers: Max Rosenberg and Milton Subotsky. Writer: Milton Subotsky. Cinematography (Technicolor): Alan Hume. Music: Elisabeth Lutyens. Starring Peter Cushing (Dr. Sandor Schreck), Christopher Lee (Franklyn Marsh), Donald Sutherland (Bob Carroll), Max Adrian (Dr. Blake), Ann Bell (Ann Rogers), Michael Gough (Eric Landor), Jennifer Jayne (Nicolle), Neil McCallum (Jim Dawson), Bernard Lee (Hopkins), Roy Castle (Biff Bailey), Alan Freeman (Bill Rogers), Peter Madden (Caleb).

WHAT IT'S ABOUT:

Five strangers clamber into a train compartment, and before the train departs, a fifth, named Dr. Schreck, joins them. Schreck is a polite but mysterious old gentleman who explains how the Tarot card deck he holds can foretell everyone's future. Each passenger is offered a tantalizing but frightening glimpse of what might lie ahead... In one case, an ancient curse unleashes a murdering werewolf. In another, creeping vines develop an evil intelligence and threaten the world. The third concerns a tune derived from voodoo rituals that has a nightmarish effect on its audience. In the fourth, a snobby art critic is stalked by the disembodied hand of a painter he tormented; the fifth involves not one, but two active vampires living in suburbia. When Schreck ultimately produces the Death Tarot card for each of the passengers, their dark fate is sealed. As they reach their destination and step out into a foggy limbo, it is clear that their train has crashed and that they all perished in the accident. Dr. Schreck's true appearance as the Grim Reaper confirms this revelation.

WHY IT'S IMPORTANT:

Snagging Hammer stalwarts like Christopher Lee, Peter Cushing and even Michael Gough, Amicus Productions used *Dr. Terror's House of Horrors* in '64 to declare full-scale war on their famous rival, upping the ante with anamorphic widescreen and a refreshing return to the anthology story format. The multi-tale gimmick, presented most famously in the 1946 British classic *Dead of Night*, works delightfully well here, inspiring a plethora of follow-ups and ultimately defining Amicus itself. Many have correctly compared *Dr. Terror*'s "nasty boy" sense of humor to the morbidly gleeful twist endings of E.C.'s celebrated comics. Ironically, Amicus would go on to produce respectable screen versions of both *Tales from the Crypt* and *The Vault of Horror* in the mid-1970s.

Turning directly to *Dead of Night* for structural inspiration, *Dr. Terror* offers five short horror tales (with efficient titles like "Vampire" and "Werewolf") tied together by a spooky bookend device, in this case strangers on a train having their dark futures foretold. The stories are all stylish one-jokers (full 'scope adding a certain freshness) and the wraparound gimmick is especially well-crafted, with portentous green light haloing Dr. Schreck as he grimly uncovers the Tarot Death card for each and every passenger. Their eventual arrival in the next world, at an abandoned, fog-shrouded

67 THE OMEN 1976

111 2.35

Poster/photos: © 1976 20th Century Fox

YOU HAVE BEEN WARNED
IF SOMETHING FRIGHTENING HAPPENS TO YOU TODAY, THINK ABOUT IT
IT MAY BE
THE OMEN
TWENTIETH CENTURY-FOX Presents
GREGORY PECK LEE REMICK
THE OMEN
A HARVEY BERNHARD-MACE NEUFELD PRODUCTION
Co-starring DAVID WARNER BILLIE WHITELAW
Directed by RICHARD DONNER
Executive Producer MACE NEUFELD Produced by HARVEY BERNHARD
Written by DAVID SELTZER Music JERRY GOLDSMITH PANAVISION® Prints by DELUXE®
R RESTRICTED
ORIGINAL SOUNDTRACK ALBUM ON TATTOO RECORDS AND TAPES. DISTRIBUTED BY R.C.A. RECORDS

WHO MADE IT:

20th Century-Fox (U.S./U.K.). Director: Richard Donner. Producer: Harvey Bernhard. Writer: David Seltzer. Cinematography (Deluxe Color): Gilbert Taylor. Music: Jerry Goldsmith. Starring Gregory Peck (Robert Thorn), Lee Remick (Katherine Thorn), David Warner (Jennings), Billie Whitelaw (Mrs. Baylock), Harvey Stephens (Damien), Patrick Troughton (Father Brennan), Martin Benson (Father Spiletto), Robert Rietty (Monk), Tommy Duggan (Priest).

WHAT IT'S ABOUT:

Robert Thorn, the U.S. Ambassador to Italy, willingly substitutes an infant given to him by a local priest after his distraught wife, Katherine, has a stillborn child. They name the child Damien and raise it as their own. But soon, bizarre and monstrous events begin to take place: Damien's first nanny hangs herself, animals in general seem terror-stricken by him, and he has a desperate panic attack whenever he's taken near a church. A mysterious new nanny, Mrs. Baylock, is actually more than she seems: Baylock is in truth part of a conspiracy that has targeted the Thorns. Little Damien is actually a literal anti-Christ, deliberately insinuated into this American family because of the political advantages...according to a prophecy from the Book of Revelation, Satan's son, baring a 666 birthmark, will rise as a powerful world leader. As Robert desperately puts the pieces of this insidious plot together, working with ill-fated allies, he becomes embroiled in more murder and mayhem. Katherine is killed, Mrs. Baylock is thwarted in a violent encounter, and Damien is nearly slain by his own foster father on the altar of God. But Thorn is shot to death, and Damien is ultimately free to grow-up as a very real threat to humankind.

WHY IT'S IMPORTANT:

Considering that it stands in the enormous creative shadow of *The Exorcist*, Richard Donner's *The Omen* is actually a better movie than it has any right to be. The very presence of Gregory Peck and Lee Remick suggests a glossy Hollywood take (Billie Whitelaw's more interesting as the literal nanny from Hell), but David Seltzer's original screenplay makes clever use of the Book of Revelation to fashion a tense, reasonably believable satanic conspiracy yarn. His mystery structure works well, most notably in the disturbing discoveries of photographer-victim David Warner and the origins of the conspiracy itself. Director Donner (who helmed the immortal *Twilight Zone* episode "Nightmare at 20,000 Feet" and would soon tackle *Superman*) uses commercial scare techniques throughout, but every set-piece is expertly realized; this is a first-class studio entertainment with all the trimmings. And given the film it's attempting to orbit, ultra-dramatic parental angst, inventive camera moves and shocking "death by the devil" scenes would appear to be creative prerequisites.

In the end, however, the relentless one-sidedness of this battle, usually a positive in films trying to be edgy, wears the viewer down. Handsomely-mounted suspense sequences inevitably give way to the repellent flavors of incessant sadism. Indeed, if *The Omen* had continued for another ten minutes, it would probably be unbearable...a widescreen, state-of-the-art snuff film without hope or humanity. Behind-the-camera plusses: composer Jerry Goldsmith delivers some arresting Gregorian chants (they won the noted composer his only Oscar), while cinematographer Gilbert Taylor is clearly having fun experimenting with wide, soft lenses, often catching the "star glow" effect (an elegant signifier of supernatural cinema since *Rosemary's Baby*).

Landis' landmark lycanthrope re-do: funny, spooky and aggressively gross...

66 AN AMERICAN WEREWOLF IN LONDON 1981

1.85

ROM THE DIRECTOR OF ANIMAL HOUSE...
DIFFERENT KIND OF ANIMAL.
AN AMERICAN WEREWOLF IN LONDON
THE MONSTER MOVIE
POLYGRAM PICTURES PRESENTS
A LYCANTHROPE FILMS LIMITED PRODUCTION
AN AMERICAN WEREWOLF IN LONDON
STARRING DAVID NAUGHTON, JENNY AGUTTER
GRIFFIN DUNNE & JOHN WOODVINE
ORIGINAL MUSIC BY ELMER BERNSTEIN
EXECUTIVE PRODUCERS PETER GUBER & JON PETERS
PRODUCED BY GEORGE FOLSEY, JR.
WRITTEN AND DIRECTED BY JOHN LANDIS
R

WHO MADE IT:

Universal Pictures/Polygram Filmed Entertainment (U.S.). Director: John Landis. Writer: John Landis. Producers: George Folsey Jr., Jon Peters, Peter Guber. Cinematography (Technicolor): Robert Paynter. Music: Elmer Bernstein. Monster make-up effects: Rick Baker. Starring David Naughton (David Kessler), Griffin Dunne (Jack Goodman), Jenny Agutter (Nurse Alex Price), John Woodvine (Dr. J.S. Hirsh), Frank Oz (Mr. Collins/Miss Piggu), John Landis (Man being smashed in window).

WHAT IT'S ABOUT:

David Kessler and Jack Goodman are two American college students backpacking across the Yorkshire moors. With the rising of the full moon, they are attacked by a mysterious large animal, and Jack is killed. Soon after, the recovering David begins to have bizarre hallucinations, with the reanimated corpse of Jack visiting him regularly and warning him that he has become a werewolf. Sure enough, Kessler soon transforms into a four-footed, furry monster, and begins slaughtering the local population of London on a nightly basis. Cared for by a pretty nurse but urged to kill himself by Jack, David suffers the tortures of the damned before he is shot to death by disbelieving police, even as the girl confesses her love for him.

WHY IT'S IMPORTANT:

Like it's kissin' cousin *The Howling*, *An American Werewolf in London* resurrects the Hollywood lycanthrope with a canny mixture of laughs and vicious monster action. In both cases, an artful horror movie geek is at the helm, ensuring plenty of tender loving care and a hip, playfully defiant 1980s sensibility that informs every frame. Taking a shot at conservative John Wayne's *The Alamo* in the very first scene is only the beginning. Undermining cinema's traditional balance between humor and horror is John Landis' key objective, and it's little wonder this film inspired none other than Michael Jackson to hire the free-spirited director as ringleader of Jackson's equally scary/funny werewolf-themed video, *Thriller*.

Digging a little deeper, Landis pays homage to Universal's horror legacy in ways he may not even have been aware of. Two pals in an exotic, remote location who share a fatal encounter with the horrific unknown forms the basis of Robert E. Howard's seminal "Pigeons from Hell," deftly filmed by Universal for their *Thriller* TV series in 1961. The fact that the slaughtered friend hangs around for informative chats in an increasingly decomposed state only adds to a surreal sense of disorientation (like the nightmare-within-a-nightmare gag, fresh in the mid-80s), playing into Landis' comedic tone while providing necessary exposition.

It was Griffin Dunne's wild make-up job, along with the titular monster's, that wound up becoming the most celebrated component of the movie, earning *Werewolf* a well-deserved Oscar for Rick Baker. Showcasing David Naughton's initial transformation in a well-lighted room took nerve - *The Howling* opted for dark chiaroscuro - as did the controversial decision to go with a four-footed wolf-beast rather than a traditional snouted humanoid a la Hull, Chaney Jr. or Reed.

Not exactly a classic but certainly audacious, *An American Werewolf in London* is finally more than just the sum of its considerable parts. Pleasures of irreverence aside, it reminds us of a specific, never-to-be-repeated era in Hollywood when make-up effects and costuming for horror movies were at their creative height.

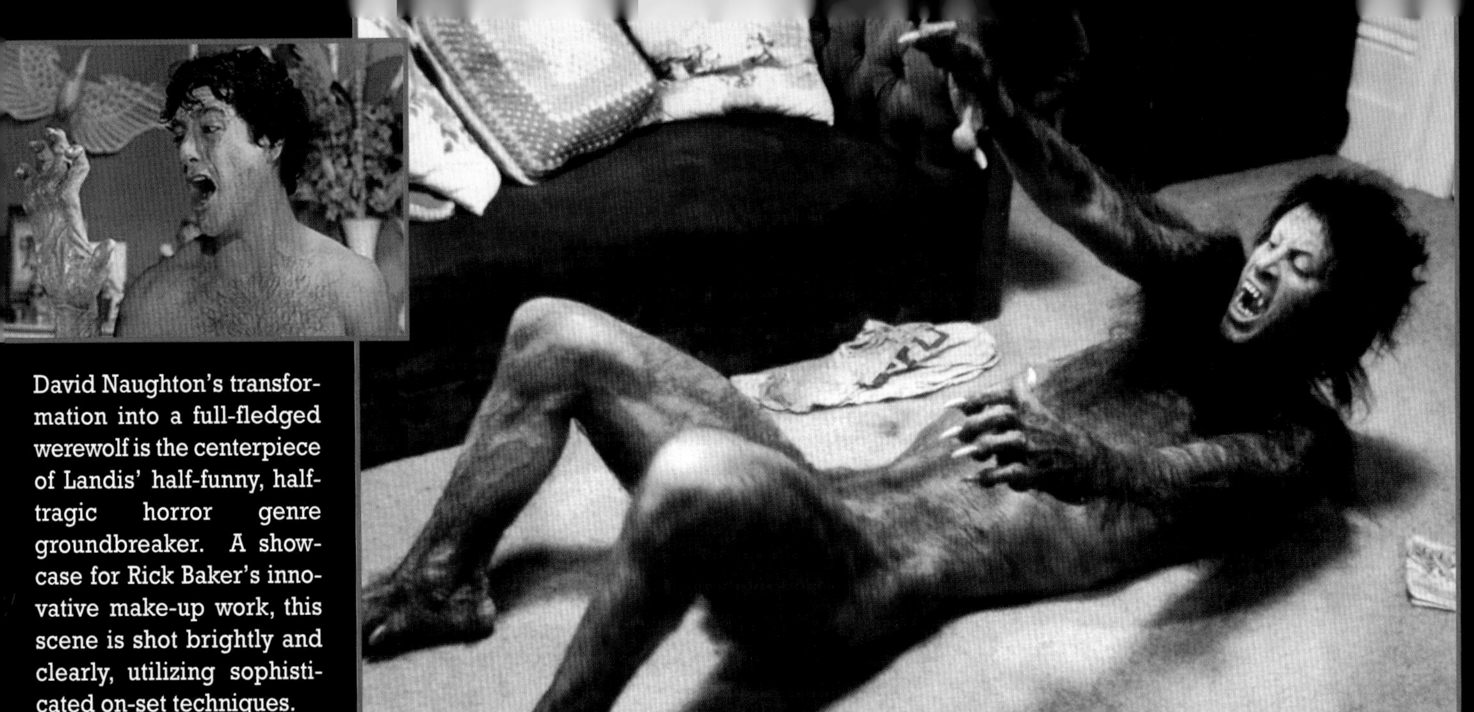

David Naughton's transformation into a full-fledged werewolf is the centerpiece of Landis' half-funny, half-tragic horror genre groundbreaker. A showcase for Rick Baker's innovative make-up work, this scene is shot brightly and clearly, utilizing sophisticated on-set techniques.

An unkind cut: This double-nightmare gag proved highly entertaining for early '80s audiences.

Some fans were turned off by the four-footed, mad dog-like werewolf dished up by Landis and company, preferring Joe Dante's *Curse of the Demon* -inspired humanoids from *The Howling*, released the same year. Monster Boomers Landis and Dante pretty much dueled to a draw in the '80s lycanthrope sweepstakes.

Gore was a part, but not the focus, of this pungent return to classic Universal horror, subtitled "The Monster Movie."

Griffin Dunne's "dead friend" routine nearly steals *American Werewolf*.

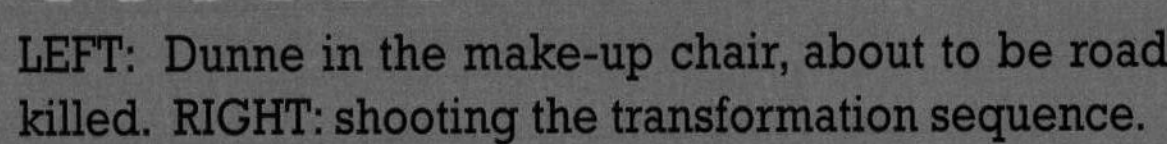

LEFT: Dunne in the make-up chair, about to be road-killed. RIGHT: shooting the transformation sequence.

Psychological horror at its most disturbing, with a Henry James pedigree...

65 THE INNOCENTS 1961

2.35

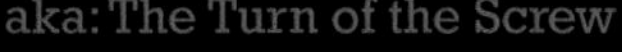

aka: The Turn of the Screw

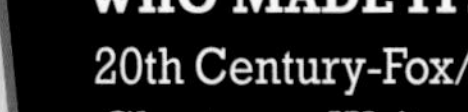

WHO MADE IT:

20th Century-Fox/Achilles (U.K.). Director: Jack Clayton. Producer: Jack Clayton. Writers: William Archibald, Truman Capote (additional dialogue), based on the novella "The Turn of the Screw" by Henry James. Cinematography (b/w): Freddie Francis. Music: Georges Auric. Starring Deborah Kerr (Miss Giddens), Peter Wyngarde (Peter Quint), Megs Jenkins (Mrs. Grose), Michael Redgrave (The Uncle), Martin Stephens (Miles), Pamela Franklin (Flora), Clytie Jessop (Miss Jessel), Isla Cameron (Anna).

WHAT IT'S ABOUT:

An inexperienced governess named Miss Giddens is interviewed by a socialite who is seeking someone to take care of his little niece and nephew. The somewhat callous employer expects Giddens to watch over the children without bothering him with questions or problems, making that stipulation part of their arrangement. At Bly House, a charming but eerily remote country mansion, young Miles and Flora meet their new governess and greet her warmly. But the house itself seems strange and filled with dark secrets. Looking into its history, Miss Giddens discovers that her predecessor, Miss Jessel, was having an affair with the valet, an evil-looking man named Quint, and apparently both of them died under mysterious circumstances. It isn't long before Giddens begins seeing their ghostly apparitions about the house and grounds: Jessel appears tragic, heartbroken, Quint diabolic and savagely lustful. As the strange manifestations continue, Miss Giddens comes to believe that these nether-world creatures are trying to possess Miles and Flora. Resolved to protect her innocent charges from harm, natural or supernatural, she ultimately winds up challenging the demonic Quint for Miles' very soul. It is a terrifying, emotionally wrenching final encounter that ends tragically.

WHY IT'S IMPORTANT:

Beating Robert Wise's *The Haunting* by a solid two years, *The Innocents* offers up a connoisseur's collection of spooky mansion views and hysterical heroines in flight, captured in all their black-and-white glory on an enormous anamorphic screen. And like Wise's film, at the heart of these ghostly goings-on is a first-rate actress, in this case international star Deborah Kerr (fresh from her award-winning appearance in Delbert Mann's *Separate Tables*).

Director Jack Clayton adheres closely to his celebrated source material, depicting ghosts as demonic manifestations of Miss Giddens' unleashed imagination. With almost professorial precision, he sets up the psychological trauma to come: Giddens is given total control of her charges by an uncle so remote he practically guarantees an emotional rebellion. Young Miles himself has a troubled history, and the entire estate reeks of other-worldly indifference. What better place for this dignified, high-strung spinster to unleash her potent sexual demons? And such exquisite demons they are: Quint, played by Peter (*Burn, Witch, Burn*) Wyngarde, is a diabolical ethereal presence, his sharp features periodically peering through windows or bathed in eerie shadows. The equally indistinct companion, Miss Jessel (Clytie Jessop), is far sadder and more sympathetic, but just as enigmatic as she appears forlornly in rainy, isolated fields, and even once – most startlingly – indoors. Meanwhile, the well-named innocents (Martin Phillips and Pamela Franklin) are compelling mini-doppelgangers, with Phillips building on an eerie presence first established in *Village of the Damned*. Ms. Franklin would grow up sufficiently to be raped by an evil spirit some ten years later in John Hough's *The Legend of Hell House*, another significant paranormal thriller.

Miles (Martin Phillips) is comforted by Miss Giddens (Deborah Kerr) in this early stage of their ill-fated relationship.

Deborah Kerr was at the peak of her professional powers in 1961, having excelled in just about every type of movie (dramas, comedies, musicals, mysteries, costume epics). She is perhaps best remembered for starring roles in *From Here to Eternity* and *The King and I*.

Giddens forces hysterical Miles to face his demonic, adult alter-ego. But is this monster real or imagined? The heart of the horror, never better played.

What is the curious relationship between snarling, ghostly Quint and the disquieting young man left in Miss Giddens' charge?

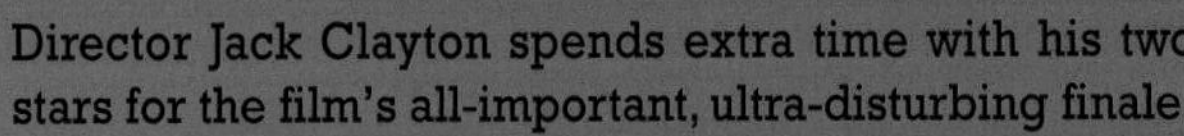

Director Jack Clayton spends extra time with his two stars for the film's all-important, ultra-disturbing finale.

64 The Texas Chainsaw Massacre 1970

83  1.85

Who will survive and what will be left of them?

America's most bizarre and brutal crimes!...

"THE TEXAS CHAINSAW MASSACRE"

What happened is true. Now the motion picture that's just as real.

THE TEXAS CHAIN SAW MASSACRE · A Film by TOBE HOOPER · Starring MARILYN BURNS, PAUL A. PARTAIN, EDWIN NEAL, JIM SIEDOW and GUNNAR HANSEN as "Leatherface" Production Manager, RONALD BOZMAN · Music Score by TOBE HOOPER and WAYNE BELL · Music Performed by ARKEY BLUE, ROGER BARTLETT & FRIENDS, TIMBERLINE ROSE, LOS CYCLONES · Story & Screenplay by KIM HENKEL and TOBE HOOPER · Producer/Director, TOBE HOOPER · COLOR · A BRYANSTON PICTURES RELEASE.

R RESTRICTED

WHO MADE IT:

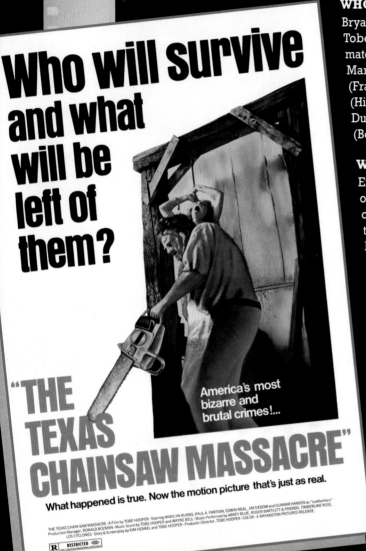

Bryanston Distributing Company (U.S.). Director: Tobe Hooper. Producers: Tobe Hooper, Lou Peraino. Writers: Kim Henkel, Tobe Hooper. Cinematography (color): Daniel Pearl. Music: Wayne Bell, Tobe Hooper. Starring Marilyn Burns (Sally Hardesty), Allen Danziger (Jerry), Paul A. Partain (Franklin Hardesty), William Vail (Kirk), Teri McMinn (Pam), Edward Neal (Hitchhiker), Jim Siedow (Old Man), Gunnar Hansen (Leatherface), John Dugan (Grandfather), Robert Courtin (Window Washer), William Creamer (Bearded Man), John Henry Faulk (Storyteller), Jerry Green (Cowboy).

WHAT IT'S ABOUT:

En route to their grandfather's possibly vandalized grave, a small group of Texas teens picks up a scary-looking hitchhiker who uses a knife both on his own hand, and against one of the teens. After ejecting this lunatic, they stop off at a small, sinister house to find gas. Instead, they are confronted by a deranged, masked murderer named Leatherface and his family of equally mad cannibals. One of the teens is impaled on a meat hook, while others have their brains bashed in or are slashed where they sit. Only fear-frenzied Sally manages to escape – barely – even as chain saw-wielding Leatherface continues his relentless pursuit.

WHY IT'S IMPORTANT:

A grindhouse mega-classic shot in 16mm, *The Texas Chain Saw Massacre* is not based on a true incident, although the opening crawl does prepare viewers for a thoroughly raw, documentary-like experience. The film boasts a masked psychotic named Leatherface as its primary attraction, the first significant bogeyman of the post major-studio horror movie era. But apart from the iconic value of this chainsaw-wielding, fast-on-his-feet hulk, director Tobe Hooper's diseased brainchild redefines relentless; it's an unapologetic excursion into rural nightmare territory that seems to continue what Wes Craven gleefully started in *Last House on the Left* two years earlier.

Young cast members served up for the slaughter are mostly serviceable and certainly game for a difficult, accident-prone shoot, with Paul A. Partin especially memorable as a wheelchair-bound whiner. The final third of the movie builds to a grueling climax where his sister Sally (Marilyn Burns), tied to a chair for "dinner" with her deranged captors, manages to escape by plunging through a window and racing to a nearby highway. After 80 minutes of bashings, hackings and impalements, director Hooper just won't let go, with stunned truck drivers who just happen to be passing by suddenly plunged into the ongoing massacre. It's almost as if the filmmaker has become obsessed with "getting" Sally as much as his single-minded mutilator is. That palpable enthusiasm is effectively transferred to viewers, who are certainly spent but weirdly exhilarated as foiled but forever elemental Leatherface exults in the morning sunshine, just before *Massacre*'s final, merciful cut to black.

Best scenes: the hitchhiker's palm-slicing demonstration, Teri's hooking and Kirk's dismemberment, Franklin's slaughter in the field, an unexpected dinner for Sally, the feeble Old Man's inability to smash her brains in, the final harrowing chase and rescue.

63 THE LOST BOYS 1987

93

2.20

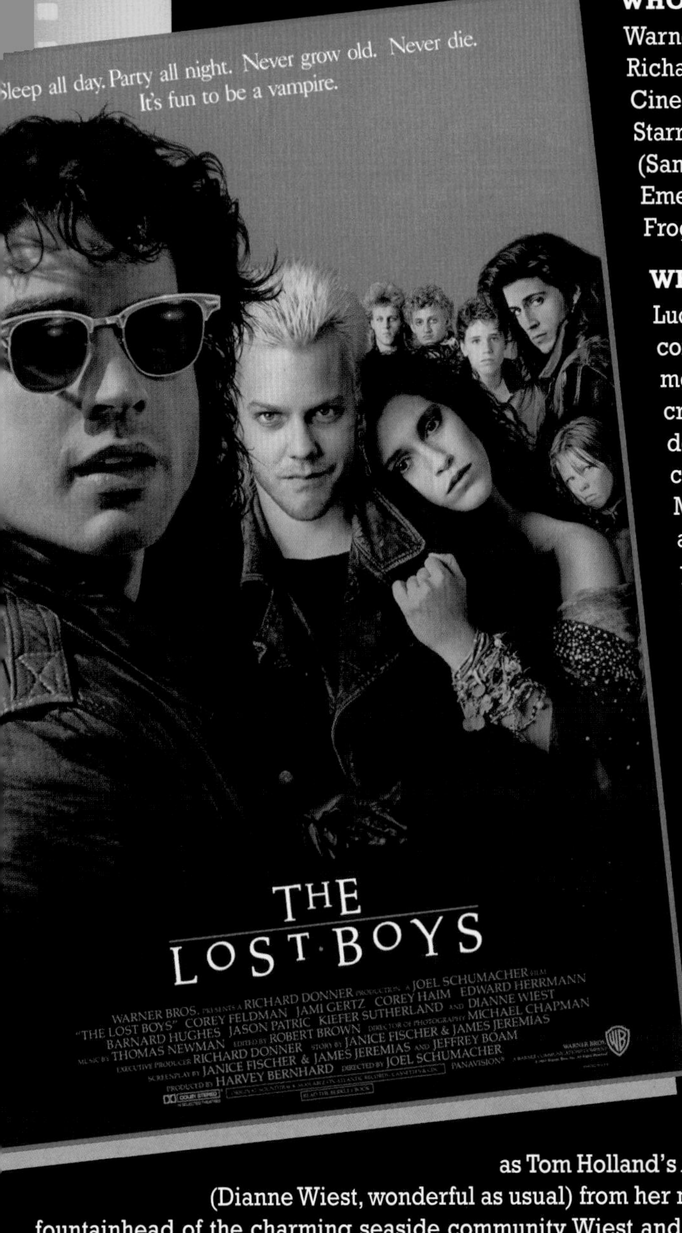

Sleep all day. Party all night. Never grow old. Never die.
It's fun to be a vampire.
THE LOST BOYS

WHO MADE IT:

Warner Bros. (U.S.). Director: Joel Schumacher. Producers: Harvey Bernhard Richard Donner. Writers: Janice Fisher, James Jeremias, Jeffrey Boam Cinematography (Technicolor): Michael Chapman. Music: Thomas Newman Starring Jason Patric (Michael Emerson), Kiefer Sutherland (David), Corey Haim (Sam Emerson), Dianne Wiest (Lucy Emerson), Barnard Hughes (Grandpa Emerson), Edward Herrmann (Max), Jami Gertz (Star), Corey Feldman (Edgar Frog), Jamison Newlander (Alan Frog), Brooke McCarter (Paul).

WHAT IT'S ABOUT:

Lucy Emerson and her two sons, Michael and Sam, relocate to a sunny seaside community and soon become involved with some curious locals. Darkly sexy members of a motorcycle gang are in truth blood-craving vampires, and before long Michael falls deeply in love with Star, gorgeous squeeze of vicious leader David. After a harrowing initiation, Michael becomes, like Star, a partial vampire; not an easy lifestyle change to adjust to. Meanwhile, younger brother Sam has befriended two local kids who are professed monster-hunters, in addition to being comic book geeks. Michael manages to vanquish David, Sam and his pals take out a few bloodsuckers on their own, and a bewildered Lucy is saved from a romantic relationship with the source of all local evil by her curmudgeonly dad...an old hand at this sort of thing.

WHY IT'S IMPORTANT:

The family that slays together, stays together. An old Forry Ackerman pun informs this weird, turbo-charged teen vampire flick that coolly foreshadows today's *Twilight* confections. By combining adolescent angst with Anne Rice-era bloodsuckers, *The Lost Boys* emerges as a semi-superficial but stylishly-mounted thriller with laughs a la John Landis. And by adding a perverse *Monster Squad* element of tweenage bike-riding Van Helsings, director Joel Schumacher and company instantly achieved cult as well as mainstream success.

In some ways, the film follows the same "it can happen to you" plot path as Tom Holland's *Fright Night*. A young man (Corey Haim) tries to protect his clueless mother (Dianne Wiest, wonderful as usual) from her new boyfriend Max (Edward Herrmann), who just happens to the vampiric fountainhead of the charming seaside community Wiest and her two sons have settled into. Max's "boys" are literal Hell's Angels, a gang of bejeweled 'cycle-riding bloodsuckers who terrorize with reckless abandon. It gets even messier when Haim's older brother Michael (Jason Patric) is drawn into the Boys' inner circle as a vampire-in-training, having fallen in love with sexy, sympathetic Star (Jami Gertz), also in the same "half vampire" stage. This promptly inspires the sadistic wrath of gang leader David, played with cool imperious glee by a young and feral Kiefer Sutherland. Toss in a foxy grandpa (Barnard Hughes) who's been putting up with this kind of "vampire crap" for years and the fresh perversity of Schumacher's spirited mix shines through. As for that pair of pint-sized monster exterminators, the brothers Frog, both Corey Feldman and Jamison Newlander redefine "cute"; they're more like feisty, in-over-their-heads anime heroes than real people. (Feldman and *Lost Boys*' fellow Cory, the late Mr. Haim, would become something of a teen flick combo in the 1980s.)

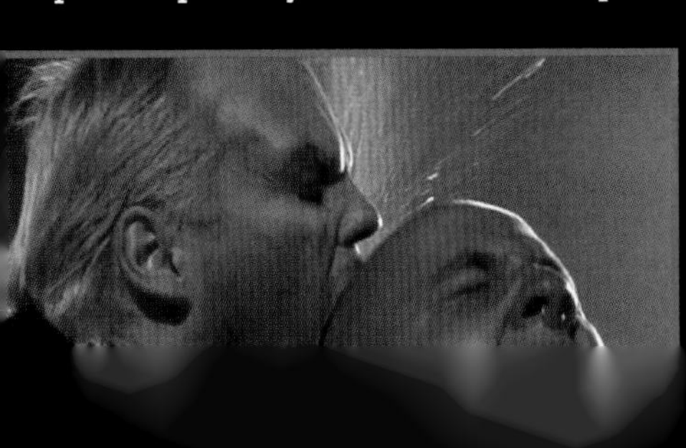

Best scenes: Michael's gross initiation/test at the bridge, fanboy Sam's first encounter with the Frogs, the bonfire slaughter, death in a holy water-filled bathtub, final aerial battle (shades of Hong Kong cinema) between David and Jason.

A classic American horror premise is sharply redefined by angst-era Brits...

62 BURN, WITCH, BURN 1962

 1.85 

aka: The Night of the Eagle

Poster/photos: © 1962 American International Pictures

WHO MADE IT:

Anglo-Amalgamated (U.K.)/American International Pictures (U.S.). Director: Sidney Hayers. Producers: Albert Fennell, Samuel Z. Arkoff. Writers: Charles Beaumont, Richard Matheson, George Baxt, based on the novel "Conjure Wife" by Fritz Leiber. Cinematography (b/w): Reginald Wyer. Music: William Alwyn. Starring Peter Wyngarde (Norman Taylor), Janet Blair (Tansy Taylor), Margaret Johnston (Flora Carr), Anthony Nicholls (Harvey Sawtelle), Reginald Beckwith (Harold Gunnison).

WHAT IT'S ABOUT:

College Professor Norman Taylor is a man on the rise professionally and socially, winning over students and faculty members alike. His wife Tansy attributes this success to the good luck charms and related talismans she keeps hidden from him. One day he accidentally stumbles upon these artifacts and demands an explanation. Tansy is convinced that they owe their happiness to her collection, and that destroying the charms could reverse good fortune and allow "enemies" to strike out at them. Even so, the religious items are burned in a fireplace, with Norman's photo accidentally burned along with them. It isn't long before Tansy's greatest fears are realized: Norman is nearly run down by a truck, his reputation is challenged by a rattled female student, and even darker dangers await. Tansy makes arrangements to destroy herself so that Norman may live, but his sudden belief in the supernatural results in a spell that calls her safely back. Taylor finally confronts the 20th-Century witch who has been tormenting him, schoolmistress Flora Carr. Using an enchanted tape recording, she transforms the college's stone eagle into a monstrous marauder...but in the end, it is she who falls dead under the stone creature's wings, not Taylor.

WHY IT'S IMPORTANT:

Often compared to *Curse of the Demon*, another tidy black-and-white British chiller from roughly the same period, *Burn, Witch, Burn* (aka *The Night of the Eagle*) deserves praise for its relatively sophisticated treatment of a far-out subject. A modern professional utilizing witchcraft to achieve greedy goals would form the basis of *Rosemary's Baby* a few years down the line, and it's interesting to watch the concept being audience-tested here by film artists who clearly know what they're doing. Star Peter Wyngarde, fresh from playing devilish spirit Quint in *The Innocents*, provides a convincing portrait of an intensely rational man driven to the brink of irrationality by paranormal events. And Margaret Johnson is equally fun to watch as the limping, vindictive schoolmistress, a closeted practitioner of black magic with schemes aplenty up her witch's sleeve. But it's female lead Janet Blair who unexpectedly steals the show as Wyngarde's superstitious wife Tansy, hopelessly addicted to her need for safeguarding talismans and exotic good luck charms. The fact that she is ultimately right about her husband's conjuring enemies makes her even more sympathetic and believable. What's worse, we wonder: living in fear of witchcraft, or being scolded by a loved one who doesn't believe in it, and is therefore vulnerable to attack?

Director Sidney Heyes handles bitchy dialogue exchanges and elaborate over-the-top terror sequences with equal precision. Stylistically, his film runs the gamut from smooth modern thriller a la *Psycho*, to atmosphere-drenched gothic horror confection, complete with misty graveyards and cobwebs. Best scenes: Tanzy's alcoholic-like confession and the destruction of her charms, the unseen eagle scratching at the door (an early use of subliminal cuts), the climactic, high-flying attack across the college grounds.

A giant stone eagle brought to life by black magic ferociously attacks college professor Norman Taylor (Peter Wyngarde), a former non-believer in the supernatural.

Miniature sets were constructed for the eagle's brief but memorable rampage.

ABOVE: Set in the upper-class world of academia, *Burn, Witch, Burn* benefits from relatable characters with petty jealousies and dark ambitions.

Tansy (Janet Blair) stands before her collection of religious talismans and charms, which may or may not be responsible for her husband's rise to prominence.

ABOVE: Horrified Tansy looks on as Taylor destroys her charms in a fireplace.

LEFT: Under the hypnotic spell of spiteful Flora Carr (Margaret Johnson), Tansy attacks her husband with a knife.

Universal filmed a 1940s version of "Conjure Wife," entitled *Weird Woman*, for their *Inner Sanctum* series of psychological horror films.

Literate, psychological take on the Burke and Hare travesties...

61 The Body Snatcher 1945

1.37

WHO MADE IT:

RKO Radio Pictures (U.S.). Director: Robert Wise. Producer: Val Lewton. Writers: Phillip MacDonald and Carlos Keith, based on the novel by Robert Louis Stevenson. Cinematographer: Robert De Grasse. Music: Roy Webb. Starring Boris Karloff (Cabman John Gray), Henry Daniell (Dr. Wolfe "Toddy" MacFarlane), Bela Lugosi (Joseph), Edith Atwater (Meg Camden), Russell Wade (Donald Fettes), Sharyn Moffett (Georgina Marsh), Donna Lee (Street singer).

WHAT IT'S ABOUT:

In 1871 Edinburgh, the renowned Dr. MacFarlane, surgeon and teacher of anatomy, has been paying a local cabman named John Gray to secretly bring him exhumed bodies of the recently deceased for classroom demonstration purposes. With cemeteries under tighter lock and key, the nefarious Gray soon becomes a murderer to provide the needy doctor with fresh bodies. Wicked and sadistic, Gray constantly taunts MacFarlane, reminding him of past indiscretions and placing him on the same moral plane as himself. This ultimately leads to a fateful battle between the two men, with MacFarlane emerging victorious. The doctor's victory over Gray is short-lived, however, as a new corpse he secures seems to possess a very familiar face. This startling revelation drives the body-snatching surgeon to madness and sudden, violent death.

WHY IT'S IMPORTANT:

Probably the most solid of the Val Lewton masterpieces of the '40s, *The Body Snatcher* is more than just a great Boris Karloff vehicle, although in the metaphoric John Gray he fashions one of his finest screen characterizations. Like the novel on which it is based, director Robert Wise's study of corruption covers the real-life horror story of ruthless surgeon Dr. Knox and his grave-robbing (and murdering) cohorts, Burke and Hare. Henry Daniell's character, the tortured, guilt-plagued Dr. McFarland, is presented as a former student of Knox's, with devilish Gray his tell-tale conscience...a living equivalent of the festering portrait depicting another famous literary "Gray." Both are hideous reminders of moral compromise, and both are symbols that the protagonists attempt to destroy with force, killing themselves in the process. It's Faust meets Edgar Allan Poe on a Hollywood sound stage, with Lewton's psychologically astute filmmaking unit ideally suited to the adaptation.

Actually, RKO had specifically wanted a Karloff-Lugosi teaming a la Universal, and Lugosi was originally cast front-and-center as McFarlane, a smarter-written version of the doctor roles he'd been playing in *The Black Cat* and *The Raven*. But director Wise preferred the more experienced and austere Henry Daniell, relegating the famous *Dracula* star to a supporting character hastily worked into the story.

Best scenes: the off-camera "burking"of the street singer; Gray's damning chat with McFarland alone in the tavern; the final, rain-soaked reveal, with Wise pushing reverb dialogue tricks to the max.

60 THE BLACK CAT 1936

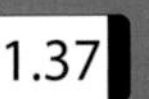

WHO MADE IT:

Universal Pictures (U.S.). Director: Edgar G. Ulmer. Producer: E.M. Asher. Writer: Edgar G. Ulmer, based loosely on the story by Edgar Allan Poe. Cinematography (b/w): John J. Mescall. Music: Classic excerpts, compiled by Heinz Eric Roemheld. Starring Boris Karloff (Hjalmar Poelzig), Bela Lugosi (Dr. Vitus Werdegast), David Manners (Peter Alison), Julie Bishop aka Jacqueline Wells (Joan Alison), Egon Brecher (The Majordomo), Harry Cording (Thamal), Lucille Lund (Karen Werdegast), Henry Armetta (Police Sergeant), Albert Conti (Police Lieutenant).

WHAT IT'S ABOUT:

Newlyweds Peter and Joan Alison are traveling by train to a European resort. En route they meet Dr. Vitus Werdegast, and since all three are headed in the same general direction, they soon engage a bus to take them the rest of the way. When the bus crashes and Joan is injured, the survivors make their way to the nearby fortress of architect Hjalmar Poelzig, an old friend of the doctor's who is actually a bitter enemy. The Alisons soon realize they are prisoners of dangerous adversaries engaged in a bizarre duel to the death. Werdegast's daughter Karen, long believed to be dead, is secretly married to Poelzig, and meets a violent end when she learns that her father has returned to rescue her. A Satanic ceremony is interrupted, the entire house is blown to bits by the vengeful Werdegast, and both young lovers manage to escape.

WHY IT'S IMPORTANT:

Although sometimes forgotten in the wake of Universal's more high profile "monster" classics, *The Black Cat* is a memorable gem in its own right, a loopy, slightly tongue-in-cheek tale of revenge, perverted love, and devil worship. Maybe it's because we've never seen Boris and Bela having so much fun together in a Hollywood fright flick. Unlike later pairings, this isn't a Karloff vehicle with Lugosi in a minor role simply for marquee value; here are they are equals, the horror heavyweights of their day, and both make the most of the juicy opportunity.

To many, however, the real star of *The Black Cat* is director Edgar Ulmer, who soon became known in the industry as a tasteful craftsman capable of transforming even the lowest-budgeted project into something resembling art. There's no doubt Ulmer "feels" his material as a poet does, from the Lugosi character's torment to Karloff's straightforward acceptance of devil worship as an alternative religion (entirely logical, given his wicked character's offbeat predilections). Transforming the villain's castle into a deco masterpiece is a brilliant reversal of expectations, and Ulmer's always-interested camera, often taking on first-person perspectives, records all the ensuing macabre events with precision and style. As always in a film by this director, background music is omnipresent, in this case melodramatic lifts from both the classics and Universal's stock library.

A tad surprised by the film's popularity, Universal immediately ordered up a semi-sequel, *The Raven*. Without Ulmer at the helm, however, the resulting movie suffers in comparison, leaving itself open to charges of sadism and violence without the safety net of legitimate artistic

DIABOLICAL DUO

Having transformed Universal Pictures into a thriving horror film factory with the mega-hits *Dracula* and *Frankenstein*, Bela Lugosi and Boris Karloff became the studio's premiere bogeymen in the early 1930s. Their first teaming in Edgar Ulmar's *The Black Cat* is arguably their finest, with Lugosi cast against type as the more sympathetic of the two. The chess game featured prominently in the film mirrored their own ongoing popularity contest with the public, studio bosses, and ultimately fans of the genre.

First of the new generation bogeyman thrillers: moody, methodical and unexpected...

59

HALLOWEEN 1978

2.35

Poster/photos: © 1978 Compass International

WHO MADE IT:

Compass International (U.S.). Director: John Carpenter. Producers: Debra Hill, John Carpenter, Kol Lusby, Irwin Yablans, Moustapha Akkad. Writers: John Carpenter, Debra Hill. Cinematography (Metrocolor): Dean Cundey. Music: John Carpenter. Starring Donald Pleasence(Dr. Sam Loomis), Jamie Lee Curtis (Laurie Strode), Nancy Kyes (Annie Brackett), P.J. Soles (Lynda van der Klok), Charles Cyphers (Sheriff Leigh Brackett), Kyle Richards (Lindsey Wallace), Brian Andrews (Tommy Doyle), John Michael Graham (Bob Simms), Nancy Stephens (Marion Chambers), Arthur Malet (Graveyard Keeper), Mickey Yablans (Richie), Tony Moran (Michael Myers age 23), Will Sandin (Michael Myers age 6), Nick Castle (The Shape).

WHAT IT'S ABOUT:

In 1963, a psychotic child named Michael Meyers murders his sister with a butcher knife. Eight years later, this deranged killer escapes from confinement, steals the hospital's transfer car, and returns "home" to Haddonfield, Illinois. There, he stalks decent teenager Laurie Strode and her friends, who live a carefree existence in this suburban community. The silent but deadly Meyers is pursued by psychiatrist Dr. Sam Loomis, who works with the sheriff in a desperate attempt to re-capture him. Wearing a grim mask, Meyers murders one teenage girl after another before cornering baby-sitting Laurie, who is determined to protect the little children in her charge. Stabbings and other retaliatory attacks fail to stop his onslaught, but the last-minute arrival of an armed Loomis sends Meyers careering over the balcony, riddled with bullets. Still, his body vanishes…it seems nothing can stop the "boogeyman."

WHY IT'S IMPORTANT:

The bridge between cheesy "slasher" films that proliferated in the late'70s and more imaginative thrillers yet to come, *Halloween* was an unexpected surprise in its day. Director John Carpenter proved himself an auteur to conjure with, crafting a deceptively simple but powerful tale of teenage life in the suburbs, suddenly shattered by the hellish return of a former "neighbor."

Ever since AIP stumbled upon the formula in the '50s, casting teen protagonists in a scary flick aimed at that demographic eliminates "the middle man," getting the audience right where it lives. Carpenter was fortunate enough to have Jamie Lee Curtis as his lead; the daughter of Tony Curtis and *Psycho* star Janet Leigh, she brings an interesting pedigree/inner maturity to the part. Her likeable, down-to-earth heroine holds Carpenter's weird narrative together. Curtis is beautifully supported by her young female co-stars, each of them given a rich and colorful character to play. Establishing this realistic trio of friends at the outset enables the girl-by-girl murder scenario to play out compellingly – later "body counts" in lesser films generally leave the audience in a state of numbed indifference.

Then there's the main adult presence, veteran "odd" actor Donald Pleasance, resolved to recapture the escaped nutjob he's been studying for years. His inclusion adds just the right touch of professorial authenticity; but he's also deliciously metaphysical in his grim ramblings, ultimately confirming Curtis' most terrifying suspicion: that the unreal murderer in their midst isn't human at all, but the oft-mentioned "boogeyman." The final shot in the movie confirms Michael Myers' supernatural status.

Best scenes: the girls chatting on their way home; Curtis spotting the masked figure near a clothesline; every one of the cleverly staged murders; Pleasance's final line.

Halloween begins with an extended POV prologue, unusual in its day, as young Michael Myers (Will Sandin) claims his first victim. Years later, the boy's doctor and keeper (Donald Pleasance) compares this soulless, apparently supernatural psychotic to evil incarnate ("He has… the Devil's eyes…").

Young Jamie Lee Curtis was an ideal choice for the frightened, but responsible heroine, baby-sitter Laurie Strode.

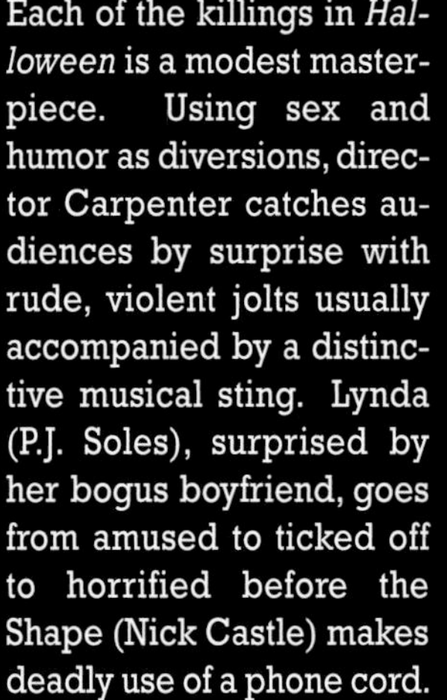

Each of the killings in *Halloween* is a modest masterpiece. Using sex and humor as diversions, director Carpenter catches audiences by surprise with rude, violent jolts usually accompanied by a distinctive musical sting. Lynda (P.J. Soles), surprised by her bogus boyfriend, goes from amused to ticked off to horrified before the Shape (Nick Castle) makes deadly use of a phone cord.

This penultimate moment of horror captures *Halloween* at its best: dark, funny, and seriously twisted. Happy holiday!

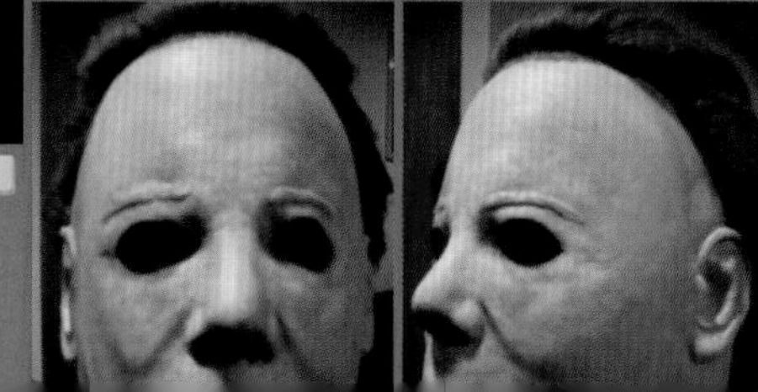

The original version of Myer's "hang dog" face appliance was adapted from a two-dollar Captain Kirk rubber mask sold to the public.

A field day for Laughton as the mad, manimal-making Dr. Moreau...

58 ISLAND OF LOST SOULS 1932

70 1.37

WHO MADE IT:

Paramount Pictures (U.S.). Director: Erle C. Kenton. Writers: Philip Wylie and Waldemar Young, based on the novel *The Island of Dr. Moreau* by H.G. Wells. Cinematography (b/w): Karl Struss. Music: Arthur Johnston, Sigmund Krumgold. Make-up: Wally Westmore. Starring Charles Laughton (Dr. Moreau), Richard Arlen (Edward Parker), Leila Hyams (Ruth Thomas), Bela Lugosi (Sayer of the Law), Kathleen Burke (Lota the Panther Woman), Arthur Hohl (Mr. Montgomery), Stanley Fields (Captain Davies), Paul Hurst (Captain Donahue), Tetsu Komai (M'ling).

WHAT IT'S ABOUT:

Stranded on an isolated South Seas island, shipwreck survivor Edward Parker is the uninvited guest of Dr. Moreau, the island's ingenious, secretive, whip-cracking owner. Through uncanny scientific means, Moreau has created a face of obedient animal-men in his operating theater, which is dubbed the "House of Pain" by all who were formed in it. Among these is Moreau's most perfect semi-human creation, Lota, who was derived from a panther. Using Parker as romantic bait, Moreau hopes to take his experiment to a whole new level by having the animal-woman procreate. These and other mad plans are finally foiled by the arrival of a modest rescue party, consisting of Parker's fiancée Ruth and a daring sea captain. Eventually Edward and Ruth manage to escape Moreau's nightmare island, aided ironically by Lota, who sacrifices her own life to protect the human male she has come to love. Moreau's well-deserved fate is more grisly: he is caught in the furious, hate-crazed revolt of the monsters he created. Free from the whip at last, they eviscerate their wicked master with his own surgical instruments in the House of Pain.

WHY IT'S IMPORTANT:

In the 1930s world of Hollywood horror, Universal had its iconic monsters, Warners its synthetic bogeymen, and Paramount seemed to specialize in mad scientists of one sort or another (ending the decade with a major Technicolor offering, *Dr. Cyclops*). The earliest and juiciest of these characterizations is the infamous Dr. Moreau, played to scene-chewing perfection by Charles Laughton.

It's said that H.G. Wells despised this movie, considering it a desecration of his famous novelette in terms of tone. Truth be told, Laughton's performance robs the good doctor of some inherent Wellsian dignity, very much the way Claude Rains and director James Whale changed the invisible man into a flamboyant scene-stealer. Yet it's this very aspect of Laughton's Moreau that transforms *Lost Souls* into a rich, fondly-remembered classic of its genre. Equally interesting in its own way is Bela Lugosi's turn as the simian Law Sayer, ringleader of the surgeon's race of monsters. Looking ahead to cheapies like *The Ape Man*, Lugosi is terrific in this small, heavily made-up but significant role. His distinctive, in this case only partially-human voice is sometimes threatening, sometimes tortured and sympathetic. And then there's the manimals themselves, no two of them exactly alike. These truly grotesque human-animal hybrids (presented in-your-face during the film's horrific climax) were accomplished with groundbreaking make-ups by Wally Westmore that seem to anticipate the *Monster on the Campus*-style sci-fi monster designs of the 1950s.

Decades later, two remakes were made, with heavyweights Burt Lancaster and Marlon Brando taking over as Moreau. But for pure, succulent Hollywood ham with all the delicious melodramatic trimmings, film buffs can't do much better than Paramount's original little *Island*.

Nominal hero Edward Parker (Richard Arlen, in bed, seen here with Arthur Holt) finds himself in a nightmarish situation after he is marooned on Moreau's off-the-map island. Arlen was a popular leading man in 1930s screen melodramas.

Dr. Moreau (Charles Laughton) is at the mercy of his monstrous man-imals, all of them hungry for revenge against their sadistic creator.

The doctor gives an order to his enthused monkeyman.

Partially a panther, Lota (Kathleen Burke) becomes the focus of Moreau's foul experiment in procreation.

LEFT: Bela's Lugosi's original, discarded make-up design was quite bizarre. ABOVE, LEFT: Lugosi (center) and friends take on Moreau.

The most famous and successful 3D horror film, a handsome, well-crafted remake...

57 HOUSE OF WAX 1953

90 1.37

Poster/photos: © 1953 Warner Bros.

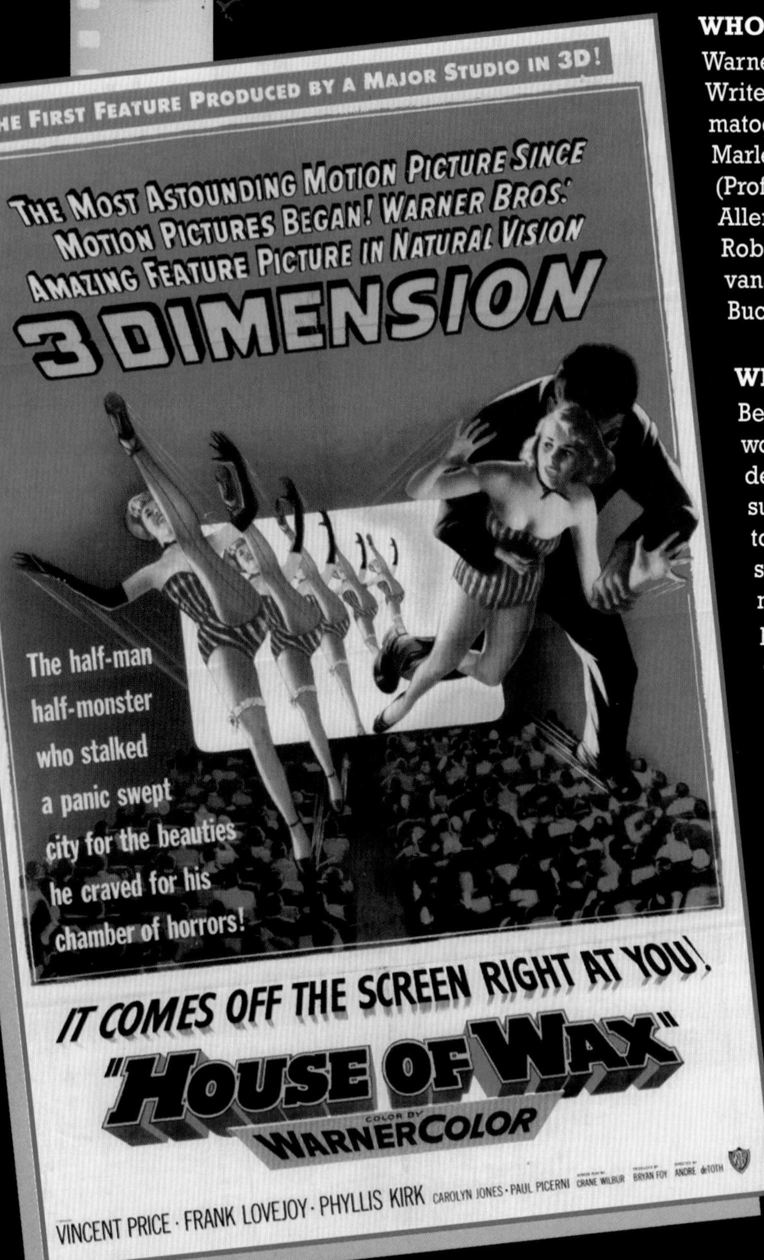

THE FIRST FEATURE PRODUCED BY A MAJOR STUDIO IN 3D!
THE MOST ASTOUNDING MOTION PICTURE SINCE MOTION PICTURES BEGAN! WARNER BROS.' AMAZING FEATURE PICTURE IN NATURAL VISION
3 DIMENSION
The half-man half-monster who stalked a panic swept city for the beauties he craved for his chamber of horrors!
IT COMES OFF THE SCREEN RIGHT AT YOU!
"HOUSE OF WAX"
COLOR BY WARNERCOLOR
VINCENT PRICE · FRANK LOVEJOY · PHYLLIS KIRK
CAROLYN JONES · PAUL PICERNI
CRANE WILBUR
BRYAN FOY
ANDRE de TOTH

WHO MADE IT:

Warner Brothers (U.S.). Director: Andre de Toth. Producer: Bryan Foy. Writer: Crane Wilbur, based on the play by Charles S. Belden. Cinematography (3D; WarnerColor/Technicolor): Bert Glennon, J. Peverell Marley, Lathrop B. Worth. Music: David Buttolph. Starring Vincent Price (Prof. Henry Jarrod), Frank Lovejoy (Lt. Tom Brennan), Phyllis Kirk (Sue Allen), Carolyn Jones (Cathy Gray), Paul Picerni (Scott Andrews), Roy Roberts (Matthew Burke), Angela Clarke (Mrs. Andrews), Paul Cavanagh (Sidney Wallace), Dabbs Greer (Sgt. Jim Share), Charles Buchinsky aka Charles Bronson (Igor), Reggie Ryman (The barker).

WHAT IT'S ABOUT:

Beauty-loving wax museum curator Henry Jarrod finds his masterworks engulfed in flames when his business partner, Matthew Burke, decides to torch their place for insurance money. Jarrod is presumed dead, a victim of the fire, and soon after a grotesque, phantom-like figure in black prowls the night, murdering Burke and stealing various bodies from the morgue. As New York cops try to nail the killer, a miraculously alive-and-well Henry Jarrod reappears and opens a new wax museum, one specializing in horror and re-creations of violent crimes. Sue Allen seems to recognize one of the wax figures as a close friend who was recently murdered, and Jarrod explains that he bases his work on subjects taken from the newspaper. It soon becomes apparent that Jarrod is indeed the crazed killer, covering his victims with wax and displaying them in the museum. Sue, who resembles Jarrod's beloved, long-lost figure of Marie Antoinette, nearly suffers the same fate before police break in on the madman's lair and surround him. After a vicious fight, the artist-turned-psychotic killer falls into his own vat of bubbling wax, and Sue is rescued.

WHY IT'S IMPORTANT:

3D came out of nowhere in 1952, convincing many in Hollywood that the cumbersome process (requiring stereoscopic glasses) would replace all traditional "flat" movie presentations. Warner Bros. dusted off their 1933 *Mystery of the Wax Museum* for a relatively lavish dimensional remake, recruiting Vincent Price as the film's energetic villain. It quickly became the most successful 3D film of its genre, establishing Price as Hollywood's greatest bogeyman in the post WWII era. In many ways, the film is an improvement over the original, tighter and more dynamic. A strong supporting cast (Frank Lovejoy as a detective, Carolyn Jones playing a flighty victim, young Charles Bronson as mute henchman Igor) lends *House of Wax* added mainstream respectability, making it one of the very few studio horror films from this sci-fi dominated period.

Warners followed the huge success of *Wax* with a similar-in-flavor period chiller, *Phantom of the Rue Morgue*, also filmed in colorful 3D. With Karl Malden replacing Vincent Price and a killer gorilla the principle threat, *Rue Morgue* failed to click with audiences, and the stereoscopic gimmick already seemed played out by late 1954.

Approximately ten years later, a third *House of Wax* feature was produced by Warners, conceived as a TV pilot but released theatrically as *Chamber of Horrors*. And in 2004, a new, ambitious adaptation hit theaters, with improved special effects and some nice horrific touches by director Jaume Collet-Serra. Still, for in-your-face thrills (literally) and solid popcorn-movie entertainment, nothing beats Price's spirited 1953 version. And don't forget to duck that persistent ping-pong ball!

Doing much of his own stuntwork, actor Vinc
Price found himself dodging flaming debris
an exciting opening set-piece built around
destruction of Henry Jarrod's first wax museu

Charles Bronson as Igor, in one of his earliest screen roles (billed as Charles Buchinsky), throttles *House of Wax*'s nominal hero, Paul Picerni.

Years later, Jarrod opens a new and improved wax emporium. This time, however, his exhibits are the wax-covered human bodies of murdered victims.

The ethereal music score for *Wax* was provided by studio composer David Buttolph, who provided the same creative service for Warners' *The Beast from 20,000 Fathoms* half a year earlier.

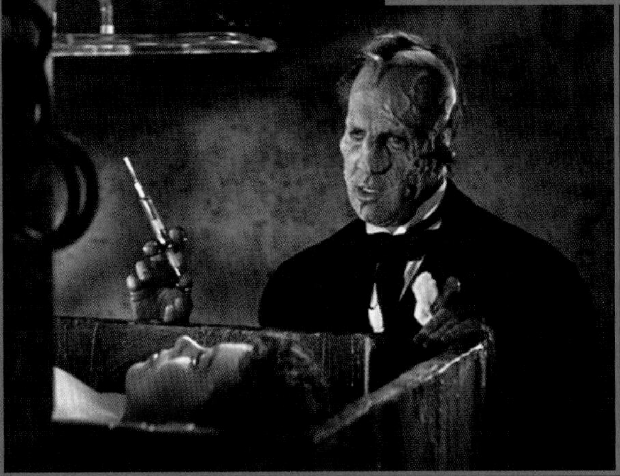

Scarred and p
chotic Henry Jar
begins his reign
terror. Star Vinc
Price followed t
showy role with
similar one in Jo
Brahm's 3D im
tion for Columb
the mostly forg
ten *Mad Magicia*

For all the scary sequences in *House of Wax*, it's the 3D ping-pong ball routine that most viewers remember!

Cronenberg makes his mark in this ghastly tale of freaks and their fabricator...

56 The Brood 1979

92 | 1.85

DAVID CRONENBERG'S
THE BROOD
THE ULTIMATE EXPERIENCE IN INNER TERROR.
THEY'RE WAITING... FOR YOU!
PIERRE DAVID and VICTOR SOLNICKI present
OLIVER REED and SAMANTHA EGGAR
in DAVID CRONENBERG'S THE BROOD with ART HINDLE

WHO MADE IT:

New World Pictures (Canada/U.S.). Director: David Cronenberg. Producers: Claude Heroux, Pierre David, Victor Solnicki. Writer: David Cronenberg. Cinematography (color): Mark Irwin. Music: Howard Shore. Starring Oliver Reed (Dr. Hal Raglan), Samantha Eggar (Nola Carveth), Art Hindle (Frank Carveth), Henry Beckman (Barton Kelly), Nuala Fitzgerald (Juliana Kelly), Cindy Hinds (Candice Carveth), Susan Hogan (Ruth Mayer), Gary McKeehan (Mike Trellan), Michael Magee (Inspector), Robert Silverman (Jan Hartog), Joseph Shaw (Coroner), Felix Silla (Creature), John Ferguson (Creature), Nicholas Campbell (Chris).

WHAT IT'S ABOUT:

Dr. Hal Raglan is an unconventional psychologist who uses unusual, rather flamboyant techniques to help his patients. One of them, Nola Carveth, may be inflicting injuries on her own child, something Nola's former husband Frank wants very much to prevent. As antagonism between Frank and Raglan increases, Nola's parents are attacked by weird, dwarf-like creatures that are ultimately revealed as mutant extensions of her own unhinged subconscious. These feral newborns become vicious and deadly-dangerous the more her wounded emotions are agitated. Summoning his courage, Frank must somehow keep his unhinged wife placated before the mini-monsters she's given birth to run amok and more ghastly murders are committed.

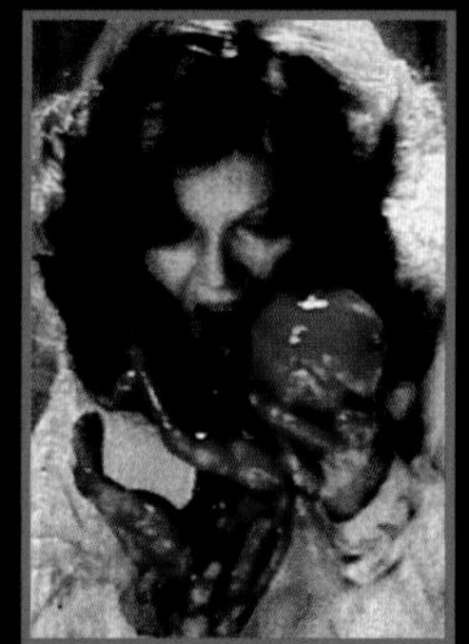

WHY IT'S IMPORTANT:

David Cronenberg has always been intrigued by potentially grotesque contortions of the human body. Limbering up for the more front-and-center sci-fi flavors of *The Fly*, he jumped wholeheartedly into this grim, highly original chiller that combines parenthood issues with a modern spin on the mad scientist formula. Coincidentally, *The Brood* was released the same year as Ridley Scott's *Alien*, establishing the ultra-disgusting, body-bursting "surprise" creature as a potent new monster in mainstream horror cinema.

But Queen Bee Samantha Eggar's third act birthing of an embryonic freak is only one of the grotesqueries offered up by Cronenberg's juicy screenplay. The red-jacketed, cleft-lipped tykes who murder mindlessly whenever their unstable mother's temper flares are the real Frankenstein Monsters of this scenario. These single-minded demonettes appear rather startlingly in homes and schoolrooms (the slaying of a young teacher before a roomful of toddlers is *Brood*'s most unsavory sequence). The end result of psychiatrist Oliver Reed's bizarre experiments in "rage shaping," the creatures are finally vanquished when their fully-crazed mother is slain by her former husband, played with understandable, long-suffering angst by Art Hindle. The final dialogue sequence between this estranged couple is especially interesting and relatable, for *The Brood* is about marital discord, self-deception and parental responsibility as much as exotic murder and mayhem. An underappreciated actress, Eggar is magnificent as the emotionally tormented and unwitting mother of these bloodlusting monsters, a concept that predates James Cameron's Queen Alien by seven years.

55 CARRIE 1976

98 1.85

IF YOU'VE GOT
A TASTE FOR TERROR...
TAKE CARRIE TO THE PROM.

"CARRIE"

If only they knew she had the power.

A PAUL MONASH Production A BRIAN DePALMA Film "CARRIE"
starring SISSY SPACEK
JOHN TRAVOLTA and PIPER LAURIE · Screenplay by LAWRENCE D. COHEN
Based on the novel by STEPHEN KING · Produced by PAUL MONASH · Directed by BRIAN DePALMA
Production Services by Carrie's Group
United Artists
R RESTRICTED

WHO MADE IT:

United Artists (U.S.). Director: Brian De Palma. Producers: Brian De Palma, Paul Monash. Writer: Lawrence D. Cohen, based on a novel by Stephen King. Cinematography (color): Mario Tosi. Music: Pino Donaggio. Starring Sissy Spacek (Carrie White), Piper Laurie (Margaret White), Amy Irving (Sue Snell), William Katt (Tommy Ross), Betty Buckley (Miss Collins), Nancy Allen (Chris Hargensen), John Travolta (Billy Nolan), P.J. Soles (Norma Watson).

WHAT IT'S ABOUT:

Raised by a psychotically religious mother, Carrie White is a painfully introverted high school student frequently tormented by her classmates. But this much-abused girl possesses a secret power: telekinesis, the ability to move objects by sheer force of will. One of the harassing students, Sue Snell, has a change of heart and asks her boyfriend to take Carrie to the upcoming prom instead of her. But Chris Hargenson, another, less forgiving student, ups the ante by hatching a wicked scheme involving pig's blood and Carrie's public humiliation. The plan backfires when White's psychic skills explode uncontrollably at the prom, turning the event into a catastrophic bloodbath. Later, attacked by her crazed mother at home, Carrie retaliates by killing Mrs. White in a mock crucifixion; then she uses psy-powers to bring their house down upon them for a final burial. Although both mother and daughter are gone, the devastating psychological effects of this experience are not soon forgotten.

WHY IT'S IMPORTANT:

Carrie is probably the most successful translation of a Stephen King story to the big screen. With a powerful premise built around two notable performances, and ably supported by a group of well-cast young people, the film manages to transcend its scare-and-shock genre, catching the agony of adolescent angst as surely as the best non-fantasy drama.

Who else but Sissy Spacek could have played Carrie with exactly the right degree of wide-eyed terror, not because of some monstrous bogeyman stalking her, but as a result of her first period? It's a hellish, humiliating scene that starts the movie, setting the tone for more personal catastrophes to come. There's no question that both King and de Palma clearly understood the gut-wrenching realities of nerd torment and unrelenting self-loathing. To provide the appropriate psychological background for our heroine's dilemma, she is given the Mom from Hell (Piper Laurie), a religious fanatic who devolves into a full-fledged madwoman as her only daughter comes of romantic age. Their scenes together are weird, appropriately over-the-top, yet disturbingly realistic; this is Laurie's best turn since her role in 1961's *The Hustler*. The assault on Carrie at the height of her social acceptance is a genuine American tragedy, culminating in a public bloodbath that is both horrific and somehow justified, as least from the numbed point of view of the abused psychic heroine. The movie's final shock moment, part of a sympathetic female friend's nightmare, is one of the greatest jolts in any horror picture, from any era.

54 THE MAN WHO LAUGHS 1928

 110 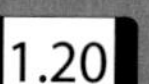 1.20 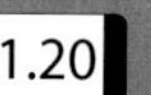

WHO MADE IT:

Universal Pictures (U.S.). Director: Paul Leni. Producer: Paul Kohner. Writers: J. Scrubb Alexander, Walter Anthony, Mary McClean, Charles E. Whittaker, based on the novel by Victor Hugo. Cinematography (b/w): Gilbert Warrenton. Starring Mary Philbin (Dea), Conrad Veidt (Gwynplaine), Julius Molnar Jr. (Child Gwynplaine as a child), Olga Baclanova (Duchess Josiana), Brandon Hurst (Barkilphedro), Cesare Gravina (Ursus), Stuart Holmes (Lord Dirry-Moir), Sam De Grasse (King James II), George Siegmann (Dr. Hardquanonne).

WHAT IT'S ABOUT:

England, 1690. A nobleman is sentenced to death, while his son, Gwynplaine, is deliberately disfigured, the boy's face transformed into a permanent rictus grin. Shunned and homeless, gargoyle-like Gwynplaine discovers an abandoned baby girl, the blind Dea, and soon both are taken in by a mountebank named Ursus. As the years go by, his traveling show allows these two a modest living: indeed, the public seems fascinated by the grotesque "Man Who Laughs." Gwynplaine truly loves Dea, but feels his hideous face makes him unworthy of her. Eventually, records are discovered which reveal his lineage and the potential inheritance of his father's position in the royal court. He is compelled to marry the Duchess Josiana, who is attracted to him in spite of herself. But rather than accept a shallow life as a Peer in the House of Lords, Gwynplaine dramatically flees the palace and escapes England with his beloved Dea.

WHY IT'S IMPORTANT:

Helmed by the greatest horror director of the silent era, *The Man Who Laughs* was Universal's follow-up to Lon Chaney's mega-hits. Like *Hunchback of Notre Dame*, it found respectable source material in Victor Hugo's popular novel, repeating the winning "formula" of a pitiable, deformed creature and a beautiful young woman who either loves or feels profound sympathy for him. Produced with all the trimmings Universal could afford (magnificent sets and costumes, as befits a prestige project), the final result was a triumph for the studio and the last great macabre film of the pre-sound period.

Dominating this opulent experience, of course, is the Man himself. A celebrated German actor, Conrad Veidt deftly combines elements of both Lon Chaney and Charles Chaplin in his heartbreaking turn as Gwynplaine, the living human gargoyle. An almost Christ-like figure, he endures wickedness off the scale, the grotesque laughing grin inflicted upon him a constant reminder of life's strange ironies and the depressing human "comedy" in general. Under Paul Leni's assured and stylish direction, his enormous personal pain is directly conveyed to viewers. Interestingly, helmer Leni and star Veidt were seriously considered for Universal's *Dracula* following Lon Chaney's death. Leni's own, far more sudden demise (a freakish tooth infection) ended that potential re-collaboration.

Final note: *The Man Who Laughs* is the first Universal movie to employ make-up artist Jack P. Pierce, who got the gig by responding to an ad in *Hollywood Reporter*. Pierce's brilliant "denture" work for Gwynplaine assured him a permanent place at the studio for close to twenty years, where he would go on to create and design the greatest movie monsters of all time.

Lesbian vampires, Hammer-style; buxom, rich-blooded and stylish...

53

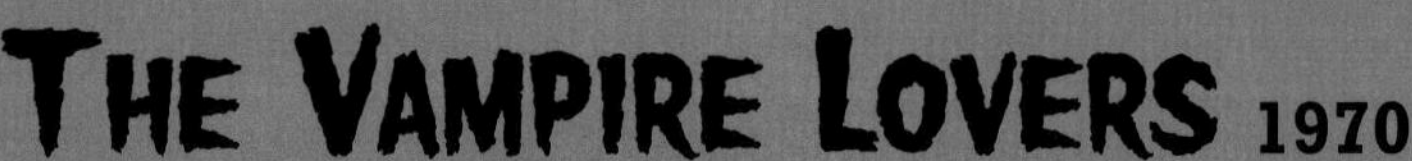

THE VAMPIRE LOVERS 1970

91 | 1.85

Poster/photos: © 1970 Hammer Films. Released by American International Pictures

YOU DARE...
te the deadly passion
of the BLOOD-
NYMPHS!
The
Vampire
Lovers
CAUTION
Not for the
mentally
immature!
AN AMERICAN INTERNATIONAL
HAMMER FILM PRODUCTION
STARRING
INGRID PITT · GEORGE COLE · KATE O'MARA and PETER CUSHING as "THE GENERAL"
GUEST STAR DAWN ADDAMS
SCREENPLAY BY TUDOR GATES · DIRECTED BY ROY WARD BAKER · PRODUCED BY HARRY FINE · CO-PRODUCER MICHAEL STYLE
COLOR BY MOVIELAB

WHO MADE IT:

Hammer Films (U.K.)/American International Pictures (U.S.). Director: Roy Ward Baker. Producers: Michael Style, Harry Fine. Writers: Harry Fine and Michael Style, Tudor Gates, from the story *Carmilla* by Sheridan Le Fanu. Cinematography (Technicolor/Movielab): Moray Grant. Music: Harry Robertson. Starring Ingrid Pitt (Marcilla/Carmilla/Mircalla Karnstein), George Cole (Roger Morton), Kate O'Mara (The Governess/Mme. Perrodot), Peter Cushing (General von Spielsdorf), Ferdy Mayne (Doctor), Douglas Wilmer (Baron Joachim von Hartog), Madeline Smith (Emma Morton), Dawn Addams (The Countess), Jon Finch (Carl Ebhardt), Pippa Steele (Laura), Kirsten Betts aka Kirsten Lindholm (First Vampire), Janet Key (Gretchin), John Forbes-Robertson (Man in Black), Charles Farrell (Landlord).

WHAT IT'S ABOUT:

In 19th-Century Styria, a seductive female vampire preys on the beautiful and innocent daughters of wealthy families. Among those stricken are the Baron Hartog (who becomes a vampire hunter to avenge the death of his sister) and General von Spielsdorf, who loses his loving daughter Laura. Now calling herself Carmilla, the guilt-ridden but insatiable vampiress becomes a fixture at the residence of Mr. Morton, where she promptly befriends and seduces young Emma Morton, making a wanton slave of the girl's governess in the process. Finally, after additional murders, General von Spielsdorf arrives with the now-aged Baron Hartog, and Carmilla's reign of bloody terror is cut short with her staking and decapitation.

WHY IT'S IMPORTANT:

Hammer Films of England revolutionized horror cinema in the 1950s, reinvigorating the moribund genre with adult, violent takes on classic terror subjects. But by the late '60s styles and tastes were changing yet again, and most dramatically. Still in the business of producing period supernatural thrillers but more than willing to experiment, Hammer turned to sex appeal for a new direction Why not do a spin on their popular vampire melodramas with a distaff version, sensual yet stylish enough to qualify as an up-to-date 1970 "prestige" item?

In Sheridan le Fanu's venerable *Carmilla* the studio found what it was looking for. Filmed last in 1960 by Roger Vadim (*Blood and Roses*), this new incarnation would take full advantage of relaxed censorship and the late '60s/early '70s mandate to be more daring. Hammer was wise to choose Ingrid Pitt as Carmilla; unlike most of the studio's starlets, Pitt was a seasoned pro who had just appeared opposite Richard Burton and Clint Eastwood in MGM's *Where Eagles Dare*. A tad more mature than her character, the actress compensates with a relatively subtle, first-rate performance and some nude scenes that are utterly jaw-dropping (Pitt would disrobe in other films as well, bless her). Ably supporting the lead are both Peter Cushing (very good as a Prussian aristocrat) and Douglas Wilmer as an aged, grimly resolved vampire hunter whose sister had been a victim many years earlier. An extremely effective opening set-piece, eventually followed by smartly-integrated flashbacks, establishes this tragic back-story.

Producers Harry Fine and Michael Style seemed determined to polish-up the studio's image with this new, tastefully wrought, decidedly sexy adaptation of the oft-filmed Fanu classic. *The Vampire Lovers* remains their modest masterpiece, a spirited reminder in 1970 that the House of Hammer was still a force to contend with.

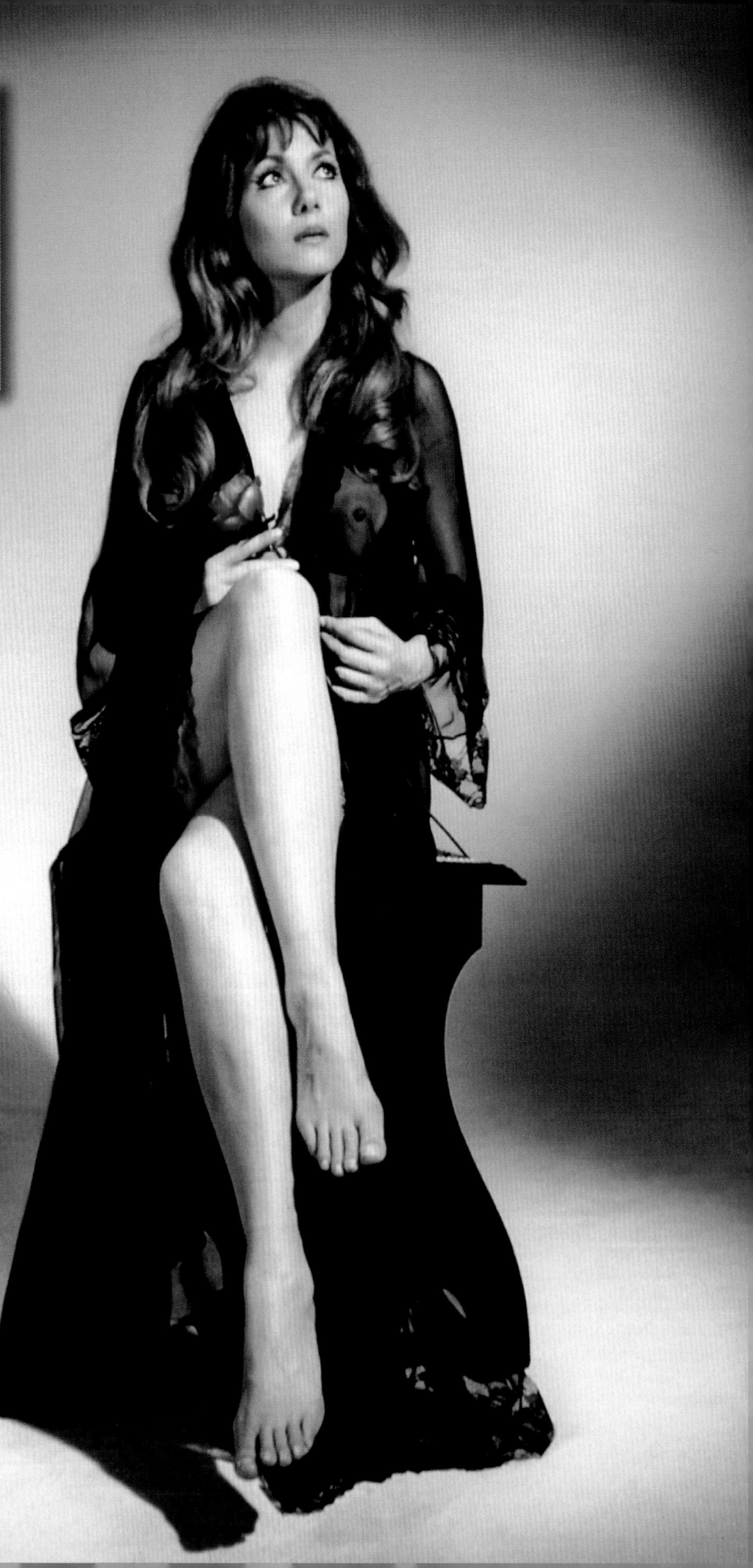

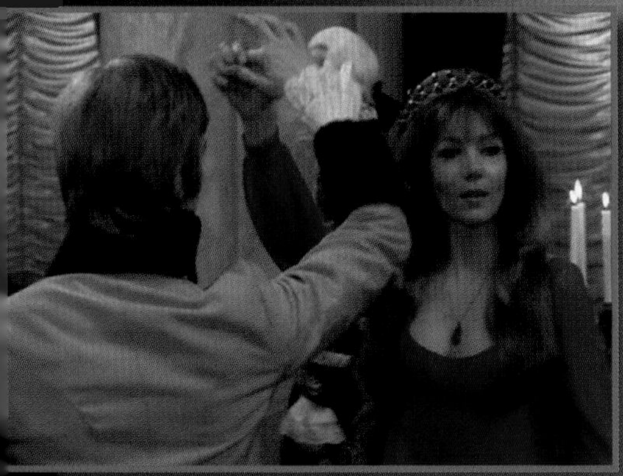

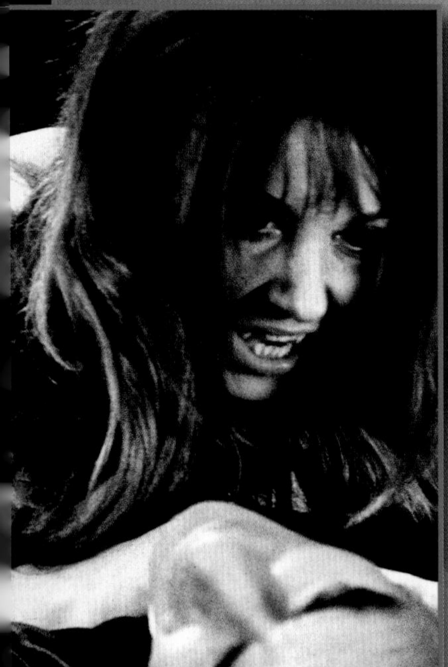

WHEN DREAMS BECOME NIGHTMARES

LEFT: Beautiful Carmilla Karnstein (Ingrid Pitt) brings joy into the lives of the families she seduces, before her predatory instincts inevitably transform bliss into sudden, fatal horror (from *The Vampire Lovers*). Just as darkly insatiable is dream demon Freddy Krueger (Robert Englund) from *A Nightmare on Elm Street*, presented here with resourceful teen antagonist/target Nancy Thompson (Heather Langenkamp).

Genuinely scary, darkly surreal teen thriller introduces an iconic bogeyman...

52 A NIGHTMARE ON ELM STREET 1984

Poster/photos: © 1984 New Line Cinema

WHO MADE IT:

New Line Cinema (U.S.). Director: Wes Craven. Producer: Robert Shaye. Writer: Wes Craven. Cinematography (color): Jacques Haitkin. Music: Charles Bernstein. Make-up: Kathy Logan, David B. Miller. Starring John Saxon (Lt. Thompson), Ronee Blakley (Marge Thompson), Heather Langenkamp (Nancy Thompson), Amanda Wyss (Tina Gray), Jsu Garcia aka Nick Corri (Rod Lane), Johnny Depp (Glen Lantz), Charles Fleisher (Dr. King), Joseph Whipp (Sgt. Parker), Robert Englund (Fred Krueger), Lin Shayne (Teacher), Joe Unger (Sgt. Garcia) Mimi Craven (Nurse).

WHAT IT'S ABOUT:

Teenagers in a small community all have the same dream: each is pursued by a sinister figure with distinctive razor-sharp knives attached to the fingers on his right hand. Soon after, these teens are savagely targeted by a mysterious, monstrous force, until one of them, Nancy Thompson, begins to suspect that the stalker from their nightmare is responsible. Visiting a dream therapy clinic confirms this: Nancy retrieves a distinctive hat, worn by the killer, during a new nightmare. This sheds light on a long-held local secret: the hat belongs on the evil head of Fred Krueger, a sadistic child murderer burned to death by vengeful parents over a decade ago. Now it seems he's manipulating local children through their dreams, exacting revenge from beyond the grave. When all adult efforts to stop Krueger's current attacks fail, it's up to a resolved Nancy to end his twisted reign of terror. Playing by "dream" rules, she turns her back on the phantasm, draining him of energy. But has this exorcism truly rid the world of Fred Krueger?

WHY IT'S IMPORTANT:

In the wake of "bogeyman" horror films like John Carpenter's *Halloween* and the *Friday the 13th* series, Wes Craven unleashed *A Nightmare on Elm Street* in 1984, introducing the most popular "slasher monster" of them all, Fred (or "Freddy") Krueger, as portrayed by Robert Englund. With his burned visage (important plot point), fedora, striped shirt and, most memorable of all, metal-clawed gloved hand, this bizarre child attacker/murdering fiend/dream demon was the icon for horror cinema during the 1980s. Well received by critics and adored by fans, Craven's little brainchild inspired a rash of profitable but increasingly campy sequels that wound up elevating New Line Cinema from feisty mini-major to formidable Hollywood studio.

This first movie, however, is a stylish and scary affair, alive with imaginative ideas and an assured directorial style. As teen heroine Nancy Thompson (Heather Langenkamp) strives valiantly to figure out the profound mystery of Krueger, one amazing murder set-piece after another unfolds, the fantasy aspect of Freddy's "dream" attacks allowing for some innovative and outrageous special effects. From his first silhouetted appearance with unnaturally extending arms to the final exorcism, film technology works hand-in-hand with psychologically-sound scripting to produce some of the most memorable moments in Reagan-era horror cinema. Indeed, Nancy's ordeal has whiffs of Ellen Burstyn in *The Exorcist*, as we follow a believable female protagonist through sterile-white doctor's offices and research labs while the hapless experts try to fathom her unprecedented, ultra-horrific dilemma. And like Sigourney Weaver in *Alien*, destroying this seemingly invulnerable monster is ultimately up to her and her alone.

Best scenes: Tina's classroom vision; Freddy's entry into our world; Glen's geyser-like demise; Nancy pulling Krueger's hat out of nowhere during a dream research experiment; the final showdown.

Super-bogeyman Fred Kreuger uses "dream warfare" to punish the unsuspecting children of his murderers.

More so than most traditional horror films, *A Nightmare on Elm Street* made use of spectacular visual concepts, from reducing youthful co-star Johnny Depp to a geyser of blood (LEFT) to providing a charred child killer from beyond the grave. Wicked, colorful Fred (or "Freddy") Krueger would go on to become bogeyman #1 in 1980s horror cinema.

Death by special effects: a reso
Nancy strips Krueger of his po
Or has she?

Like Karloff, *Nightmare* star Robert Englund spent hour
up chair enduring his transformation into an iconic mov

Surprisingly effective MGM take on the daring Oscar Wilde morality play...

51 THE PICTURE OF DORIAN GRAY 1945

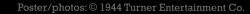

WHO MADE IT:

Metro-Goldwyn-Mayer (U.S.). Director: Albert Lewin. Producer: Pandro S. Berman. Writer: Albert Lewin, based on the novel by Oscar Wilde. Cinematgraphy (b/w with Technicolor inserts): Harry Stradling Sr. Music: Herbert Stothart. Starring George Sanders (Lord Henry Wotton), Hurd Hatfield (Dorian Gray), Donna Reed (Gladys Hallward), Angela Lansbury (Sibyl Vane), Peter Lawford (David Stone), Lowell Gilmore (Basil Hallward), Richard Fraser (James Vane), Douglas Walton (Alan Campbell), Morton Lowry (Adrian Singleton), Miles Mander (Sir Robert Bentley), Lydia Bilbrook (Mrs. Vane).

WHAT IT'S ABOUT:

In Victorian London, wealthy aristocrat Dorian Gray makes a most unusual wish after his portrait is finished, a kind of deal with the devil: he will remain young forever, even as the man in the picture grows old and corrupt, bearing the weight of his multiple sins. At the behest of amoral friend Lord Henry Wooten, Dorian even puts his innocent fiancée Sibyl Vane to a unfair personal test. When she fails, he abruptly ends their engagement, and the heartbroken young woman commits suicide. As the years fly by, Gray continues to have disastrous effect on all those in his orbit. He eventually murders artist Basil Hallward, the painter of his portrait, then proposes to Hallward's beautiful young niece Gladys, a girl he's genuinely cared for since she was a child. Finally disgusted with his loathsome existence, Dorian decides to destroy the portrait in a desperate attempt to find salvation. But when the knife he used on Hallward plunges into the painting, Gray realizes that he has struck a mortal blow against himself. Wooten and Gladys burst into Dorian's nursery and find Hallward's magnificent portrait just as it was when he originally painted it. On the floor beside it is the dissipated corpse of Dorian Gray, grotesquely reflecting a ruined lifetime of sin and depravity.

WHY IT'S IMPORTANT:

Produced roughly around the same time as their high-profile remake of *Dr. Jekyll and Mr. Hyde*, Albert Lewin's *The Picture of Dorian Gray* was an unexpected success for MGM commercially and critically. Many observers were amazed that the picture was made at all, given the daring nature of Wilde's narrative. But in the best tradition of golden age Hollywood, censorship restrictions inevitably left a great deal to the viewer's imagination, enabling Dorian's vaguely depraved acts to register rather effectively without being spelled out.

Newcomer Hurd Hatfield plays Dorian as reserved and alienated but still charming enough to earn our sympathy; he'd be typed as "weird" for the rest of his movie career. In many ways, the film really belongs to George Sanders as Lord Henry Wooten, amoral philosopher and lovable cad-about-town. Wooten is indirectly responsible for *Gray*'s destruction and several tragic deaths, yet we're still rather taken with him, making this witty troublemaker more Dorian than Dorian in some respects. Angela Lansbury as the ill-fated Sybil Vane and Donna Reed as Gladys hold their own in this mostly male-dominated morality play.

Lewin is to be commended for a number of impressively handled horror sequences. Hallward's stabbing is staged with a swinging lamp casting ominous, moving shadows, a cinematic gag re-visited by Alfred Hitchcock in the climax of *Psycho*. The final transformation of the painting into its former self while other visual elements are moving in the frame is a masterpiece of special effects construction.

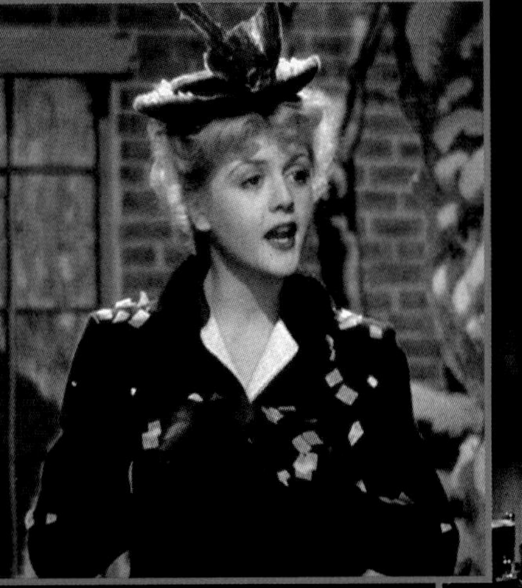

The multi-talented Angela Lansbury (here singing "Little Yellow Bird") was a fresh face at MGM when she was cast as the apple of Dorian Gray's eye.

The amazing "before and after" portraits for the film, presented as Technicolor inserts, were handled by two different artists: Henrique Medina rendered Dorian as a handsome young man, while Ivan Le Lorraine Albright painted him as a dissipated monster.

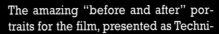

It is Lord Henry (George Sanders, ABOVE RIGHT) who leads unsuspecting Dorian to his moral doom (BELOW, makeup by Jack Dawn).

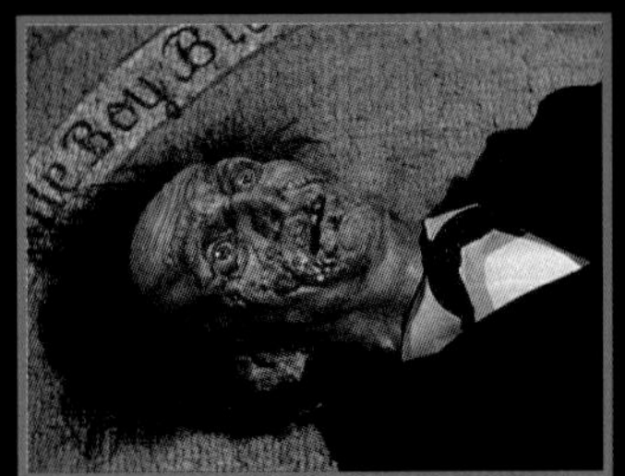

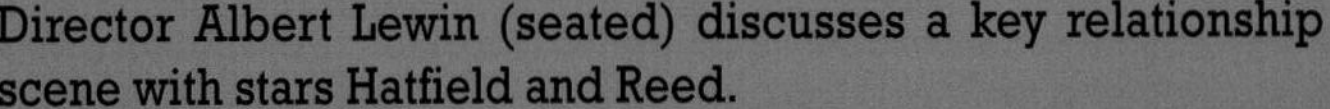

Director Albert Lewin (seated) discusses a key relationship scene with stars Hatfield and Reed.

Tod Browning's over-the-top circus creepshow, unique and unnerving...

50 FREAKS 1932

 1.37

Poster/photos: © 1932 Turner Entertainment Co.

WHO MADE IT:

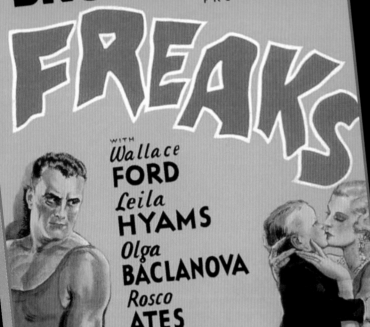

Metro-Goldwyn-Mayer (U.S.). Director: Tod Browning. Producers: Tod Browning, Harry Rapf, Irving Thalberg (uncredited). Writer: Tod Robbins, based on the story "Spurs." Cinematography (b/w): Merritt B. Gerstad. Starring Wallace Ford (Phroso), Leila Hyams (Venus), Olga Baclanova (Cleopatra), Roscoe Ates (Roscoe), Henry Victor (Hercules), Harry Earles (Hans), Daisy Earles (Frieda), Rose Dione (Madame Tetrallini), Daisy Hilton (Siamese Twin), Violet Hilton (Siamese Twin), Schlitz (Himself), Josephine Joseph (Half-Woman, Half-Man), Johnny Eck (Half Boy), Peter Robinson (Human Skeleton), Prince Randian aka Randion (The Living Torso).

WHAT IT'S ABOUT:

In a traveling sideshow, voluptuous, scheming trapeze artist Cleopatra marries one of the circus' midgets, Hans, after learning of his large inheritance. Hans and the other deformed sideshow performers, who range from various pinheads to a cigarette-smoking "human torso," tend to watch after each other in a generally hostile world of unsympathetic "normal" people. When they learn that Cleopatra has not only been unfaithful to poor Hans, but is actually planning to murder him in a scheme with her lover, the sideshow strongman, they decide to take especially grisly action. During a violent thunderstorm, they band together and surround the wicked couple, finally chasing them into the night. Some time later, Cleopatra's monstrous fate is revealed to a new crowd of sideshow gawkers: tongue cut out, one eye gouged and both legs hacked off, she has been surgically transformed into a squawking "human chicken" by the vengeful Freaks.

WHY IT'S IMPORTANT:

A one-of-a-kind movie if ever there was one, *Freaks* is Tod (*Dracula*) Browning's deliciously malformed baby, a decidedly weird outing that prestige studio MGM wanted absolutely nothing to do with. But with the success of Browning's vampire groundbreaker over at Universal, Metro had very little choice: *Freaks* would indeed go before the cameras, even if its nauseated parent studio would barely promote and support the finished product. And this isn't a case where the horror-craving public came to the film's rescue. Browning was simply ahead of his time with his unapologetically bizarre hybrid of circus melodrama and lurid horror film. The fact that these mini-"monsters" were in truth an often-maligned minority group made some viewers queasy (the finale's ludicrous "bird-woman," apparently the end product of their mysterious arcane skills, only added to the problem). Ostensibly a love rectangle, with two of the participants being little people, *Freaks* was promptly forgotten after its abortive major studio release. The film's memory was kept alive by dedicated cinema buffs over the years, until a revival in art houses and on video introduced it to a whole new generation of fans...who were, needless to say, far more open to the movie's oddball excesses than 1932 audiences. As for director Browning, MGM endorsed his barely-disguised redo of *Dracula* (*Mark of the Vampire*) a few years later, providing them with a mainstream Lugosi scarefest audiences could sink their teeth into.

In the final analysis, *Freaks*' offbeat pleasures ultimately outweigh a few significant drawbacks. We ultimately care about the decent, sinned-against midget protagonist, Hans, and are pleased to see him re-united with his true and loyal love in the re-inserted final scene. And the titular *Freaks* themselves, from drooling pinheads to abused gender-benders, are startling, never-to-be-forgotten screen personalities (the cigarette-smoking human torso being my personal favorite).

Celebration turned sour: The freaks recoil when they are rudely rejected by Hans' new wife, the off-screen Cleopatra. This is one of the best-remembered scenes of the film. Gooble-gobble, everyone!

Of the various human aberrations that make up the cast of *Freaks*, perhaps none is more bizarre than Prince Randian, the living torso.

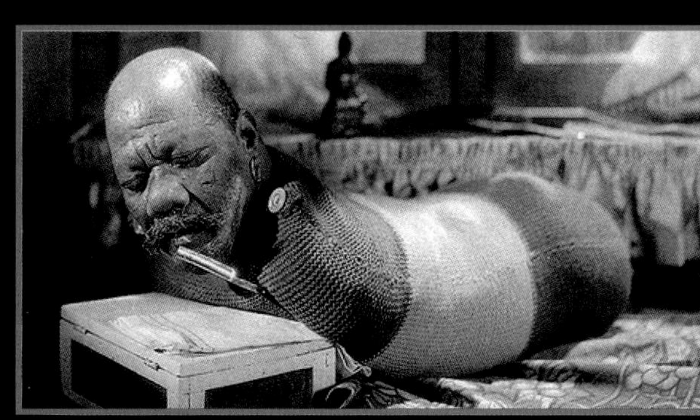

Love-smitten Hans (Harry Earles) only has eyes for the worthless, scheming trapeze artist Cleopatra (Olga Baclanova).

Cleopatra's foul fate: from queen of the air to quacking monstrosity, the weird result of freak-inflicted revenge.

Among the freaks is familiar face Wallace Ford, eight years before *The Mummy's Hand*.

Macabre master Tod Browning relaxes on set with several key members of his offbeat cast.

49 THE BIRDS 1963

197  1.37

Poster/photos: © 1963 Universal Studios

WHO MADE IT:

Universal Pictures/Alfred J. Hitchcock Productions (U.S.). Director: Alfred Hitchcock. Producer (uncredited): Alfred Hitchcock. Writer: Evan Hunter, based on the short story by Daphne du Maurier. Cinematography (Technicolor): Robert Burks. Editor: George Tomasini. Soundscape: Oskar Sala, Remi Gassmann, Bernard Herrmann. Starring Rod Taylor (Mitch Brenner), 'Tippi' Hedren (Melanie Daniels), Jessica Tandy (Lydia Brenner), Suzanne Pleshette (Annie Hayworth), Veronica Cartwright (Cathy Brenner), Ethel Griffies (Mrs. Bundy), Charles McGraw (Sebastian Sholes), Ruth McDevitt (Mrs. MacGruder), Lonny Chapman (Deke Carter), Joe Mantell (Traveling salesman), Doodles Weaver (Fisherman), Malcolm Atterbury (Deputy Al Malone), Karl Swenson (Drunk Doomsayer), Richard Deacon (Mitch's city neighbor).

"It could be the most terrifying motion picture I have ever made!"—

"...and remember, the next scream you hear may be your own!"

ALFRED HITCHCOCK'S "The Birds"

TECHNICOLOR®

STARRING ROD TAYLOR · JESSICA TANDY SUZANNE PLESHETTE and Introducing 'TIPPI' HEDREN

A Fascinating New Personality

Based on Daphne Du Maurier's Classic Suspense Story!

Screenplay by EVAN HUNTER · Directed by ALFRED HITCHCOCK

Universal Release

WHAT IT'S ABOUT:

On a whim, socialite Melanie Daniels follows brash lawyer Mitch Brenner to his isolated home in the small seaside community of Bodega Bay. Encounters with Mitch's brittle, overprotective mother Lydia, former girlfriend Annie Heywood, and younger sister Cathy precede a bizarre and savage series of avian attacks. For no apparent reason, birds of all species swoop down upon the unsuspecting community, terrorizing fleeing schoolchildren and finally attacking main street en masse. After schoolteacher Annie is killed trying to protect a child, the Brenners and Melanie take refuge in the Brenner home, which they fortify as best they can. After surviving a harrowing evening, Melanie is savagely attacked by avian invaders while investigating some mysterious upstairs sounds by herself. Ultimately, they all manage to slip away in their car and escape Bodega Bay, even as the birds prepare for what may be a final wave of attacks.

WHY IT'S IMPORTANT:

After the phenomenal success of *Psycho*, Hitchcock pushed even further into horror-fantasy territory with Universal's *The Birds*, upping the visual ante with spectacular special effects and a generous amount of relatively tasteful gore. Viewed superficially, it's a simple story of our feathered friends running amok for no discernable reason, and woe to anyone caught in the middle of their terrifying attacks. While there's tremendous irony in the notion of harmless creatures we smug humans take for granted (and continually mistreat) turning on us in such a monstrous, perhaps even apocalyptic way, that's actually not enough to support a two-hour narrative. So, for subtext, Hitchcock seizes upon the metaphoric power of birds as symbols of unsettled, "fluttery" emotions: unhappy Melanie is in desperate need of a mother figure for stability; disenfranchised Lydia requires an adult daughter to care for and love, making her acceptable for son Mitch. Until their clearly defined personal problems are resolved, all hell breaks loose in the form of the inexplicable bird attacks. Once these inner furies are quelled at the film's conclusion (Hitch gives each woman a significant close-up and they look at each other acceptingly), the family unit is saved and permitted to leave Bodega Bay safely. While the destructive "birds" may attack again, we screwed-up humans at least have a chance...

Best scenes: Lydia's discovery of the dead farmer in his bedroom; the schoolhouse and main street attacks; Marion's final encounter with avian monsters in an upstairs Brenner room.

In the 1990s, Universal decided to revive *The Birds* as a made-for-TV movie, hoping to extend their high-profile franchise a la the various *Psycho* sequels and re-dos. Needless to say, this unwise creative experiment didn't fly.

Classic shot: first one bird, then another, until the entire frame is filled with winged monsters!

In a move reminiscent of James Whale, Hitchcock covers the gruesome discovery of the dead farmer with three successive shots, culminating in a bloody close-up.

This film was based on a story by Daphne du Maurier, whose classic novel *Rebecca* provided the basis of one of Alfred Hitchcock's greatest pre-war successes. Although *The Birds* has no music score, composer Bernard Herrmann served as soundscape consultant.

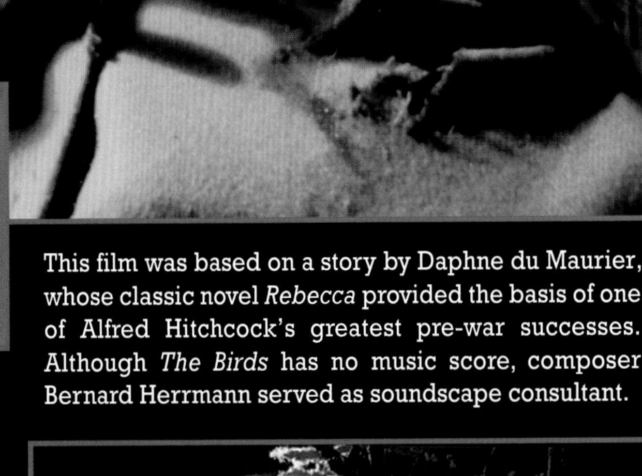

"Hitch" on set during production. *The Birds* contained more special effects than any previous Hitchcock film.

Corman's second swing at Poe earns big bucks and mainstream validation...

48 Pit and the Pendulum 1961

2.35

WHO MADE IT:

American International Pictures/Alta Vista Productions (U.S.). Director: Roger Corman. Producers: Roger Corman, James H. Nicholson, Samuel Z. Arkoff. Writer: Richard Matheson, based on a story by Edgar Allan Poe. Cinematography (Pathecolor): Floyd Crosby. Music: Les Baxter. Starring Vincent Price (Nicholas/Sebastian Medina), John Kerr (Francis), Barbara Steele (Elizabeth), Luana Anders (Catherine), Antony Carbone (Doctor Leon), Patrick Westwood (Maximillian), Lynette Bernay (Maria), Larry Turner (Nicholas as a child), Mary Menzies (Isabella).

WHAT IT'S ABOUT:

Investigating the sudden and unexpected death of his sister Elizabeth, Francis Barnard goes to Spain for an audience with Nicholas Medina, her widowed husband. Nicholas explains that his late wife succumbed to the "heavy atmosphere" of their imposing castle by the sea and went mad. Frances is not satisfied with this explanation, although he feels sorry for his host after learning of the man's childhood demons: Medina witnessed his beloved mother being tortured to death by his own wicked father, Sebastian Medina. The situation repeats itself when Nicholas is driven to madness and mayhem by scheming Dr. Leon, in cahoots with the still-alive Elizabeth. Innocent Francis is drawn into the fray, ultimately imprisoned in a pit and subjected to a massive, swinging pendulum. Nicholas/Sebastian is finally overpowered, and Francis is rescued from this death device in time.

WHY IT'S IMPORTANT:

The most commercially successful of all the AIP/Roger Corman/Edgar Allan Poe adaptations of the early '60s, *Pit and the Pendulum* is perhaps the most acceptable as a mainstream entertainment (it was the only entry in the series to play on prime-time network television). Fresh from the unexpected success of *House of Usher*, director Corman reveled in an increased budget and a better-than-usual cast, experimenting with audacious new cinematic techniques while building on the stylistic devices and themes he set in place with the first movie.

At the heart of the horror as usual is Vincent Price, showcased effectively as a decent, rational, even sympathetic nobleman. Guilt-plagued Nicholas Medina is sinned against by supposed loved ones until he finally loses his mind and becomes a depraved sinner himself. Corman would re-use the "best friend conspiracy" scenario a year later in *The Premature Burial*, putting star Ray Milland through similar paces. But here the idea is fresh and well-played, especially with AIP's recently crowned Scream Queen goddess Barbara (*Black Sunday*) Steele as Medina's wickedly scheming, supposedly deceased first wife.

Everything about the melodrama builds to Price's bravura turn as a full-fledged nut job, subjecting innocent visitor John Kerr to the titular device of extreme torture. Recognizing his special obligation to "wow" audiences, showman Corman pulls out all the cinematic stops for this much-anticipated finale: it is colorful, exciting and terrifying, a thoroughly impressive rollercoaster ride by a talented young director at the peak of his powers.

As usual, cinematography (Floyd Crosby) and art direction (Daniel Haller) are first rate, and Les Baxter's jolting, semi-electronic music score is equally memorable.

Already a staple element of Corman's Poe series for AIP: the magnificent establishing shot, in truth a breathtaking matte painting. This image and variations would re-appear continually as stock footage in other films.

Nicholas goes nuts: star Vincent Price has a field day exploring emotional extremes in his colorful *Pit* characterization(s), ranging from kind-hearted and considerate to sadistic, insane and diabolical. Price and Corman would repeat this split personality motif in another Poe adaptation, *The Haunted Palace* (1963).

The film's titular climax is an unforgettable set-piece, arguably the high point of Roger Corman's directorial career. BELOW: The widescreen master shot from this sequence is an amazing fusion of painted elements and live-action.

TOP: A terrifying discovery in the crypt. LEFT: Price turns the tables on tormentor Steele.

Standing beside his enormous Pendulum prop, Roger Corman prepares star John Kerr for a thrilling brush with death.

POLTERGEIST 1982

WHO MADE IT:

MGM/UA/SLM Production Group (U.S.). Director: To Frank Marshall, Steven Spielberg, Kathleen Ken Spielberg, Michael Grais, Mark Victor. Cinemat Matthew F. Leonetti. Music: Jerry Goldsmith. St (Steve Freeling), Jobeth Williams (Diane Freel (Dr. Lesh), Dominique Dunne (Dana Freeling), Freeling), Heather O'Rourke (Carol Ann Freeling), Tuthill), Virginia Kiser (Mrs. Tuthill), Martin Ca Lawson (Ryan), Zelda Rubinstein (Tangina), Jame

WHAT IT'S ABOUT:

The Freeling family sees the American dream e of nightmares when their suburban home is in into a hotbed of hostile ectoplasmic activity. Fro youngest daughter Carol Ann to the terrorizing of invited paranormal investigators, events go from bad to worse until a most unusual psychic "house cleaning" expert manages to guide the desperate parents into the successful retrieval of their daughter. Eventually it's revealed that this house was built over what was once a local cemetery. The buried bodies of the deceased were supposed to be removed and re-located, but never were. Now, returning as angry spirits seeking retribution for this affront, they take revenge b mansion to pieces. The rattled Freelings, middle of this cosmic tandrum, manage to

WHY IT'S IMPORTANT:

1982 was Steven Spielberg's summer at th both the insanely popular sci-fi family immensely entertaining re-imagining of t for mainstream moviegoers. *Poltergeis* same kind of first-class production values, directorial tech art visual effects that had characterized recent sci-fi epics like *Star Wars*, *Superman*. Now it was the bone-chilling (but family-friendly) ghost story that would receive this kind of lavi Recruiting horror movie director Tobe Hooper as titular helmer (shades of Christian Nyby/Howard Hawks an provides a suburban canvas that is so unmistakably his in terms of content and style that pretending he wasn't in downright foolish. Although regular composer John Williams wasn't available, Jerry Goldsmith delivered a sup "warmth" score that fully captured producer Spielberg's barbeque-and-firefly sensibility. In terms of the story its Richard Matheson whips up a serviceable b over a cemetery, but since the bodies of the located as promised, their ghosts wreak havo new owners. By plopping this powerful idea la Spielberg, the film makes its case in a relat that austere psychic investigator thrillers lik *Legend of Hell House* just can't touch. Ultimat both a smart and deftly-filmed supernatur addicts and also as a colorful mass-appeal

Intangible dreamlike fantasy offers an early, uncommon female vampire...

46

VAMPYR 1932

Poster/photos: © General Foreign Sales Corp.

WHO MADE IT:

Tobis Filmkunst (Germany)/General Foreign Sales Corp. (U.S.). Director: Carl Theodor Dreyer. Producers: Carl Theodor Dreyer, Julian West. Writers: Christen Jul, Carl Theodor Dreyer, based on the novel by Sheridan Le Fanu. Cinematography (b/w): Rudolph Mate, Louis Nee. Music: Wolfgang Zeller. Starring Julian West (Allan Gray), Rena Mandel (Gisele), Sybille Schmitz (Leone), Jan Hieronimko (Village Doctor), Henreiette Gerard (Marguerite Chopin), Jane Mora (The Nurse), Maurice Schutz (Lord of the Manor), Albert Bras (Servant).

WHAT IT'S ABOUT:

Traveling in the French countryside, a young occult investigator named Allan Gray experiences a series of bizarre and inexplicable events while staying at an inn in the vicinity of a solitary chateau. An unexpected night visitor, a mysterious book about vampirism, ghost-like shadows, and a pair of young girls tormented by some mysterious, life-draining force bewilder and intrigue Gray. Finally, the culprit is exposed as an extremely evil old woman, Marguerite Chopin, who died in mortal sin and caused similar occurrences a quarter of a century before. After a surreal encounter with his own premature burial, Allan Gray joins forces with a family servant to drive an iron stake through Marguerite's heart as she lies in her grave. Meanwhile, the vampire's henchman, an evil doctor, is buried alive by falling flour in a nearby mill.

WHY IT'S IMPORTANT:

Be forewarned: Carl Dreyer's early talkie *Vampyr* requires a great deal of patience, and a primer on the Dutch director's work and unique style wouldn't hurt either. Deliberately designed to deconstruct cinematic storytelling while the form was still in its infancy, this "fantastique" chiller is an outlandish assault on convention in just about every way. Shadows dance about madly, eventually rejoining their unfazed casters, gravediggers work in reverse motion, phantoms flit in and out of bedrooms, and best of all, real vampires apparently walk the earth, seeking and claiming innocent victims. Is this truly a dreamlike universe populated by weird, nightmare creatures, or are we merely trespassing on the fertile imagination of the film's dour hero, Allen Gray, a man in search of supernatural sensations? Even by the picture's finale we really aren't sure.

Naturally, any movie this audacious has to be applauded on general principles, and there is much in *Vampyr* that truly borders on the brilliant. It still offers the best premature burial ever put on film, and the tale's central threat, the battleaxe lesbian female vampire, is eerie and disturbing, even by today's standards. Her mesmerized victim Leone's insidious grin as she is overtaken by evil is a standout moment, and the wicked doctor's demise in an avalanche of flour is weird in exactly the right way. Moreover, Dreyer's camera moves with almost supernatural fluidity through rooms and hallways, infusing *Vampyr* with a curious visual energy lacking in most of the early sound features. But again, we're dealing with an eccentric filmmaker who deliberately wants to trash logical expectations at every turn. This kind of movie can either exhilarate an audience, or baffle it to the point of utter frustration. I say: summon your courage, light up that joint and give *Vampyr* a whirl.

Lavish, literate, exciting adaptation boasts Laughton's centerpiece performance...

45 THE HUNCHBACK OF NOTRE DAME 1939

WHO MADE IT:

An RKO Radio Picture (U.S.). Director: William Dieterle. Producer: Pandro S. Berman. Writer: Bruno Frank, based on the novel by Victor Hugo. Cinematography (b/w): Joseph H. August. Music: Alfred Newman. Quasimodo make-up: Perc Westmore. Starring Charles Laughton (Quasimodo), Cedric Hardwicke (Frollo), Thomas Mitchell (Clopin), Maureen O'Hara (Esmeralda), Edmond O'Brien (Gringoire), Alan Marshal (Phoebus), Walter Hampden (Archdeacon), Harry Davenport (King Louis XI), Katherine Alexander (Madame de Lys), George Zucco (Procurator), Fritz Leiber (Old Nobleman), Etienne Giradot (Doctor), George Tobias (Beggar).

WHAT IT'S ABOUT:

In 1482 Paris, Quasimodo ("semi-human"), the deformed bellringer of Notre Dame cathedral, is at the heart of political intrigue, widespread social unrest and spiritual/personal strife. His secretly-depraved adopter, Claude Frollo, orders him to abduct beautiful young gypsy Esmeralda, a crime for which Quasimodo is publically pilloried. Ironically, it is his intended victim, not Frollo, who comforts the tormented hunchback and gives him water. Returning the favor, Quasimodo rescues Esmeralda from execution when she is framed for the murder of her lover, Captain Phoebus, by Frollo, now literally mad with jealousy. Soon all forces converge on the imposing cathedral, and Quasimodo responds with a spectacular counterattack, spilling a downpour of molten lead on a rabble led by rebellious Trouillefou. In contrast, Gringoire the poet has found a more peaceful method of solving France's social problems by appealing to the relatively open-minded Archdeacon. Frollo, fully deranged and menacing Esmeralda from within the cathedral, attacks a rescuing Quasimodo, who finally turns on his evil master and hurls him to his doom. The gypsy eventually rides off with Gringoire, leaving lonely Quasimodo to ponder his place in a chaotic and bewildering, often unjust world.

WHY IT'S IMPORTANT:

Only partially a horror film, *The Hunchback of Notre Dame* is arguably the greatest adaptation of a literary classic in Hollywood history. Masterful screen direction, an amazing ensemble cast, spectacular sets and a rousing, unforgettable music score make this RKO epic one of those oft-mentioned classics from that magical movie year, 1939.

At the heart of Victor Hugo's enduring story, of course, is the titular character, a certain cathedral bellringer more monster than man in appearance, but endowed with an elemental sense of morality. Taking nothing away from Lon Chaney's groundbreaking portrayal of Quasimodo in the silent version, or even Anthony Quinn's brawny approach in 1957, it is Charles Laughton who is forever identified with this colorful, supremely challenging role. His genius for conveying pathos transcends an especially heavy monster make-up (kept hidden in all advance studio publicity), crafted by Perc Westmore. The star's lovely and spirited young protégé, Maureen O'Hara, shines in her screen debut as gypsy dancer/inadvertent political agitator Esmeralda. And it's the "beauty and the beast" aspect of their relationship that justifies this movie's classification as a "monster" or "horror" experience. (That, and the fact that the silent version launched Lon Chaney's career as a fright star.)

But a picture with this level of depth doesn't stop there: it has a plethora of social, fraternal and religious themes to explore, and it does so confidently without once forgetting its primary obligation as a mass-market Hollywood entertainment. Literally above it all in the film's final shot, sharing the frame with a stone gargoyle before the camera pulls away for a full view of the cathedral, Quasimodo becomes nothing less than humanity's humble conscience, cursed with emotions and an inconvenient need for love. Like the film itself, the moment is a triumph for director William Dieterle, star Laughton, and the long-gone studio system approach to making motion pictures.

sually tute, intellectually ound, d emotionally tisfying r viewers of any age, *The Hunchback of Notre Dame* is as ose as it gets to a perfect movie experience. BOVE: RKO craftsmen brought the cathedral of otre Dame to life by combining miniatures with ass paintings. The film begins and ends with a full ot of the majestic edifice.

BOVE: playing opposite Laughton is his lovely otégé, Maureen O'Hara. Orson Welles was nearly the running to portray Quasimodo, having just rived at RKO for his landmark (and much envied) mmaking deal.

"Water!" the pilloried Hunchback begs, and only the woman he abducted has the humanity to relieve his suffering. Always a dramatic high point of this story, it was never better staged, played or photographed than here.

A monster movie, a love story, and a literary epic with spectacular action sequences…they all add up to RKO's much-celebrated 1939 classic.

The first great actor to play Quasimodo on screen was Hollywood's Man of a Thousand Faces, Lon Chaney.

A unique and experimental return to the fundamentals of fear...

44 THE BLAIR WITCH PROJECT 1999

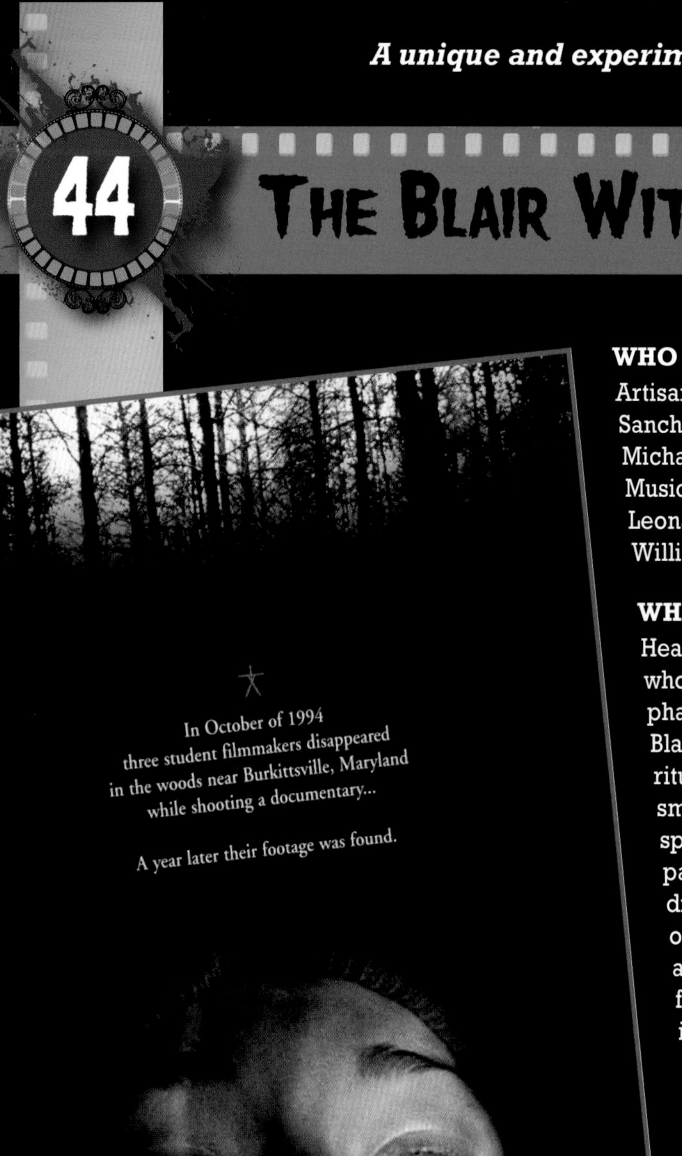

In October of 1994
three student filmmakers disappeared
in the woods near Burkittsville, Maryland
while shooting a documentary...
A year later their footage was found.
THE BLAIR WITCH PROJECT
www.blairwitch.com

WHO MADE IT:

Artisan Entertainment (U.S). Directors/Writers: Daniel Myrick, Eduardo Sanchez. Producers: Robin Cowie, Gregg Hale, Bock Eick, Kevin J. Foxe, Michael Monello. Cinematography (color and b/w): Neal Fredericks. Music: Tony Cora. Starring Heather Donahue (Heather Donahue), Joshua Leonard (Joshua 'Josh' Leonard), Michael C. Williams (Michael 'Mike' Williams), Bob Griffith (Short Fisherman), Jim King (Interviewee).

WHAT IT'S ABOUT:

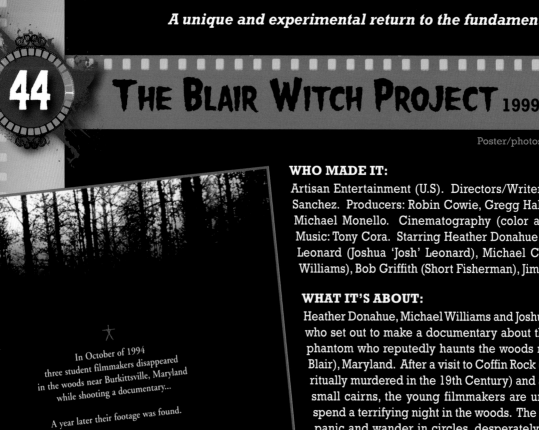

Heather Donahue, Michael Williams and Joshua Leonard are film students who set out to make a documentary about the Blair Witch, a legendary phantom who reputedly haunts the woods near Burkittsville (formerly Blair), Maryland. After a visit to Coffin Rock (where five men were found ritually murdered in the 19th Century) and an old cemetery with seven small cairns, the young filmmakers are unable to find their car and spend a terrifying night in the woods. The following day they begin to panic and wander in circles, desperately heading south. Then Josh disappears. Another terrifying night is endured, filled with the sounds of children and the sensation that someone or something is prowling around their tent. On the third night, they hear Josh's agonized cries for help and follow them to an abandoned old house. What they find in the basement leads to what appear to be Heather's death screams.

WHY IT'S IMPORTANT:

Made for next to nothing by a pair of semi-professionals, *The Blair Witch Project* introduced videocam cinema to mainstream audiences, a fake-out approach to storytelling that provides a "you are there" sense of reality traditional movies simply can't match. It's all POV from an amateur hand-held camera, complete with the inevitable shakes and what appears to be an arbitrary filming style. But it all works beautifully, harking back to Val Lewton's worthy goal of terrifying audiences by merely suggesting something unthinkably horrific without ever showing it.

Reducing plot and conflict to elemental simplicity, *Blair* has something in common with the classic fable *Hansel and Gretel*, as a small group of likeable teenage film students find themselves lost in mysterious woods reputedly haunted by an old, legendary witch. Somehow, without benefit of map or compass, they must find their way out before nightfall. It's that basic. Adding to their growing anxiety are local myths of murdering serial killers and other strange disappearances, the discovery of portentous burial grounds, and the eventual disappearance of their own crewmates. While it's hard to judge acting in a production of this kind, all of the featured kids are believable, some even sympathetic (ambitious protagonist Heather takes the blame for their ordeal in a final, moist-eyed video recording). Her ill-fated "project" results in a primal nightmare anyone of today's techno-savvy generation can easily relate to. When all is said and done, there is nothing more terrifying than huddling in a tent while listening to one of your missing friends screaming his head off somewhere in the blackened woods. It also helps that *Project*'s canny young producers simultaneously prepared a mock documentary about the Blair Witch herself, filling in some pertinent facts for viewers seeking a little more story content.

Ultimately, you either go with a picture like this or you don't. Many civilians and even a few horror fans find this shaky hand-held technique extremely irritating, ditto the built-in limitations of POV coverage from a single camera. But for brave viewers with an imagination and a willingness to forgo certain traditional movie pleasures for an unprecedented, harrowing brush with reality, *The Blair Witch Project* is a unique gem and one of the scariest horror movies ever made...on any budget.

Early two-color urban thriller establishes an evocative milieu...

43 MYSTERY OF THE WAX MUSEUM 1933

Poster/photos: © 1933 Turner Entertainment Co.

WHO MADE IT:

Warner Brothers/Vitaphone (U.S.). Director: Michael Curtiz. Producer: Henry Blanke. Writers: Carl Erickson and Don Mullaly, from a story by Charles S. Belden. Cinematography: Ray Rennahan (two-strip Technicolor) Starring Lionel Atwill (Ivan Igor), Fay Wray (Charlotte Duncan), Glenda Farrell (Florence Dempsey), Frank McHugh (Jim), Allen Vincent (Burton), Gavin Gordon (George).

WHAT IT'S ABOUT:

In 1921 London, sculptor Ivan Igor watches his beloved wax museum go up in flames after his unscrupulous business partner sets fire to the place for insurance money. Years later, in 1933 New York, a badly crippled Igor opens a new wax museum, employing various shady characters as assistants. Meanwhile, a feisty reporter named Florence Dempsey begins investigating mysterious suicides and murders, even as the corpse of a beautiful woman is stolen from the morgue. It's ultimately revealed that Igor is the monstrous figure who has been killing people, stealing their bodies, and covering them with wax to create life-like statues for his museum. His face is in reality a mask, eventually smashed by Dempsey's pretty roommate Charlotte. The hideous sculptor-turned-fiend is finally gunned down by the police, and he collapses into a giant vat of wax.

WHY IT'S IMPORTANT:

If Universal had mythical monster characters like Frankenstein, Dracula and the Mummy under studio contract, gangster studio Warner Bros. apparently held the copyright on wax museums...their ultimate legacy in the spooky genre. It all began with this modest but innovative little crime thriller spiced effectively with horror and fantasy elements. Like companion oddity *Doctor X*, *Mystery of the Wax Museum* was directed by WB's legendary Michael Curtiz, and shot in early, glowing two-strip Technicolor. Heightened by ghoulish green and waxy amber, it's a visual palette perfectly suited to the macabre subject.

As in *X*, a grotesque monster is at the heart of horrific doings, although this time the synthetic flesh is wax, and it's the flawless human face of Lionel Atwill that is the false, mask-like persona. Both pictures also offer comedy relief newshounds to follow the plots and participate in climactic suspense and action sequences. Glenda Farrell, whose wise-cracking city reporter is room-mated with demure Fay Wray, was semi-reprised by a bawdy Carolyn Jones in the 1953 *House of Wax*. Without question, her earthly character is handed the film's wildest and most quotable dialogue ("Dry up, you soap bubble!"; "He made Frankenstein look like a lily!")

Mystery was a lost film for several decades, and when it finally resurfaced in the late '60s, many fans considered it slow-moving and generally inferior to *Doctor X*, let alone the beloved Vincent Price 1953 remake. Viewed now with more objectivity, Curtiz's oddball what-done-it seems a tad low-key at times, but the sets, art direction and use of color set it apart. And Queen Screamer Fay Wray's"unmasking" of Igor - cracking a human face to reveal a hideous fiend inside - is a striking variation on Erik the Phantom's signature set-piece.

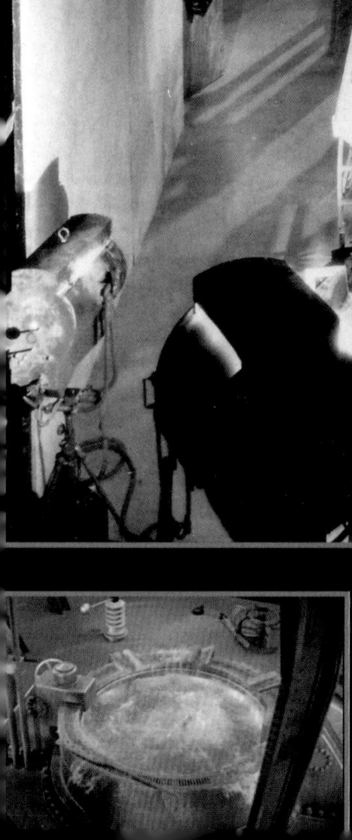

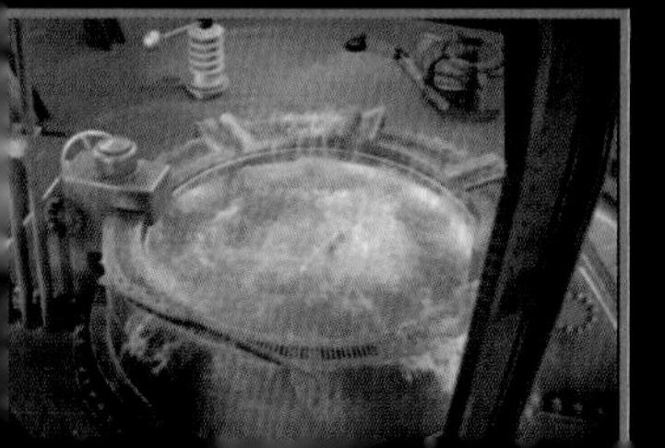

EXTREME MADNESS

ABOVE/LEFT: Warner Bros. spared no expense with this vast set for *Mystery of the Wax Museum*, which included a working vat of boiling liquid. Notice stars Fay Wray and Lionel Atwill on an upper platform being directed by Michael Curtiz. RIGHT: Just as insane as Atwill's mass-murderer was *The Lodger*, aka Jack the Ripper, played to the hilt by Laird Cregar (holding Merle Oberon hostage before George

Cregar's center stage in this lively, atmospheric take on the Ripper story...

42 THE LODGER 1944

84

1.37

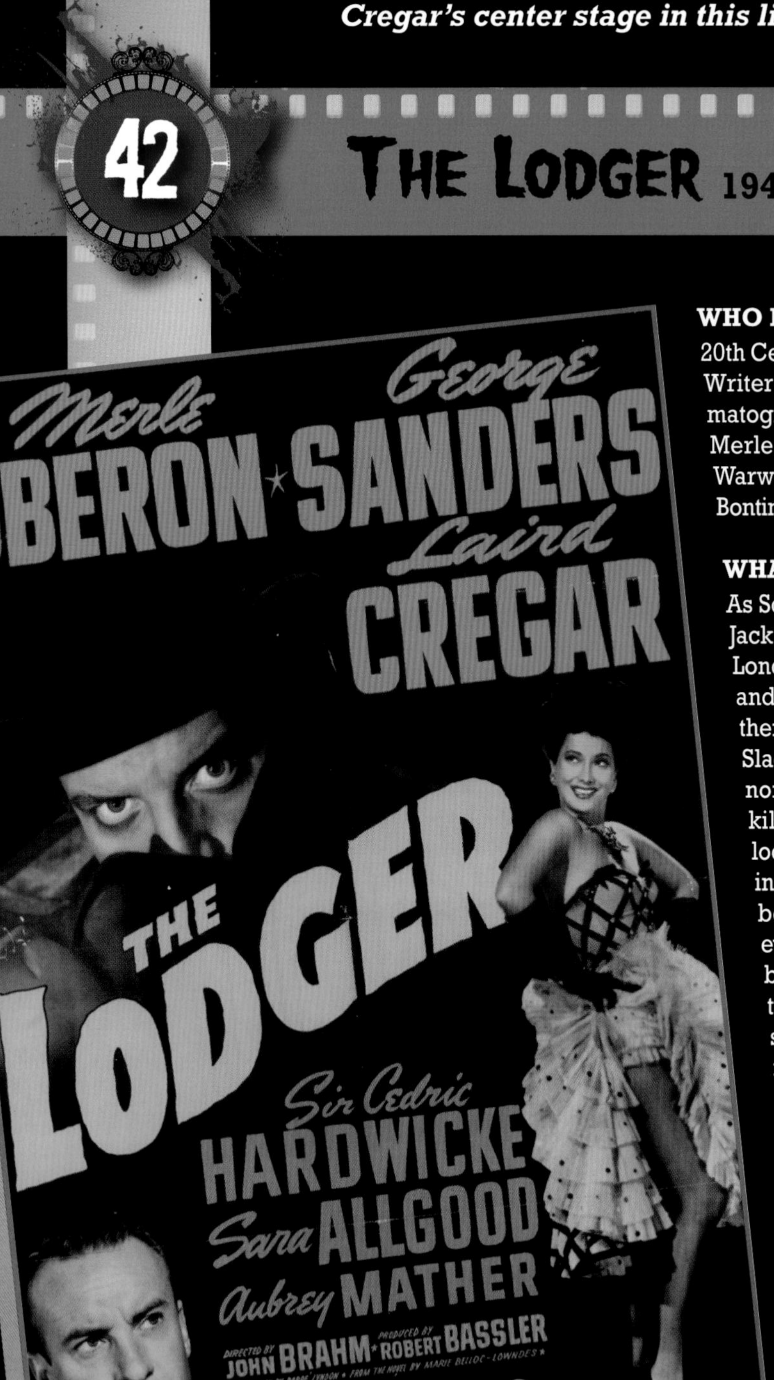

WHO MADE IT:

20th Century-Fox (U.S.). Director: John Brahm. Producer: Robert Bassler. Writer: Barre Lyndon, from the novel by Marie Belloc-Lowndes. Cinematographer (b/w): Lucien Ballard. Music: Hugo Friedhofer. Starring Merle Oberon (Kitty Langley), George Sanders (Inspector John Warwick), Laird Cregar (Mr. Slade), Cedric Hardwicke (Robert Bonting), Sara Allgood (Ellen Bonting), Aubrey Mather (Supt. Sutherland).

WHAT IT'S ABOUT:

As Scotland Yard police strive desperately to apprehend serial killer Jack the Ripper, a pathologist named Slade walks the foggy streets of London in search of new lodging. He winds up renting both a room and an attic belonging to the Bontings, an elderly couple who live there with their beautiful young niece Kitty Langley, a local showgirl. Slade, remote and mysterious, appears to despise actresses, but is nonetheless drawn to Kitty, who treats him kindly. As the Ripper killings continue, Mrs. Bonting begins to suspect that her new lodger may indeed be the culprit. Inspector John Warwick is called in; he checks out Mr. Slade's mysterious but ultimately explainable behavior, amorously pursuing Kitty in the process. But it's eventually established that Slade's artist brother was led to ruin by drink and a beautiful woman; this apparently prompted the twisted pathologist to "even the score" by slaughtering one sexy showgirl after another. Alone with Kitty in her theater dressing room, a tormented Slade is finally besieged by waiting police, but manages to escape into the building's catacombs. He leads Warwick and his minions on a harrowing chase before they eventually corner him in the upper level, by a window. Staring down his antagonists like a trapped animal, the knife-wielding Ripper spins about, crashes through the glass and plunges several stories into the river below.

WHY IT'S IMPORTANT:

Is Jack the Ripper a "monster"? Hollywood seems to think so, treating the Father of all Serial Killers as something so larger-than-life, he might as well be supernatural... a very close cousin of Mr. Hyde's, perhaps. Hitchcock's silent take on this subject focused on the suspicion a mysterious new "lodger" inspires: is he or is he not the notorious Ripper? He isn't. But when 20th Century-Fox embarked on their own version of *The Lodger* in the early '40s, they made no bones about the fact that the man suspected of being England's most notorious killer was indeed the genuine Jack.

Fox mostly avoided horror movies, but a low-budget programmer called *The Undying Monster* had propelled director John Brahm to a certain prominence in the studio as their "go to" helmer of atmospheric chillers. Although under contract, George Sanders had refused to appear in Brahm's *Monster* (a nifty werewolf story), but apparently had no problem playing second fiddle to personal friend Laird Cregar in the same director's *The Lodger* one year later. And this film truly is Cregar's showcase. Whether quoting the Bible or throttling beautiful actresses, his hulking menace, coupled with a soft-spoken guardedness, provides a portrait of the Ripper that is grandly theatrical in the extreme and completely convincing at the same time.

Delighted with the film's performance, Fox ordered Brahm and company to do it all over again (sort of) in a similar gaslit-vehicle called *Hangover Square*. The film turned out well -- it anticipates Hitchcock's *Psycho* in several curious ways -- but Cregar wound up accidentally killing himself near the end of production with an ill-advised crash diet. Ironically, Fox's resident Sydney Greenstreet though he'd be a more commercial Hollywood commodity if he lost weight. All he succeeded in doing was losing his life, depriving fans of a wonderful actor and a truly unforgettable screen personality.

Best scenes: The opening alley attack (ABOVE; originally designed to appear later, but moved up because it was so good); the handheld POV murder of Annie and just about anything from the climax at the theater which amounts to a veritable catalogue of expressionistic angles and compositional set-ups.

Shadowy "lines" ripple through the injured Ripper as he hobbles toward another killing during the movie's thrilling climax.

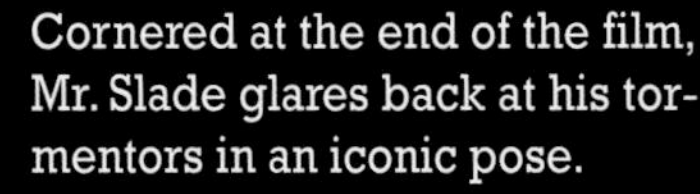

Cornered at the end of the film, Mr. Slade glares back at his tormentors in an iconic pose.

Laird Cregar re-teamed with George Sanders in John Brahm's *Hangover Square*, a 1945 semi-sequel.

The "Masterpiece Theatre" of Hammer vampire flicks; austere, stylish, gory...

41 THE KISS OF THE VAMPIRE 1963

1.66

WHO MADE IT:

Hammer Films/Rank (U.K.)/Universal-International (U.S.). Director: Don Sharp. Producer: Anthony Hinds. Writer: John Elder. Cinematographer (Eastman Color): Alan Hume. Music: James Bernard. Starring Clifford Evans (Professor Zimmer), Noel Willman (Dr. Ravna), Edward De Souza (Gerald Harcourt), Jennifer Daniel (Marianne Harcourt), Barry Warren (Carl Ravna), Jacquie Wallis (Sabena Ravna), Peter Madden (Bruno), Vera Cook (Anna), Isobel Black (Tania).

WHAT IT'S ABOUT:

Young newlyweds stopping off at a small isolated community are befriended by a charming nobleman and his followers. Before long it's established that these locals belong to a mysterious cult and have insidious plans for the unsuspecting visitors. Only a defiant but frequently drunken doctor, an occult expert, has the knowledge and courage to deal with this elite clan of vampires, having been forced to stake his own daughter in order to exorcize their evil influence. When the visitor's young bride disappears in the nobleman's castle after a masked ball, her very existence is denied by everyone connected to the event. Desperate, the young man joins forces with the well-prepared doctor and eventually manages to rescue his wife, even as the vampires become trapped within their own mansion walls. At the same time, an ancient spell brings forth hundreds of bloodthirsty bats from Hell, which swoop down on the vampires and savagely end their unnatural lives.

WHY IT'S IMPORTANT:

The Kiss of the Vampire marks the end of Hammer's golden period, sometimes called their "magic hour"; from 1957 to 1964, the little British film company changed the face of horror cinema, defining the modern, reality-based, action-oriented fright scenario. From this point on, most of their movies would be warmed-over retreads of earlier success, with only a handful of notable exceptions (*The Devil's Bride*, *The Vampire Lovers*) breaking the pattern of steady decline.

But *Kiss* is very much a Hammer thriller of classic vintage, groundbreaking, adult and stylishly decadent. Wisely giving veteran "vampire movie" director Terence Fisher a break, the studio turned to Don Sharp, who would be back for Hammer's interesting but less-satisfying *The Reptile* two years later. *The Kiss* plot borrows elements from Universal's mid-'30s cult classic *The Black Cat*, with an innocent young couple at the mercy of stylish devil worshippers living in a remote fortress. This time, these Satanists are also vampires...a connection frequently on display in early '60s horror films (Mario Bava's *Black Sunday*). With the aid of a "fallen" Van Helsing-type (Clifford Evans) and his magical exorcism formula, goodness ultimately triumphs, and the infernal vamps are dramatically ripped apart by a swarm of attacking ...bats! ("...evil against evil..."). It's a great conceptual reversal, helped enormously by an impressive, animated matte painting (see opposite page).

When Universal eventually sold the film to NBC in the late '60s for a prime-time airing, "family friendly" re-shooting was performed by U's TV unit, and an entire, totally unnecessary subplot was added (the same weird fate befell Hammer's *The Evil of Frankenstein*). Retitled *Kiss of Evil*, this bizarre hybrid played on TV for decades but was thankfully retired in recent years, and the well-crafted original is once again available for our pleasure. As the last of the great Hammers and a deft elitist thriller in its own right, it's certainly worth checking out.

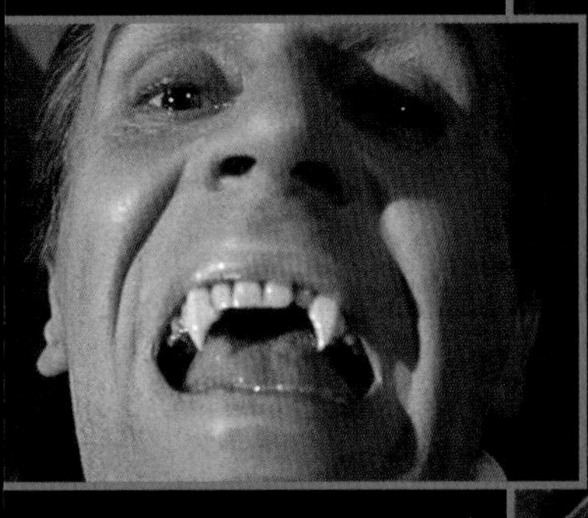

Lead vampire Dr. Ravna (played impressively by Noel Willman) began life in *The Brides of Dracula* treatments; both Hammer films swapped plot/character elements before going into production.

A more fallible Van Helsing, Professor Zimmer (Cliffords Evans) grimly instructs a deflated Gerald-Harcourt (Edward de Souza).

The movie's unique finale was a stylish blend of animated special effects, bat props on wings, and actors with blood all over their faces, shot at interesting angles and with distorted lenses.

A tad more than usual (even for Hammer), *Kiss* focused on the erotic possibilities of the vampire theme.

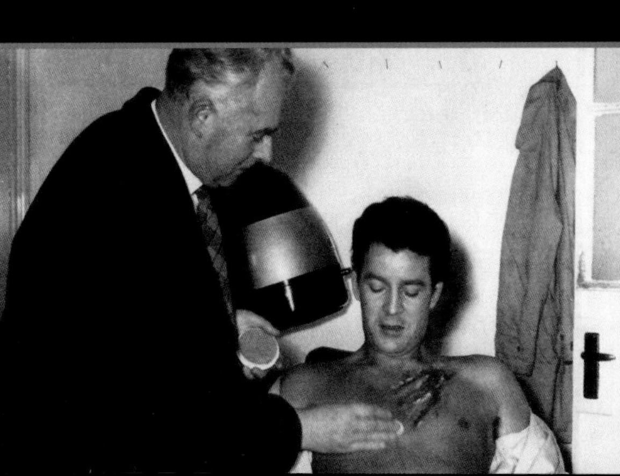

Edward De Souza (previously seen in *Phantom of the Opera*) receives some finishing touches for his chest wound make-up.

Stylishly colorful horror anthology, Italian-style, provides Boris with a juicy role...

40

BLACK SABBATH 1964

92 1.85

Poster/photos: © 1964 Alfredo Leone Trust

WHO MADE IT:

Galatea Film (Italy) and Alta Vista/American International (U.S.). Director: Mario Bava. Producers: Salvatore Billiterri, Polo Mercuri. Writers: Mario Bava, Alberto Bevilacqua and Marcello Fondato, based on stories by Ivan Chekhov, Aleksei Tolstoy and F.G. Snyder. Cinematography (Technicolor): Ubaldo Terzano. Music: Roberto Nicolosi (Italy); Les Baxter (U.S). Starring Boris Karloff (Gorca "The Wurdalak"), Mark Damon (Vladimire d'Urfe "The Wurdalak"), Michele Mercier (Rosy "The Telephone"), Jacqueline Pierreux (Helen Chester "The Drop pf Water"), Lidia Alfonsi (Mary "The Drop of Water"), Massimo Righi (Pietro "The Wurdalak"), Milly Monti (Maid "The Drop of Water").

WHAT IT'S ABOUT:

Boris Karloff hosts three tales of the supernatural. In "The Drop of Water," a nurse who prepares dead bodies for final disposition is called in to take care of a recently deceased old crone believed to have occult powers. When no one is looking, she steals the hag's ring, and later that night is haunted by mysterious sounds (drops of water from a faucet) and weird, terrifying phenomena. The dead old woman herself finally pays a call, reclaiming her property and frightening the sorry thief to death. In "The Telephone," two women are terrorized by a mysterious phone caller who may or may not be the dead man both had been involved with. He winds up murdering one and attacking the other before he himself is brutally slain by the desperate survivor. But a final telephone message seems to indicate that this supernatural killer can't be destroyed, and will return again and again. Finally, in "The Wurdalak," a family is horrified when their patriarch returns home darkly changed after slaying a local bandit. Now a remorseless blood-lusting vampire, he preys on his loved ones and promptly transforms them into what he is.

WHY IT'S IMPORTANT:

So successful was *Black Sunday* for American International Pictures that they asked director Mario Bava for another movie very much along the same lines, stylistically...only this time, the cobwebbed ruins and light-strobed faces would be in eye-popping color, playing to the director-artist's ultimate area of speciality.

And most prominent among these brilliantly-lighted faces is that of Boris Karloff. Doing a variation of his hosting duties on TV's *Thriller* (*Black Sabbath* is a three-story anthology probably inspired by the previous year's *Tales of Terror*), Big K the actor is at the heart of the film's most lavish and praised episode, "The Wurdalak." Playing a juicy role that ultimately led to ill health (he'd be seen in a wheelchair for the rest of his screen career), old pro Karloff delivers the goods with relish, as always.

Apart from "The Wurdalak," director-visualist Bava gets the most out of "A Drop of Water" (another gothic containing unforgettable set-pieces and imagery) and "The Telephone," a modern ghost story with unexpected lesbian overtones that were played down with dubbing and careful editing in the American version.

Best scenes: the ghostly corpse in her rocking chair; approaching the thief with hands raised (both from "Drop"); the dark arrival of the patriarch; the "Why did you leave us?" chorus in the ruins; the final, fatal seduction of Vladimir (all "Wurdalak").

Rocking chair witch: one of the iconic nightmare images from "The Drop of Water," first of the three tales of terror in AIP's re-edited U.S. version of Bava's colorful anthology. RIGHT: Boris Karloff as "The Wurdalak," his last great horror characterization.

Blood ties: Like *Black Sunday*, the American release of *Black Sabbath* featured an evocative Les Baxter music score that seemed an ideal match for Bava's richly textured visuals.

Gorca (Karloff) displays the severed head of a local bandit.

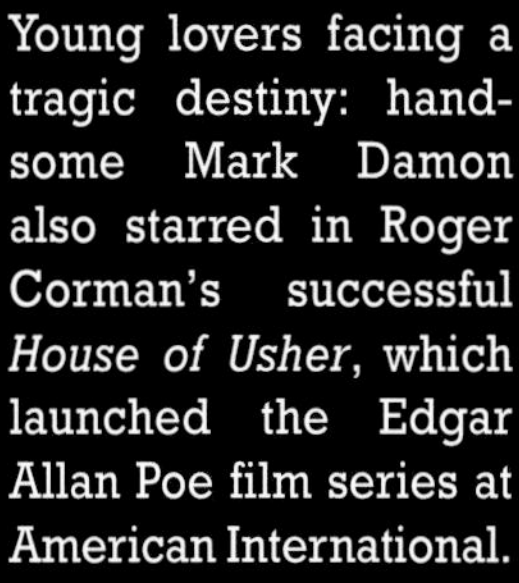

Young lovers facing a tragic destiny: handsome Mark Damon also starred in Roger Corman's successful *House of Usher*, which launched the Edgar Allan Poe film series at American International.

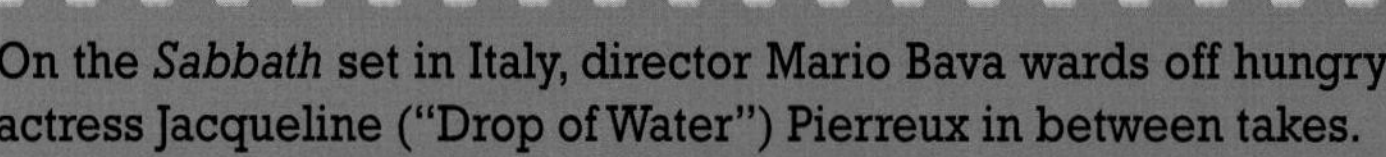

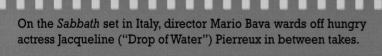

On the *Sabbath* set in Italy, director Mario Bava wards off hungry actress Jacqueline ("Drop of Water") Pierreux in between takes.

Tim Burton's fearless, gleefully horrific adaptation is gloriously on target...

39 SWEENEY TODD 2007

116 1.85 

WHO MADE IT:

DreamWorks/Warner Bros. (U.K./U.S.) Director: Tim Burton. Producers: Richard D. Zanuck, John Logan, Walter F. Parkes, Laurie MacDonald. Writer: John Logan, based on the play by Christopher Bond with music by Stephen Sondheim and Hugh Wheeler. Cinematography: Dariusz Wolski. Music: Stephen Sondheim. Starring Johnny Depp (Benjamin Barker/Sweeney Todd), Helena Bonham Carter (Mrs. Lovett), Alan Rickman (Judge Turpin), Jamie Campbell Bower (Anthony Hope), Timothy Spall (Beadle Bamford), Sacha Baron Cohen (Davie Collins/Signor Adolfo Pirelli), Ed Sanders (Tobias "Toby" Ragg), Laura Michelle Kelly (Lucy Barker), Jayne Wisener (Johanna Barker).

WHAT IT'S ABOUT:

In Victorian London, barber Benjamin Barker changes his name to Sweeney Todd and returns after fifteen years in exile to exact revenge on corrupt Judge Turpin. This corrupt official had framed Barker for a crime he didn't commit and took custody of Barker's young wife and child in the process. Todd now works with the smitten but slightly deranged Mrs. Lovett, owner of a local meat-pie shop, to complete his sacred mission of murder, which escalates far beyond his initial target to include all who have caused him great pain. Along the way, Todd tries to rescue his daughter Johanna from Turpin's clutches, winds up shoving Mrs. Lovett into a furnace, and accidentally slays his long-lost beloved wife. Todd then allows his own throat to be cut by the adopted son of a former victim, thus ending his agony.

WHY IT'S IMPORTANT:

After three decades of fascinating but frequently uneven fantasy/horror confections, director Tim Burton finally hit a bullseye with this letter-perfect film adaptation of Stephen Sondheim's infamous stage thriller. It's one of those lightning-in-a-bottle experiences: the right director, the ideal leads, a horror sub-genre (the grand guignol) surprisingly suited for Broadway-style musical counterpointing. And while this material certainly isn't for all tastes, if you'll forgive the expression, it brilliantly achieves what a great horror experience is designed to do: push audience endurance to the max with audacious, imaginative violence and pathos.

As the single-minded Demon Barber of Fleet Street, Burton's favorite performer Johnny Depp has never been more solemnly electric. His grim, mostly understated commitment to vengeance soars to life during the musical numbers, which are filmed with a self-assurance that echoes Sondheim's own *West Side Story*. Depp is nicely matched by another Burton muse, Helena Bonham Carter, as pie-making criminal soulmate Mrs. Lovett. Her desperate need for companionship leads to the creation of a makeshift family (Ed Sanders' Toby, orphaned by Todd's eager blade, assumes the role of dutiful son), but eventually collides with her reluctant husband's mad maneuverings. The final, accidental slaying of Todd/Barker's original great love, the person who inspired his insane vendetta to begin with, is tragedy at its most darkly compelling.

Best scenes: Pirelli's murder in the trunk, both of Judge Turpin's sessions in the barber chair, the slaughter montage, Todd's gut-wrenching discovery of his beloved wife's slaying, Mrs. Lovett's fiery fate in the furnace.

Todd's breathless toying with his hated nemesis Judge Turpin (Alan Rickman) provides Burton's madhouse of a musical with its most suspenseful sequence.

"At last my arm is complete!" sings an exultant Benjamin Barker, aka Sweeney Todd (Johnny Depp).

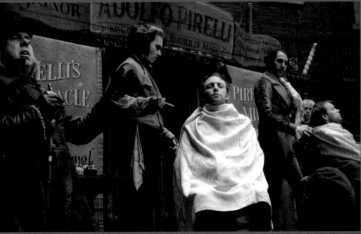

Battle of the blades: Launching his intricate revenge scheme, Todd challenges barber extraordinaire Pirelli (Sasha Baron Cohen) to a public shaving contest.

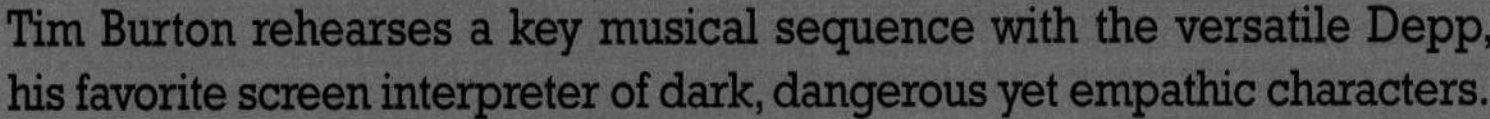

Tim Burton rehearses a key musical sequence with the versatile Depp, his favorite screen interpreter of dark, dangerous yet empathic characters.

38 MAD LOVE 1935

WHO MADE IT:

Metro-Goldwyn-Mayer (U.S.). Director: Karl Freund. Producer: John W. Considine Jr. Writers: John L. Balderston and Guy Endore, from the novel *Les Mains D'Orlac,* by Maurice Renard. Cinematography (b/w): Chester A. Lyons, Gregg Toland. Music: Dimitri Z. Tiompkin. Starring Peter Lorre (Dr. Gogol), Frances Drake (Yvonne Orlac), Colin Clive (Stephen Orlac), Ted Healy (Reagan), Sara Haden (Marie, Yvonne's maid), Edward Brophy (Rollo the Knife Thrower), Henry Kolker (Prefect Rosset), Keye Luke (Dr. Wong), May Beatty (Francoise).

WHAT IT'S ABOUT:

In Paris, the great surgeon Dr. Gogol, a man obsessed with dark fetishes, falls insanely in love with stage performer Yvonne Orlac, who is married to the famous concert pianist Stephen Orlac. When Orlac's hands are badly crushed in a train accident, Yvonne overcomes her repulsion for Gogol and begs him to help Stephen. Gogol surgically grafts the hands of executed knife-throwing murderer Rollo onto Orlac, but soon the pianist develops a bizarre fixation on his new appendages, insisting that they have a murderous mind of their own. Realizing he can push his rival over the edge, Gogol even dresses up as a bizarre "former patient," a man with his head restored. Now completely mad and about to kill Yvonne, Gogol is finally stopped by a knife thrown by Orlac...the deadly hands of Rollo finding their fatal mark.

WHY IT'S IMPORTANT:

MGM, Hollywood's "prestige" studio, rarely made fright films, but the few they did produce had curious, offbeat charms. *Mad Love* not only provides a nifty showcase for pseudo-horror star Peter Lorre; it's a rather daring-for-its-day depiction of alternate lifestyles (the S&M scene) that must have seemed awfully bizarre for conventional audiences of the 1930s. Dr. Gogol's perverse sexual obsessions are every bit as "horrific" as the implied fantasy-terror scenario the plotline shares. Maurice Renard's venerable "are a dead killer's transplanted hands taking on a murderous life of their own?" concept really doesn't need an S&M angle to hold our interest, but with a darkly sensitive actor like Lorre at the heart of the melodrama (shades of *M*), this unique portrait of personal perversion winds up dominating the film.

And there are other creative pleasures on display as well. Memorable, clever dialogue isn't generally associated with golden age horror films (Whale and Lewton aside), but Balderston/Endore's script for *Mad Love* has more than it's share of juicy quotables: "Impossible? Napoleon said that word isn't French," "I've conquered life...why can't I conquer love?" and even simple lines like"I repulse you" and "You despise me!" cut through the heart like daggers when delivered so perfectly by the self-loathing Gogol.

Pleasing fans of the genre, *Mad Love* not only serves up the wonderful Peter Lorre, but a pair of likeable Universal horror stars as well: Dr. Frankenstein himself, Colin Clive, portrays pianist Orlac with his usual high-strung conviction, while Francis Drake (Karloff's wife in *The Invisible Ray*) goes from pop-submissive to doting spouse to the wax figure of Galetea before final fade-out, looking ravishing in every incarnation.

Best scenes: Gogol's first visit to the S&M theater; the operating room breakdown, neck-braced Gogol's big reveal to Orlac; maniacal Gogol laughing uncontrollably as he walks up the stairs; his final, highly emotional confrontation with Yvonne/Galetea.

Mad Love broke new ground by introducing American moviegoers to the realities of live horror theater and the S&M scene.

Surgeon saves pianist by replacing his hands with those of a killer…but who controls their actions?

Gogol's grotesque reveal of mechanical hands and a neck brace are among the film's highlights.

Star Peter Lorre had a special talent for creating incredibly creepy yet sympathetic screen villains. As seen here, in the climax of *Mad Love*, he jumps from maniacal wickedness to anguished heartbreak without missing a beat.

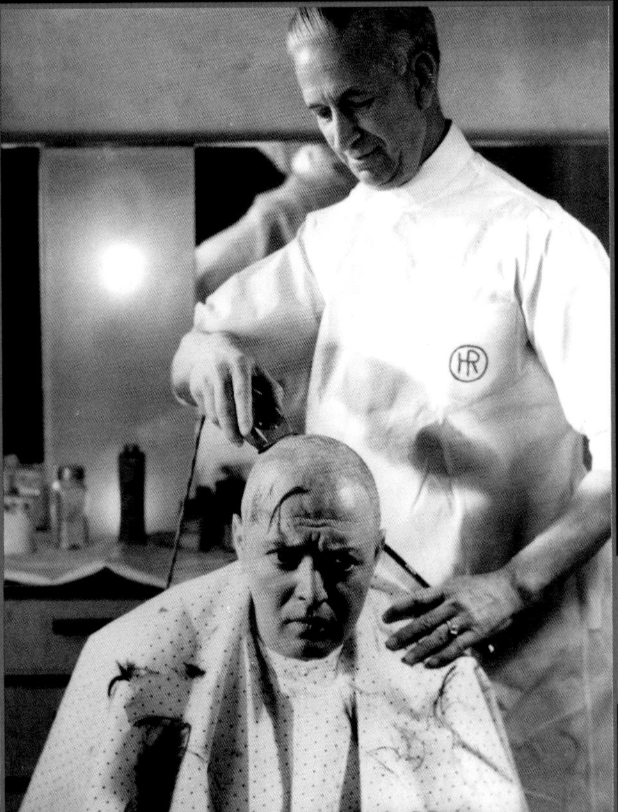

MGM's resident make-up guru Jack Dawn gives star Peter Lorre an all-too necessary haircut for his *Mad Love* role.

The first zombie movie is a peculiar visual poem, bolstered by Bela...

37

WHITE ZOMBIE 1932

 1.37

WITH THESE ZOMBIE EYES
he rendered her powerless

WHITE
ZOMBIE

WITH THIS ZOMBIE GRIP
he made her perform his every desire!

WHO MADE IT:

United Artists (U.S.). Director: Victor Halperin. Producer: Edward Halperin. Writer: Garnett Weston. Cinematography (b/w): Arthur Martinelli. Music: Guy Bevier, Xavier Cugat, Gaston Borch, Nathaniel Dett, Nem Herkin, H. Maurice Jacquet, Leo Kempinski, Hugo Riesenfeld. Starring Bela Lugosi ("Murder" Legendre), Madge Bellamy (Madeleine Short Parker), Joseph Cawthorn (Dr. Bruner), Robert Frazer (Charles Beaumont), John Harron (Neil Parker), Brandon Hurst (Silver the butler), George Burr Macannan (Von Gelder), Frederick Peters (Chauvin).

WHAT IT'S ABOUT:

Neil Parker and Madeline Short, a young couple American couple in Haiti, are invited by a casual acquaintance, Charles Beaumont, to visit his plantation and be married there. On the way over they encounter a mysterious, evil-looking figure known as Murder Legendre, leader of a group of hollow-eyed men identified as zombies. Complicating matters, the plantation owner is very much in love with Madeline, although his romantic advances are rebuffed. With no honest way to win her affection, Beaumont turns to the risky black magic of local voodoo master Legendre, who temporarily transforms her into one of his zombies. The plan is to have Madeline declared legally dead, so that Neil can return to the states and Beaumont can have her secretly revived, in order to woo her once again. But the devil-like Legendre has dark plans of his own for the beautiful young woman, and soon Beaumont, transformed into a semi-zombie himself, becomes a helpless prisoner in his seaside castle. Neil joins forces with a knowledgeable missionary named Dr. Bruner, and eventually this daring duo manage to penetrate Legendre's fortress. Battling both zombies and the voodoo master's unending bag of tricks, the rescuers find an unexpected ally in repentant Charles Beaumont, who manages to break through Legendre's voodoo spell and attack him. Both men go hurtling from the castle parapet to the rocky beach far below. With Legendre's demise, Madeline emerges from her death-like zombie state and is re-united with loving husband Neil.

WHY IT'S IMPORTANT:

The earliest important zombie movie of the sound era, *White Zombie* is a rare visual poem, an unusual Hollywood presentation of an indie that gave star Bela Lugosi his second most important role in the early '30s. Many buffs consider Murder Legendre to be Dracula, literally, in one of his many incarnations over the centuries, an amusing and entirely logical notion that adds flavor to the film.

And it's a curious, bittersweet flavor to begin with; *White Zombie* is more fairy tale than reality-based thriller. Using dreamlike atmosphere and a surfeit of imaginative optical tricks, the Halperin brothers set about defining "zombie cinema" as, in addition to horrific: exotic, fragile, indistinct, and poetic. Love and unrequited love are central themes. Legendre is Satan as much as he is Count Dracula, corrupting susceptible mortals at every turn with typical Lugosi relish. But for all the classic horror iconography on display, is *White Zombie* really a supernatural story? The foul Legendre's control over comatose men is self-evident, but are they actually dead, or just under exotic hypnotic control? Only a few "gunshots-being-absorbed" close-ups say with certainty that something literally fantastic is going on, stamping these vacant-eyed shamblers as the real thing.

Boasting Lugosi in his prime and a high-road treatment of B-movie ingredients, *White Zombie* remains a peculiar little gem, never to be duplicated (not even by game filmmakers Victor and Edward Halperin, who will revisit the genre with less success ten years later).

ABOVE: an innovative glass painting of Legendre's castle. The Halperins were fortunate to have Universal's sets at their disposal, elevating the low-budget film's production values several notches with pre-existing, expensively-wrought environments.

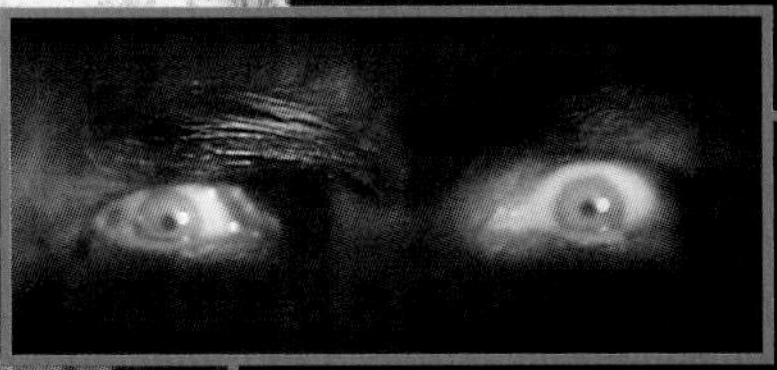

LEFT: Butler Silver (Brandon Hurst) looks on suspiciously as Legendre (Bela Lugosi) and Beaumont (Robert Frazer) vie for control of zombified victim Madeleine (Madge Bellamy).

Lugosi's satanic character, happily sculpting another wax figure, torments his now-spellbound employer (Frazer).

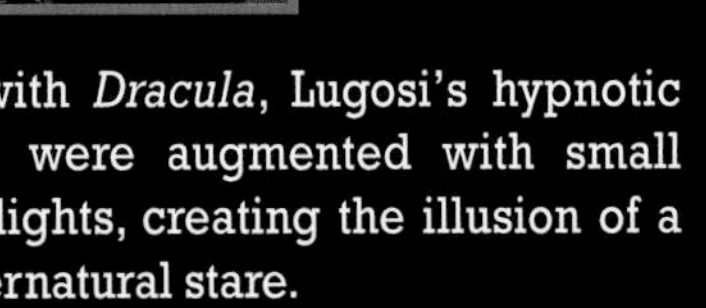

As with *Dracula*, Lugosi's hypnotic eyes were augmented with small spotlights, creating the illusion of a supernatural stare.

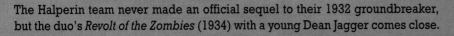

The Halperin team never made an official sequel to their 1932 groundbreaker, but the duo's *Revolt of the Zombies* (1934) with a young Dean Jagger comes close.

Chaney II rejuvenates Universal horror with the screen's most iconic werewolf...

36 THE WOLF MAN 1941

 1.37

Poster/photos: © 1941 Universal Studios

WHO MADE IT:

Universal Pictures (U.S.). Director: George Waggner. Producer: George Waggner. Writer: Curt Siodmak. Cinematography: Joseph Valentine. Music: Charles Previn, Hans J. Salter, Frank Skinner (all uncredited). Starring Lon Chaney Jr. (Larry Talbot/The Wolf Man), Claude Rains (Sir John Talbot), Warren William (Dr. Lloyd), Evelyn Ankers (Gwen Conliffe), Ralph Bellamy (Col. Montford), Patric Knowles (Frank Andrews), Bela Lugosi (Bela), Maria Ouspenskaya (Maleva), Fay Helm (Jenny Williams), Forrester Harvey (Mr. Twiddle), Ottola Nesmith (Mrs. Bally).

WHAT IT'S ABOUT:

Larry Talbot returns home after many years and is reunited with his father, Sir John Talbot. Although the two men have had personal difficulties in the past, both resolve to start their relationship anew, with Larry set to run the vast Talbot estate. While enjoying a pleasant evening out with attractive Gwen Conliffe, daughter of a local shop owner, Larry rushes to the aid of Gwen's girlfriend Jenny Williams when a wolf attacks her in the forest. Larry's bitten by the beast, but the following morning there is no trace of a wound...only the bodies of Jenny and Bela, a traveling gypsy fortune-teller, who was beaten to death by the silver-topped cane Talbot was using as a weapon. Distraught and perplexed by the bizarre tragedy, Larry is eventually told by Maleva, Bela's gypsy mother, that her slain son was a werewolf; Larry, bitten during the struggle, is now doomed to become one himself every time the full moon rises. Indeed, Talbot winds up seeing the fabled pentagram in the palm of Gwen Conliffe's hand, a sure sign that she's his next victim. But before the fully-transformed Wolf Man can murder Gwen, he is confronted by his own father, Sir John, wielding Larry's silver-tipped cane. Defending himself against the savage night monster, Sir John slams him repeatedly with the formidable stick, finally beating him into submission. And as the Wolf Man lies dying on the foggy forest ground, his grotesque, inhuman facial features revert to those of Larry Talbot. A horrified Sir John, realizing that he has killed his own son, can only look on in stunned silence.

WHY IT'S IMPORTANT:

After failing artistically and commercially with *Werewolf of London* in the mid-'30s, Universal created an original, more relatable lycanthrope in the form of Larry Talbot, aka *The Wolf Man*, just before the outbreak of World War II. This time, the movie magic was there: U's newly-minted horror star Lon Chaney Jr. would eventually portray the hyper-tragic character in a total of five movies, from '41 to '48.

Anticipating the more sophisticated "psychological" approach to horror melodrama that RKO's Val Lewton would soon embrace, *The Wolf Man* tries to have it both ways. Everyone tells poor Larry that his own troubled mind is creating these dark transformation fantasies, even as the viewing audience witnesses him morphing into a full-fledged werewolf. Originally, screenwriter Curt Siodmak showed the titular monster only from Talbot's point of view, glimpsed briefly in mirrors and pools of water. But Universal insisted on a more tangible bogeyman in the tradition of their past successes. So makeup artist/resident creature creator Jack Pierce really went to town on Chaney Jr., improving the more modest, batlike look he had developed for *Werewolf of London* with an aggressive, truly animalistic re-imagining.

Although Hammer's *The Curse of the Werewolf* (1961) would eventually score as the definitive lycanthrope saga, *The Wolf Man* remains a legitimate triumph in its own right, the best horror movie Universal made in the '40s and a satisfying vehicle for yet another of their iconic "mon-stars."

"Even a man who is pure in heart..." Agreeable Larry Talbot (Lon Chaney Jr.) buys a wolf-crowned walking stick from potential sweetheart Gwen Conliffe (Evelyn Ankers). It's his first brush with lycanthropy.

Universal Pictures surrounded new horror star Chaney Jr. with a supporting cast to die for: Claude Rains, Maria Ouspenskya (both were recently cast in Warners' prestigious *Kings Row*), Ralph Bellamy, Warren William (left), and even Bela Lugosi as the tragic gypsy-werewolf Bela, who puts his fateful bite on Larry.

The Wolf Man gets a yak-hair trim from Universal's resident make-up impresario, Jack Pierce.

Weird mystery-horror hybrid with stylized color and a first-rate monster...

35 DOCTOR X 1933

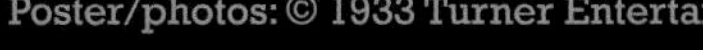

WHO MADE IT:

First National and Vitaphone through Warner Brothers (U.S.). Director: Michael Curtiz. Producers (uncredited): Hal B. Wallis, Darryl F. Zanuck. Writers: Robert Tasker & Earl Baldwin, based on the play by Howard W. Comstock & Allen C. Miller. Cinematography: (two-strip Technicolor): Ray Rennahan. Music: Bernard Kaun. Starring Lionel Atwill (Dr. Jerry Xavier), Fay Wray (Joanne 'Joan' Xavier), Lee Tracy (Lee Taylor), Preston Foster (Dr. Wells), John Wray (Dr. Haines), Harry Beresford (Dr. Duke), Arthur Edmund Carewe (Dr. Rowtz), Leila Bennett (Mamie), George Rosener (Otto), Robert Warwick (Police Commissioner Stevens).

WHAT IT'S ABOUT:

Mysterious and grisly murders occur on nights with a full moon, prompting enterprising, brash young city reporter Lee Taylor to investigate. The police are also on the trail of the flesh-eating serial killer, and their search leads to the laboratory of renowned surgeon Doctor Xavier...is one of the esteemed scientists on his staff the mass murderer? To aid in the solving of this mystery, Xavier stages re-creations of the various crimes, using his servants and sometimes even his beautiful daughter Joanne as players. The true killer is ultimately revealed as the armless, mild-tempered Dr. Wells, who uses his own bizarre creation, synthetic flesh, to make his body whole again while transforming into a grotesque, gargoyle-like fiend. Only an unexpected attack from the hidden reporter halts Wells' strangling of Xavier's captive daughter. Their struggle ends with the killer fiend, set on fire by a hurled lamp, crashing through a window and falling to his doom over a cliff.

WHY IT'S IMPORTANT:

Although best known for their gangster melodramas of the '30s and '40s, Warner Bros. occasionally took a tentative dip in the horror movie pool. *Doctor X* is an early success story, which, like the same year's *Mystery of the Wax Museum*, was shot in two-strip Technicolor. This process-in-progress (three-strip Tech would come along a couple of years later) imbues both pictures with a unique, high contrast luminosity well-suited to the subject matter.

The casting of Lee Tracy as a wisecracking reporter (kind of a pre-war Kolchak) suggests that *Doctor X*'s producers were concerned about the unsavory aspects of the horror content, and hoped to take the edge off with an overtly comical hero. Also kept around for annoying "humor relief" is Leila Bennet (Mamie the maid), who performed similar duties in *Mark of the Vampire*.

But whatever demerits the film gets for its dependence on laughs are wiped out instantly in the face of *Doctor X*'s tour de force finale...and what a face it is! Preston Foster using "synthetic flesh" to transform himself into a living gargoyle is one of the high points of horror cinema, from any era. Obviously inspired by this opportunity, director Michael Curtiz pulls out all the creative stops, dissolving from imaginative close-ups (viewed from within the flesh dish!) to offbeat overhead angles, and back again. The Technicolor lighting actually becomes a character in this truly amazing landmark sequence, an ideal showcase for Perc Westmore's macabre, innovative make-up design.

Ironically, most of the nation saw *Doctor X* in black and white, with only large cities being privy to the two-color version. But either way, this well-filmed thriller resonates, with Foster's ultra-sick reading of the line "synthetic flesh!" forever burned into the brains of every frightened patron who bought a ticket.

The operating theater in Dr. Xavier's mansion is used to re-create various "moon killer" crimes, and ultimately flush out the true culprit. A minimal set, it benefitted greatly from early, dye-transfer Technicolor.

"Synthetic flesh!": a phrase that, once heard, is never forgotten.

In most venues, *Doctor X* was presented as a black-and-white movie (above); the film played in color only in large cities. Notice the difference in psychological flavor when comparing both images.

The mysterious moon killer (Preston Foster, in all his synthetic glory) menaces Joan Xavier (Fay Wray) during the film's tense climax.

The unquestioned highlight of *Doctor X* is Preston Foster's ghoulish transformation into a monstrous, murdering fiend. While color is generally a negative in classic horror films, it was used brilliantly by director Michael Curtiz in this case. The same year, Curtiz, Atwill, Wray and two-strip Technicolor were re-united for a similar thriller, *Mystery of the Wax Museum*, eventually remade as *House of Wax*.

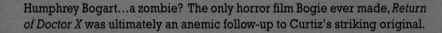

Humphrey Bogart…a zombie? The only horror film Bogie ever made, *Return of Doctor X* was ultimately an anemic follow-up to Curtiz's striking original.

Stylish, energetic sequel to "Horror of Dracula" packs a Freudian punch...

34 THE BRIDES OF DRACULA 1960

85  1.66

WHO MADE IT:

Hammer Films (U.K.)/Universal-International (U.S.). Director: Terence Fisher. Producer: Anthony Hinds. Writers: Jimmy Sangster, Peter Bryan, Edward Percy. Cinematography (Technicolor): Jack Asher. Music: Malcolm Williamson. Starring Peter Cushing (Dr. Van Helsing), Martita Hunt (Baroness Meinster), Freda Jackson (Greta), Yvonne Monlaur (Marianne), David Peel (Baron Meinster), Miles Malleson (Dr. Tobler), Henry Oscar (Herr Lang), Mona Washbourne (Frau Lang), Victor Brooks (Hans), Michael Ripper (Coachman), Andree Melly (Gina), Fred Johnson (Cure), Norman Piere (Landlord).

WHAT IT'S ABOUT:

Stranded in a small village, an attractive young teacher named Marianne spends the night at the mysterious mansion of Baroness Meinster and her half-mad servant. Soon she meets and frees the chained Baron Meinster, a handsome, charming young man who is, in truth, a ravenous vampire kept in hiding by his heartbroken mother. Marianne manages to escape with her life after Meinster turns on the Countess, and finds support in the form of Dr. Van Helsing, who has been summoned to the area to combat a recent outbreak of vampirism. Van Helsing fails to destroy Baron Meinster during their first encounter, but brings peace to his now-vampiric mother, who confesses that she encouraged his wicked ways and feels tragically responsible for what has happened. Ultimately tracking his quarry to an old windmill, Van Helsing himself is bitten, and must agonizingly burn out the evil contagion with a red-hot poker. Meinster is halted by a faceful of holy water, which scars and infuriates him, and the flames that he himself causes when he kicks over the poker coals. Racing from the fiery scene, he is destroyed by the shadow of a giant crucifix – in truth, the shadow of the windmill blade, turned cross-wise by the resourceful Van Helsing.

WHY IT'S IMPORTANT:

Hammer's eagerly-anticipated sequel to *Horror of Dracula* had the audacity not to feature Dracula at all, but a "pretty boy" disciple known as Baron Meister (David Peel) in his place. Considering that Christopher Lee had become an international star playing the bloodthirsty Count, this was something of a calculated risk.

Calculated, that is, because the film does retain Peter Cushing as steadfast Dr. Van Helsing, repeating one of his finest characterizations. It was also produced during the period where it seemed Hammer could do no wrong...and sure enough, *The Brides of Dracula* is the second-best vampire movie they ever made, just behind *Horror*. And it's light years ahead of the later Dracula sequels Lee made for the studio.

One of the reasons the film works so well is that the original Hammer mandate was still in place: justify shocking bloodshed and sexuality with sophisticated, mature, and unprecedented explorations of the psychological motivations of "monsters" or similarly tainted characters. If Christopher Lee's Dracula was the fallen artistocrat, David Peel's Meinster is the perverted offspring of an equally tragic member of high society (Martita Hunt), and their mother-son relationship suggests an unnatural intimacy not lost on critics and viewers. With more lavish production values at their disposal and a larger cast (made up of wonderful British character actors), it was pretty obvious that Hammer's talented artisans had done it again, even without the considerable services of Mr. Lee.

Peter Cushing's Van Helsing, introduced in *Horror of Dracula*, was a dedicated, athletic and earnest soldier of Christ, a perfect nemesis for Hammer's stylish vampires.

Half-mad servant Greta (Freda Jackson) helps a fresh young female vampire rise from her grave.

Best scenes: all the early material between *Great Expectations* veterans Martita Hunt (above) and Freda Jackson; Van Helsing's first confrontation with Meinster at his castle; the desperate doctor using a red-hot poker on himself to burn out a vampire bite; his holy water revenge against the Baron.

Fearsome females: In the United States, Universal released Hammer's relatively lavish, Technicolored *Brides of Dracula* with a cheaply-made American co-feature.

MARKED BY THE DEVIL

LEFT: Dracula's young disciple Baron Meinster (David Peel) carries on his master's unholy tradition in *The Brides of Dracula* (Hammer, 1960). ABOVE: A monstrous creature from Hell as it appears in Columbia's *Night* (*Curse*) *of the Demon* ABOVE INSERT: Off-screen *Demon* protagonist Dana Andrews is marked for extinction by a band of rural devil worshippers.

Tidy, supernatural noir embraces the unseen, but also provides an iconic demon...

33 CURSE OF THE DEMON 1958

95 1.66

aka: Night of the Demon

WHO MADE IT:

Sabre Film Productions/Columbia Pictures (U.K.) Director: Jacques Tourneur. Producer: Hal E. Chester. Writers: Charles Bennett and Hal E. Chester, based on story by M.R. James. Cinematography (b/w): Edward Scaife. Music: Clifton Parker. Starring Dana Andrews (Dr. John Holden), Peggy Cummins (Joanna Harrington), Niall MacGinnis (Dr. Julian Karswell), Athene Seyler (Mother Karswell), Liam Redmond (Professor Mark O'Brien), Ewan Roberts (Lloyd Williamson), Peter Elliot (Professor K.T. Kumar), Reginald Beckwith (Mr. Meek), Rosamund Greenwood (Mrs. Meek), Maurice Denham (Professor Harry Harrington), Brian Wilde (Rand Hobart).

WHAT IT'S ABOUT:

When Professor Harry Harrington threatens to expose a devil cult, he is targeted for death, a mission carried out by an enormous, winged, fire-breathing demon. Investigating this mysterious killing are his determined niece Joanna, along with scientific researcher/supernatural debunker Dr. John Holden, who is visiting England for an occult-themed convention. It appears the professor was given a parchment containing ancient Runic symbols from the cult's leader, Julian Karswell, and this is what drew the murderous demon to him. Dr. Karswell is a charming but brittle scientist/magician, a former entertainer who lives richly at the expense of his followers. Holden, at first totally skeptical, comes to accept the real presence of demonic evil when he himself is slipped a parchment. Putting the pieces of this bizarre puzzle together through a series of interviews, demonstrations, and even a séance instigated by Karswell's guilt-ridden mother, Holden realizes that he must pass the parchment back to the man who passed it to him or face the same fate as Professor Harrington. This he succeeds in doing, aboard a train, but the symbols slip away again, this time down the railroad tracks. Current "owner" Karswell desperately gives chase, but the parchment burns before his eyes on some coal. This prompts the return of the gigantic fire demon, who picks up the frantic magician in his talon, swats him to death and then hurls him on the tracks. Everyone assumes Karswell was hit by a passing train, but, as Holden and Joanna agree, it's probably "better not to know."

WHY IT'S IMPORTANT:

As horror began to replace science fiction films in the late '50s, one of Val Lewton's premiere directors from the previous decade, Jacques Tourneur, returned with a vengeance. *Night* (*Curse*) *of the Demon* is a direct outgrowth of the "suggested terror" school so effectively on display in Lewton/Tourneur's *Cat People*, *I Walked with a Zombie*, et al. But, since movie monsters were still in high demand, it hedges its bets with the best damn demon ever created for the movies (please forgive me, *Pumpkinhead*!).

Ostensibly, the tale is about the conversion of stubborn realist Dr. John Holden (Dana Andrews) into a true believer, his mind now open to a world he "never thought possible." But in actuality, the main focus of the story is magician-turned-cult leader Karswell (Niall MacGinnis). Trapped by his Faustian bargain, he must pass on the damning parchment not only to eliminate dangerous enemies, but to protect his own life from infernal retribution. One can easily picture a whole movie about this interesting character's rise and fall, with the semi-colorless "investigator" reduced to a supporting role.

As is, *Curse* (*Night*) *of the Demon* provides a welcome return to the best style of horror to be produced on screen, conjuring a one-of-a-kind classic for lucky fans of the occult.

Stalwart ghostbreaker Dr. Holden faces a genuine challenge in Julian Karswell, here posing as a clown-magician for local youngsters.

Yep, that's really Dana Andrews checking out runic symbols at Stonehenge.

Karswell's parchment threatens Dr. Holden (Dana Andrews) , who nevertheless continues with his hypnosis experiment with demon attack survivor Rand Hobart (Brian Wilde).

The Demon was accomplished with a full-figure puppet and a larger, more detailed and articulated headpiece, complete with talon.

The full-size Demon headpiece, fresh from Les Bowie's make-up lab. Some fans hate the idea of Tourneur "showing the monster."

32

Eyes Without A Face 1960

84

1.66

aka: Horror Chamber of Dr. Faustus

WHO MADE IT:

Champs-Elysees Productions and Lux Film (France)/Lopert Pictures (U.S.) Director: Georges Franju. Producer: Jules Borkon. Writers: Pierre Boileau Thomas Narcejac, Jean Redon, Claude Sautet, Georges Franju Cinematography (b/w): Eugen Schufftan. Music: Maurice Jarre. Starring Pierre Brasseur (Dr. Genessier), Alida Valli (Louise), Juliette Mayniel (Edna Gruber), Edith Scob (Christiane Genessier), Francois Guerin (Jacques) Alexandre Rignault (Inspector Parot), Beatrice Altariba (Paulette).

WHAT IT'S ABOUT:

Baffling the police, noted surgeon Dr. Genessier is responsible for the abduction, murder and mutilation of young women, using his lover/former patient, Louise, as seductive bait. The goal is to restore the face of Genessier's tormented young daughter, Christiane, disfigured in a car accident that the doctor was responsible for. Now, she views life through a mask, enduring a series of sophisticated, grotesque skin/face transplants instigated by driven Genessier. One girl after another is lured into their trap, and for a while it seems Christiane may have the new face she's been praying for. But after a final failure and resulting degeneration, all hope seems lost. A bogus victim planted by the authorities brings the doctor's gruesome operations to a halt Ultimately, he is torn to shreds by the dogs he's been using in his transplant work, released from their kennel by thoroughly mad peace-seeking Christiane.

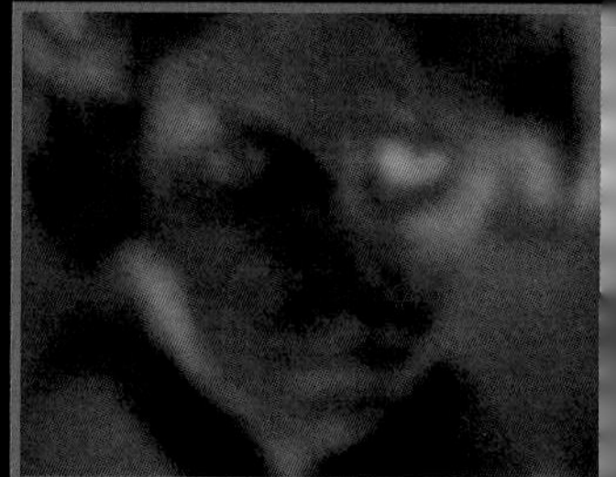

WHY IT'S IMPORTANT:

French critics were horrified by *Eyes Without a Face* when it was first released in 1959. The shock-and-scare genre had received little respect from New Wave-oriented reviewers during this post-war, Hammer-dominated renaissance period. Perhaps intrigued by the challenge, director Georges Franju managed to combine the most graphic of horrors with a seemingly objective, almost documentary-like study of obsessive pride and sanity-challenging guilt. Not surprisingly, *Eyes* left everyone open-mouthed (and in many cases, sick to their stomachs). The film's most notorious set-piece – a methodical surgical operation involving the removal of a human face – is beyond excruciating, undiluted by musical scoring or distractions of any kind. This off-the-scale assault on audience endurance is presented so nonchalantly that the raw, primal horror of the experience rises straight to the top. Love/guilt tends to dictate the murderous actions of the film's principals, but the procuring of pretty young girls by seductive Alida Valli (a full ten years after *The Third Man*) becomes something of a stylish ritual, especially with Maurice Jarre's tart harpsicord score counterpointing her nefarious efforts.

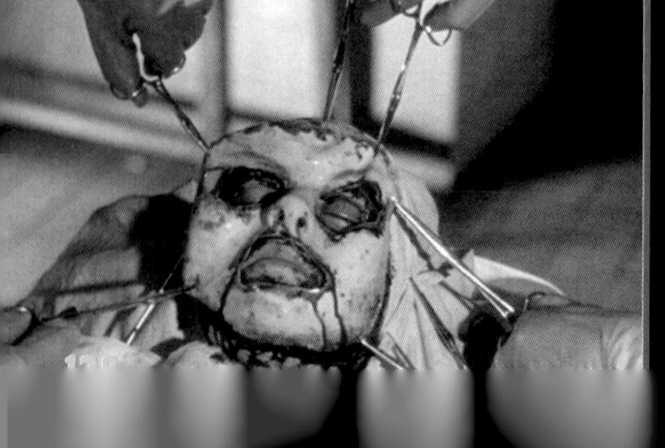

The real villain of the story, of course, is Pierre Brasseur as grimly resolved, low-key egomaniac Dr. Genessier, behind the wheel in an auto accident that disfigured his gentle, almost angelic daughter Christiane. Together with mistress/former patient Louise (Valli), these three form something of a dysfunctional family unit, albeit an exotic one, with the doctor and his lover amorally going about their bloody business under the noses of vaguely interested cops. It is only Juliette's conscience and inevitable descent into madness that halts the ongoing horror.

Best scenes: unmasking before a victim, the infamous "face-lift" operation, Juliette's tragic degeneration conveyed in a series of photos, Dr. Genessier's well-deserved demise.

Fun, wildly inventive genre-buster brings Asian action-fantasy to a global audience...

31 A CHINESE GHOST STORY 1987

98 1.85

Poster/photos: © 1987 Hong Kong Legends

WHO MADE IT:

Hong Kong Legends (China). Director: Ching Siu-tung. Producers: Tsui Hark, Claudie Chung Chun, Zhong Zheng. Writer: Yun Kai-chi, based on the novel by Po Songling. Cinematography (color): Yongheng Huang, Tom Lau, Sander Lee, Jiaogao Li, Putang Liu, Hang-Sang Poon, Wing-Hung Wong. Music: Romeo Diaz, James Wong. Starring Leslie Cheung (Ling Choi Sin), Joey Wang aka Tsu-hsien Wang (Lit Sin Seen), Ma Wu (Yin Chek Hsia), Siu-Ming Lau (Tree Devil), Zhilun Xue (Ching).

WHAT IT'S ABOUT:

Young, humble tax collector Ning Tsai-Shen arrives in a small town to carry on his money-gathering work, which is not exactly popular with the locals. As no one wishes to give him shelter for the evening, Tsai-Shen takes refuge from a downpour by spending the night in the eerie, whispered-about Lan Ro temple, which is said to be haunted. At Lan Ro, he meets up with the volatile Taoist swordsman Yin Chek-Hsia, who warns him rather forcefully to stay out of trouble. He also encounters Nieh Hsiao-Tsing, a beautiful young girl who is more than a mere human – she is a ghost, condemned to lure young men to their doom. But Hsiao-Tsing falls in love with the young tax collector, and vice-versa, starting a chain reaction of supernatural events neither one of them can control. With the aid of swordsman Yin, the young lovers take on Tsing's unearthly captor, a hideous tree spirit. Although this monstrous evil is thwarted, a mortal and a ghost are not intended for love, and lovely Nieh Hsiao-Tsing must leave the earthly realm forever.

WHY IT'S IMPORTANT:

Perhaps the most joyous (and conversely, the saddest) horror movie of all time, *A Chinese Ghost Story* was like a blast of fresh Asian air back in 1987, at least to Western film viewers. Although flying supernatural heroes and madly choreographed martial arts movies from Hong Kong had been experienced before, no film blended these over-the-top elements together so engagingly, with a heartbreaking love story and a seemingly endless succession of wildly imaginative fantasy elements elevating the experience to new heights. Unlike more traditional Asian ghost tales, there is nothing quaint or languorous about *A Chinese Ghost Story* – it's hip, fast, funny and a canny challenge to preconceived filmgoer expectations. The lightning-swift editing by David Wu is appropriately breathtaking but rarely confusing, often a problem with exaggerated action films of this kind. Although alive with elaborate special effects (fast and slow motion, rapid tracking shots a la Raimi, full-size horror props), director Ching Siu-Tung also proves himself a master of traditional visual techniques, such as the Ray Harryhausen-inspired stop-motion zombies that provide bizarre comedy relief mid-way through the movie. But at the heart of this mad potpourri of ghost vanquishers and transvestite tree monsters is a bittersweet love story that transcends all elements. Leads Leslie Cheung and Joey Wang are so charming it actually hurts to realize they can never be together; indeed, their underwater kiss in the temple pool tends to overshadow all the wildly imaginative action sequences, no easy feat. Ma Wu compliments these young lovers perfectly as grumpy-but-wise master swordsman Yin...he even gets his own show-stopping musical number, a kind of martial arts ghost-killer version of "My Way."

A Chinese Ghost Story spawned a number of sequels and imitations, none of them capturing the special magic of Ching's mini-epic. How could they? This groundbreaking classic draws strength from its fiercely original, never to be duplicated mix of myriad genre elements that miraculously come together to engage all of our emotions. The result is one of the most visually stimulating and heartfelt horror-fantasy experiences ever put on celluloid.

The first of the "serious" haunted house thrillers, a ghostly chick flick...

30 THE UNINVITED 1944

1.33

WHO MADE IT:

Paramount Pictures (U.S.). Director: Lewis Allen. Producer: Charles Brackett. Writers: Frank Partos, Dodie Smith, from the novel by Dorothy Macardle. Cinematography (b/w): Charles B. Lang. Music: Victor Young. Starring Ray Milland (Roderick Fitzgerald), Ruth Hussey (Pamela Fitzgerald), Gail Russell (Stella Meredith), Donald Crisp (Commander Beech), Cornelia Otis Skinner (Miss Holloway), Dorothy Stickney (Miss Bird), Barbara Everest (Lizzie Flynn), Alan Napier (Dr. Scott), David Clyde (Ben), Elizabeth Russell/Lynda Grey (Ghost of Mary Meredith).

WHAT IT'S ABOUT:

Brother and sister Rick and Pamela Fitzgerald stumble upon a beautiful old mansion named Winwood and decide to buy it. A young, sweet local named Stella Meredith claims her mother died there, and now haunts the place, watching over Stella and protecting her from afar. Even so, visiting Winwood proves dangerous for Miss Meredith; at one point, an unseen force drives her from the house and nearly causes her to fall from a high cliff. A séance conducted at Winwood puts Stella in a trance, and it soon becomes clear that the girl's complicated past is directly connected to the current haunting. Ultimately it's revealed that Stella's mother was not the austere and reserved Mary Meredith, but Meredith's discredited servant Carmel, who continues to guard her vulnerable daughter from Mary's icy, ectoplasmic clutches. In the end, Fitzgerald, who has fallen in love with Stella and plans to marry her, defies the enraged female ghost with a hurled candelabra and a demand that she leave Winwood forever. It was indeed a close call for Rick, as he glibly points out, since the now-exorcized evil spirit might have been his mother-in-law!

WHY IT'S IMPORTANT:

For many years, *The Uninvited* was deemed the quintessential "serious" ghost story, at least from Hollywood's golden era. Eventually, prestigious films like *The Innocents*, *The Haunting*, and *The Legend of Hell House* came along to challenge that position, each offering its own special pleasures in the "spectral" arena.

But *The Uninvited* still holds up. The storytelling is solid, characters are playfully endearing yet intelligent, and supernatural ghosts are not presented whimsically (usually the case in the 1940s), but as deadly-dangerous monsters from another world in the best tradition of bone-chilling horror.

There are great little touches throughout. Abandoning the cliché, this "haunted house" is no cobwebbed castle, but a rather lovely seaside residence that just happens to have warring spirits living within in. The business with local pets sensing the ghosts before humans can is well-handled, as is the sudden, poetic "death" of a flower in a room deflated by supernatural ill-will.

On the subject of how much is too much, would the movie be more powerful if all we got to see were our heroes' reactions to the malevolent spirit of Mary Meredith? Frankly, opinions change on this from decade to decade. But as long as the decision was made to "show the damn ghosts," Paramount certainly handled this unique creative challenge well; the animated wisp-wraiths, presented sparingly in atmospheric set-pieces, are like nothing ever seen on the screen.

So successful was this major-league ecto-fest that the studio swiftly ordered up a quasi-reworking of the idea called *The Unseen*, which faded fast. But its inspiration, copied and updated many times since the 1940s, continues to impress ghost story mavens of every generation.

Was it a good idea to visualize the ghosts? Val Lewton wouldn't; but unlike the majority of movies in this sub-genre, *The Uninvited* is no psychological horror story. The film makes no bones about the fact that its spirits are real, and out for blood.

Alan Napier (aka Alfred the butler from TV's *Batman*) assists haunted house-owners Ray Milland and Ruth Hussey in a séance centering around Gail Russell.

Unlike most "spooky" movies from the '40s, *The Uninvited* was an A-production with major studio assets. RIGHT: Sinister Miss Holloway (Cornelia Otis Skinner) comforts Stella (Gail Russell).

Young Stella's fate is linked to the evil phantasm haunting Winwood .

Rick (Milland) comes face-to-ghostly face with Mary Meredith in the memorable climax.

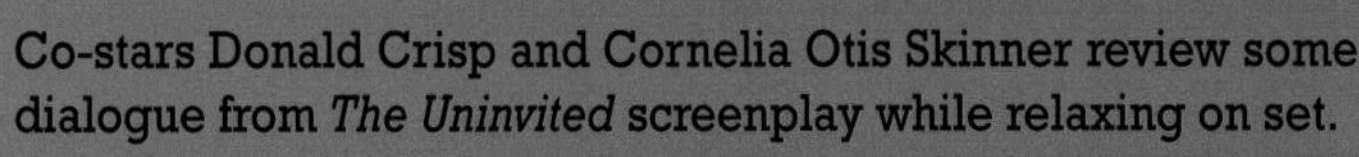

Co-stars Donald Crisp and Cornelia Otis Skinner review some dialogue from *The Uninvited* screenplay while relaxing on set.

29

I Walked With A Zombie 1943

67  1.37

Poster/photos: © 1942 RKO Pictures

I WALKED WITH A ZOMBIE

with JAMES ELLISON · FRANCES DEE · TOM CONWAY

Produced by VAL LEWTON

Directed by JACQUES TOURNEUR

SCREEN PLAY BY CURT SIODMAK & ARDEL WRAY BASED ON AN ORIGINAL STORY BY INEZ WALLACE

WHO MADE IT:

RKO Radio Pictures (U.S.). Director: Jacques Tourneur. Producer: Val Lewton. Writers: Curt Siodmak and Adele Wray, based on an original story by Inez Wallace. Cinematography (b/w): J. Roy Hunt. Music: Roy Webb. Starring James Ellison (Wesley Rand), Frances Dee (Betsy Connell), Tom Conway (Paul Holland), Edith Barrett (Mrs. Rand), James Bell (Dr. Maxwell), Christine Gordon (Jessica Holland), Theresa Harris (Alma), Sir Lancelot (Calypso singer), Darby Jones (Carrefour).

WHAT IT'S ABOUT:

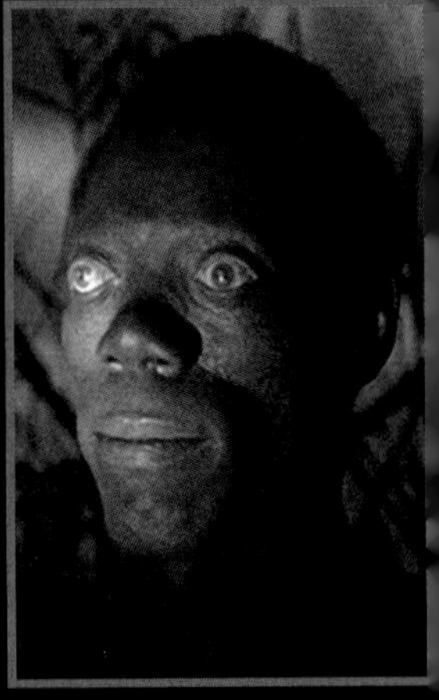

Canadian nurse Betsy Connell travels to the Caribbean island of Saint Sebastian to care for Jessica Holland, the victim of a strange sleepwalking condition that makes her appear zombie-like to superstitious locals. Jessica is the wife of Paul Holland, owner of the local sugar plantation. Holland has a tumultuous relationship with his charming but alcoholic half-brother, Rand, who blames Paul for Jessica's fate. When Alma the maid tells Betsy of how a Voodoo priest brought a woman out of a similar state of catatonia, the daring nurse escorts her silent patient to the houmfort, a sinister dwelling where the local voodoo worshippers assemble. Eventually, convinced his brother's wife is indeed a zombie, unhinged Rand plunges an arrow into Jessica's heart, and carries her lifeless body into the sea. Their bodies are discovered by fishermen and returned home.

WHY IT'S IMPORTANT:

Val Lewton's first horror film after his enormously successful *Cat People*, *I Walked with a Zombie* provided parent studio RKO with what it had been asking for all along: an exploitable bogeyman (Darby Jones) worthy of Universal's "monster" pantheon. It also enabled director Jacques Tourneur to explore a remote, dreamlike milieu of arcane religious beliefs, fatal jealousy and a picturesque descent into madness.

As in all of Lewton's horror films, there is nothing tangibly supernatural depicted; in spite of local voodoo hexing, a bug-eyed "zombie" sentry, and the exotic location, every bizarre development has a tangible explanation. Thematically, Lewton supplies some interesting subtext right from the start: the guilt of this slave-derived community is visited upon the current white plantation owners, ultimately resulting in madness and tragedy. As usual, psychological terror abounds in almost every scare sequence: sets are designed and lit for their symbolic power, with stairways leading into forbidding blackness and the eerily humming cane fields taking on an ethereal life of their own.

Worth mentioning are supporting players Edith Barrett as the family matriarch (she'd be cast in a genuine adaptation of *Jane Eyre* one year later), Sir Lancelot as a portentous Calypso singer and Christine Gordon as the silent, enigmatic female Zombie of the title.

Although well-received by critics, *I Walked with a Zombie* was most likely a disappointment at the box office, as Lewton and Tourneur were back with another "cat or human?" scenario in their next horror offering, *The Leopard Man*.

28 DR. JEKYLL AND MR. HYDE 1932

Poster/photos: © 1931 Turner Entertainment Co.

WHO MADE IT:

Paramount Pictures (U.S.). Director: Rouben Mamoulian. Producer: Rouben Mamoulian. Writers: Samuel Hoffenstein, Percy Heath, based on the novel by Robert Louis Stevenson. Cinematography (b/w): Karl Struss. Music: Herman Hand. Starring Fredric March (Dr. Henry Jekyll/Mr. Edward Hyde), Miriam Hopkins (Ivy Pearson), Rose Hobart (Muriel Carew), Holmes Herbert (Dr. Lanyon), Halliwell Hobbe (Brig. General Danvers Carew), Edgar Norton (Poole, Jekyll's butler), Tempe Pigott (Mrs. Hawkins, Ivy's landlady).

WHAT IT'S ABOUT:

Kindly, well-respected Dr. Henry Jekyll is a practicing medical doctor, scientist and academician. He startles his colleagues with a theory alleging that every man has a good and evil side, and that if man's darker nature could be properly controlled, it would add to the betterment of society. Jekyll uses drugs to experiment on himself, bringing forth a vicious, sadistic, simian-like alter-ego named Mr. Hyde. This volatile creature escapes into London's seamy night-life and terrorizes an unsuspecting party girl named Ivy Pearson. Horrified at what he has brought forth, Dr. Jekyll stops taking the drug, but transforms into Hyde anyway, eventually murdering Ivy and running afoul of the police. Shot down, Hyde's contorted features revert to those of Henry Jekyll as his life ebbs.

WHY IT'S IMPORTANT:

Generally regarded as the best adaptation of Stevenson's classic novel, Rouben Mamoulian's *Dr. Jekyll and Mr. Hyde* has been rightfully praised for its audacious, rather hyper style of visual storytelling. From the startling first-person introduction of Dr. Jekyll to innovative split-screens (cannily mirroring the protagonist's split personality) and meaningful dissolves that take forever to complete, the film is a cinema scholar's delight. And with a first-rate, simian-like "monster" worthy of Jack Pierce's creations over at Universal, success at the box office was all but assured.

Just as impressive as Mamoulian's camera tricks and Perc Westmore's make-up work is Fredric March as the driven, ill-fated scientist, bringing the dignity of a first-rate performer to an extremely demanding and challenging part. March is completely convincing as a handsome visionary scientist one moment, a sadistic, repulsive, cane-brandishing rabble-rouser the next. Equally memorable is sexy, sympathetic Miriam Hopkins as Hyde's streetwalker lover-turned-tragic victim.

Best scenes: Jekyll's initial transformation into Hyde (no lap dissolves, just color filters that accomplish a flawlessly smooth metamorphosis when photographed in black-and-white), the doctor's unexpected change into Hyde under the streetlamp, and the final, furious confrontation with police, actor March's eye sockets literally stretched to painful extremes.

Dr. Jekyll and Mr. Hyde was out of circulation for decades as a result of MGM's 1941 remake, which featured Spencer Tracy as the ill-fated chemist, finely supported by Ingrid Bergman and Lana Turner (whose roles were switched at the last minute). But Mamoulian's original, early sound classic is once again available for viewing on DVD or cable, enabling fans of the genre to revel in March's convincing histrionics and the filmmaker's innovative, never quite matched cinematic techniques.

Robert Wise deftly combines psychological terror with paranormal exploration…

27 THE HAUNTING 1963

112

2.35

WHO MADE IT:

Metro-Goldwyn-Mayer/Argyle Enterprises (U.K.). Director: Robert Wise. Producers: Robert Wise, Denis Johnson. Writer: Nelson Gidding, based on the novel *The Haunting of Hill House* by Shirley Jackson. Cinematography (b/w): Davis Bolton. Music: Humphrey Searle. Starring Julie Harris (Eleanor Lance), Claire Bloom (Theodora), Richard Johnson (Dr. John Markway), Russ Tamblyn (Luke Sanderson), Lois Maxwell (Grace Markway), Fay Compton (Mrs. Sanderson), Rosalie Crutchley (Mrs. Udley), Valentine Dyall (Mr. Dudley).

WHAT IT'S ABOUT:

Setting his sights on a legendary haunted mansion, anthropologist/psychic investigator Dr. John Markway descends upon New England's infamous Hill House for a focused scientific study. To agitate whatever occult forces may be present there, he invites two unique individuals to join him: Eleanor Lance, an emotionally volatile woman with poltergeist experience, and Theodora, a modern-day "witch" whose ESP skills are legendary. Also joining them for a harrowing, nightmarish weekend is the house's eventual inheritor, a brash American named Luke, and Markway's disbelieving wife, who promptly disappears while sleeping in the much-feared nursery. At one point, Eleanor and Theodora are trapped in their room by a mysterious unseen presence, and it becomes clear that it is the unhinged, unloved Lance that the evil mansion seeks to claim. Slamming her car into an old tree while leaving the premises, Eleanor's soul now joins the others condemned to "walk alone" in the dark corridors of Hill House.

WHY IT'S IMPORTANT:

Although director Robert Wise is often praised for his versatility as a filmmaker (everything from *The Sound of Music* to *Somebody Up There Likes Me*), he does have one area of speciality cultivated during his early apprenticeship with Val Lewton: psychological horror. After *West Side Story*'s tremendous success and *Two for the Seesaw*'s positive notices, he decided to fashion a haunted house story very different from anything previously seen on the screen, starting with the Panavision aspect ratio…a rare opportunity for a film of this kind to be made with A-list talent.

At the heart of MGM's grown-up fright fest is psychically sensitive Eleanor (Julie Harris), receiving able support from co-stars Claire Bloom, Richard Johnson and Russ Tamblyn. Probing the unknown with the enthusiasm of a privileged schoolboy, Johnson's Dr. Markway is a smooth and handsome ghostbreaker, though he is henpecked by his non-believing wife (played by Miss Moneypenny herself, Lois Maxwell). Making use of many Lewton-honed tricks of low-key suggestive horror, Wise throws in exciting widescreen/wide angle thrills that had critics of the time comparing it (favorably) to a rollercoaster ride. Ultimately, the film seems to be making a case that "the haunting" may be in Eleanor's mind, like Deborah Kerr's character in the somewhat parallel *The Innocents*. But whether it's a visually flamboyant study of a spinster run amok, or actually the genuine paranormal thriller it purports to be, *The Haunting* is generally regarded as one of the best ghost operas of all time.

Coolest scenes: all that pounding in hallways and against bedroom walls; Eleanor's hand being squeezed by a ghost; descending the spiral staircase.

Facing haunted house terrors (and an especially risky spiral staircase) are ghost hunters Claire Bloom, Russ Tamblyn, Julie Harris and Richard Johnson.

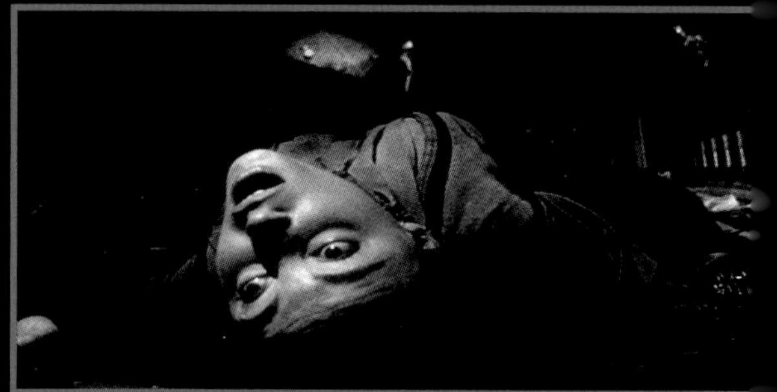

Harris and Bloom experience the film's best-remembered set-piece, the "invisible monster" pounding at the door.

A third-act surprise, disbeliever Lois Maxwell is put through Hill House hell.

Wise's film is part historical overview, part psychological character study.

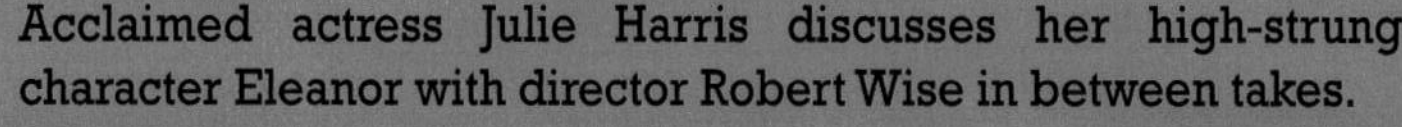

Acclaimed actress Julie Harris discusses her high-strung character Eleanor with director Robert Wise in between takes.

An elegant, original love story with decaying horror around the edges...

26

The Mummy 1932

WHO MADE IT:

Universal Pictures (U.S.). Director: Karl Freund. Producer: Carl Laemmle Jr. Writer: John L. Balderston. Cinematography (b/w): Charles Stumar. Music: James Dietrich (uncredited). Starring Boris Karloff (Im-Ho-Tep/Ardath Bey), Zita Johann (Helen Grosvenor/Princess Ankh-es-en-amon), David Manners (Frank Whemple), Arthur Byron (Sir Joseph Whemple), Edward Van Sloan (Doctor Muller), Bramwell Fletcher (Ralph Norton), Noble Johnson (the Nubian), James Crane (the Pharoah), Kathryn Byron (Frau Muller).

WHAT IT'S ABOUT:

An archeological expedition headed by Sir Joseph Whemple discovers the mummy of Im-Ho-Tep in an Egyptian tomb. When one member of the party reads aloud the Scroll of Life, which was also found in the tomb, the 3,700-year-old dead man returns to life. Years later, a strange-looking Egyptian named Ardath Bey directs another expedition, this one led by Whemple's son Frank, to the tomb of an ancient princess. The recovered mummy and other artifacts are soon housed in the Cairo museum, where Bey, in truth Im-Ho-Tep, tries to bring his beloved Ankh-es-en-amon back to life. Although he fails, a modern-day woman named Helen Grosvenor, who is the very image of the princess, hears his call. She goes to the museum at night, tries to get in and falls senseless at the front door, only to be helped by the Whemples. It becomes obvious that Helen has been acting under a powerful hypnotic spell, and occult expert Dr. Muller is resolved to break it. Believing Helen to be the reincarnation of his ancient love, Im-Ho-Tep lures her to his nearby home so that she may remember her previous life – and their love -- in days of old. He eventually decides to kill the young woman; after death, she'll be restored to life everlasting, and they can be reunited. As he raises his dagger, desperate Helen prays to a nearby statue of Isis. Frank and Dr. Muller arrive to see the living mummy destroyed by Isis' wrath and the Scroll of Life set afire.

WHY IT'S IMPORTANT:

Unlike Universal's previous horror films, *The Mummy* was an original concept for the screen, not an adaptation of a seminal novel or popular play. Inspired by the real-life "curse" that allegedly befell the discoverers of King Tut's tomb, screenwriter John L. Balderston culled story structure and character elements from *Dracula* to provide star Boris Karloff with a memorable vehicle, one that embraces everlasting love as much as it does timeless evil.

Karloff actually plays multiple versions of the same character during the course of the story. He's first seen as the rotted, bandage-swathed "mummy proper," inadvertently restored to life in an unforgettable opening set-piece. Next, he re-appears as the gaunt and wrinkled Ardath Bey, and finally, in flashbacks, as Im-Ho-Tep, a proud, heartbroken ancient Egyptian prince. Seizing this unique opportunity to demonstrate his dramatic range, Karloff tackles each of these incarnations with gusto. Equally game is exotic co-star Zita Johann as the bewildered object of his eternal love, although virtually all of her "past lives" flashback footage was left on the cutting room floor.

Director Karl Freund is perhaps best remembered as a world-class cinematographer (he shot the ultra-atmospheric *Dracula* for Universal). Not surprisingly, his slow-moving camera and precise compositions are ideally suited to this strangest of all love stories.

"He went out for a little walk! You shoul seen his face!" Archeologist Ralph N (Bramwell Fletcher) loses his mind in laughing jag after witnessing the mu rebirth.

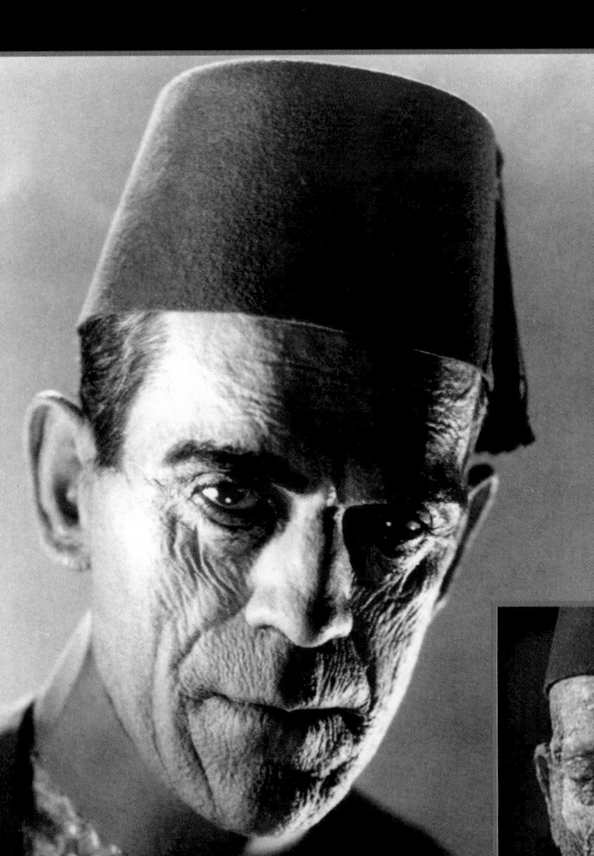

Re-appearing in human form, Im-Ho-Tep directs a later expedition to the location of his buried princess. Soon, she will be reincarnated as Helen Grosvenor (Zita Johann).

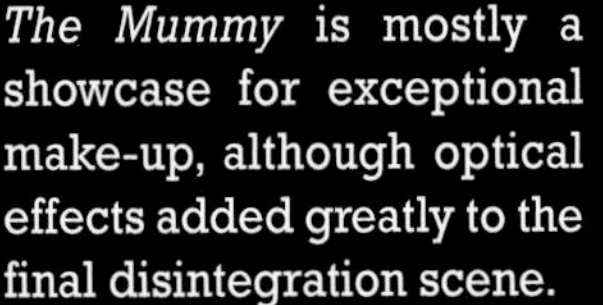

The Mummy is mostly a showcase for exceptional make-up, although optical effects added greatly to the final disintegration scene.

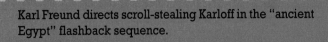

Karl Freund directs scroll-stealing Karloff in the "ancient Egypt" flashback sequence.

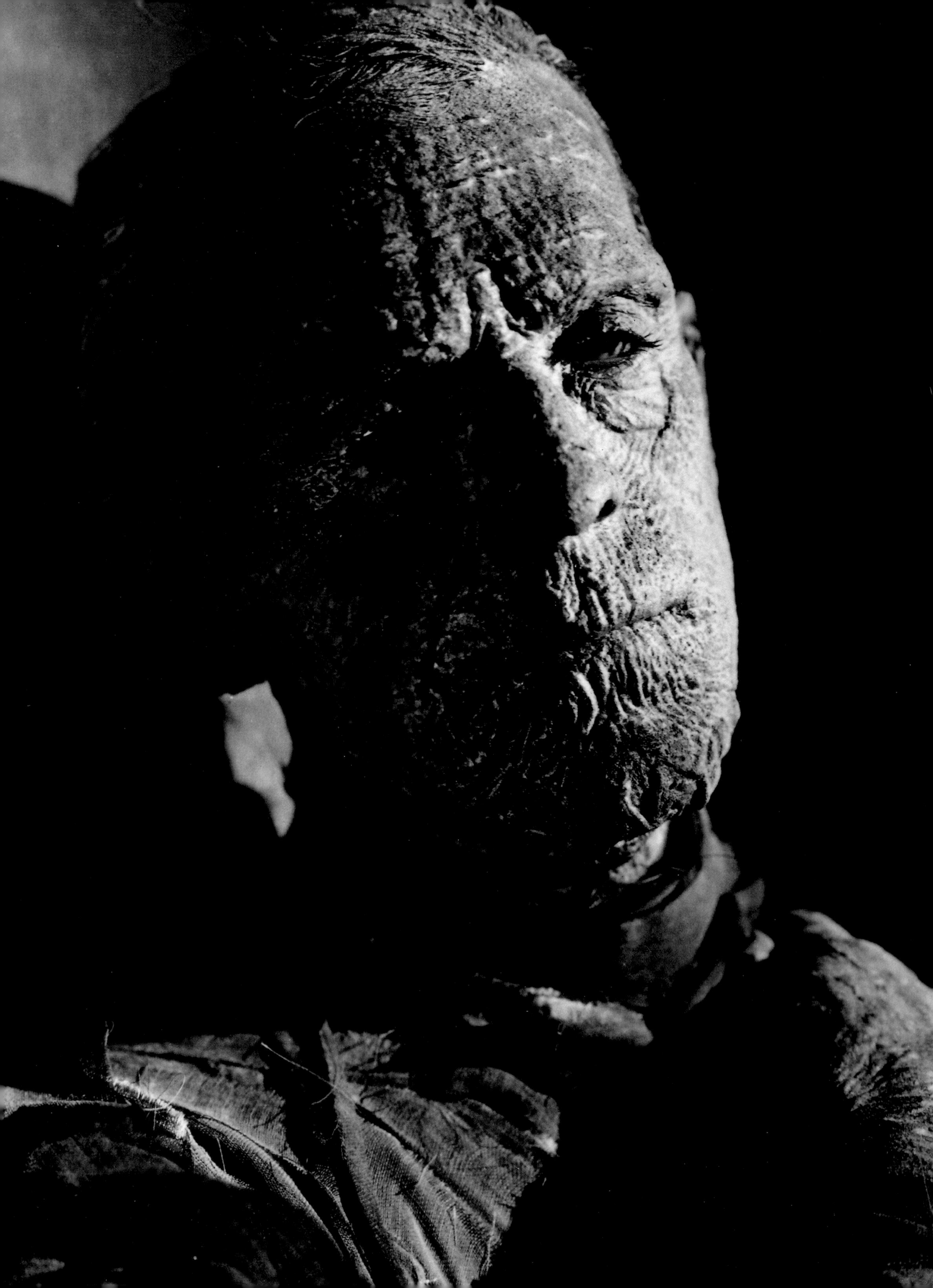

A MAKE-UP MASTERPIECE

Two, actually; the crumbling mummy of Im-Ho-Tep (LEFT) and his 20th-Century reincarnation, the ancient-looking Ardath Bey (ABOVE, being touched-up), who can nevertheless pass for a normal human being. Heir to Lon Chaney's immortal legacy in Hollywood, makeup artist Jack Pierce started a significant one of his own in '31 by transforming Boris Karloff into the square-headed

25

BLACK SUNDAY 1960

aka: The Mask of Satan

STARE INTO THESE EYES
discover deep within them the unspeakable terrifying secret of
BLACK SUNDAY
...it will paralyze you with fright!
PLEASE NOTE
The producers of BLACK SUNDAY recommend that it be seen only by those over 12 years of age!
starring BARBARA STEELE · JOHN RICHARDSON
IVO GARRANI · ANDREA CHECCHI
A GALATEA-JOLLY FILM PRODUCTION · Directed by MARIO BAVA · AN AMERICAN-INTERNATIONAL PICTURE

WHO MADE IT:

Galatea Film/Jolly Film (Italy)/Alta Vista Productions/American International Pictures (U.S.). Director: Mario Bava. Producer: Massimo de Rita. Writers: Ennio de Concini, Mario Serandrei, based loosely on Nikolai Gogol's short story "Viy." Cinematography: Mario Bava. Music Roberto Nicolosi (Italy); Les Baxter (U.S.). Starring Barbara Steele (Katia Vajda/Princess Asa Vajda), John Richardson (Dr. Andre Gorobec) Andrea Checchi (Dr. Thomas Kruvajan), Ivo Garrani (Prince Vajda) Arturo Dominici (Igor Javuto), Enrico Olivieri (Prince Constantine Vajda), Antonio Pierfederici (Priest), Tino Bianchi (Ivan), Clara Bind (Inn Keeper), Mario Passante (Coachman), Renato Terra (Boris) Germana Dominici (Sonya, Inn Keeper's daughter).

WHAT IT'S ABOUT:

In 17th-Century Moldavia, the evil Princess Asa is condemned for vampirism and devil-worship, along with her equally tainted servant, Javuto. Both have the horrendous "mask of Satan" driven into their faces, and defiant Asa is burned alive by the frightened townspeople. Before the flames claim her, she places a vengeful curse against the descendents of those who dared to defy her and her dark master. Two hundred years later, two doctors en route to a medical convention stumble upon the princess' ancient crypt and inadvertently resurrect her. With the aid of the also-reborn Javuto and others placed under her hypnotic spell, Asa makes plans to possess the body of her own twin descendent, Princess Katia. She is thwarted by the younger of the two doctors, whose love for Katia eventually exposes Asa's monstrous plot. Javuto falls into a pit during a life-and-death struggle, Katia is finally released from her ancestor's diabolical hold, and Asa the vampire-witch is again burned alive for her various sins.

WHY IT'S IMPORTANT:

1960 was a banner year for horror cinema. Roger Corman introduced his Poe series with *House of Usher*. Hammer gave us their second vampire thriller, *The Brides of Dracula*, another instant classic. Hitchcock hatched his immortal *Psycho*. And over in Italy, a certain cinematographer-turned-director was about to unleash his own unforgettable vision in a genre perfectly suited to his special talents.

Given Mario Bava's fame as a brilliant director of color, it's ironic that *Black Sunday* (aka *The Mask of Satan*) wound up being the film tha gained him an international following. Kind of like an old Universal, studio-bound fog-fest with perverse Euro-expressionist angles and other juicy excesses, *Sunday* allows Bava free reign to overwhelm us with atmosphere. He even makes use of the red-filter technique (mos famously utilized in 1932's *Dr. Jekyll and Mr. Hyde*) to achieve flawless facial transformations, something only possible with black-and-white photography. Unforgettable in the dual role of Asa the witch (bad girl) and victimized descendent Princess Katia (good girl) Barbara Steele became the first official Scream Queen for a new generation of drooling fans. In the U.S., an additional pleasure was Les Baxter's energetic and inventive music, which matched Bava's flamboyant visual style better than the movie's original, rather spare score

Best scenes: scorpions spilling out of Asa's ...

The opening set-piece of *Black Sunday* establishes the rich gothic mood of the film, along with the sadism and ultra-violence that would soon become its trademarks. An overnight international horror star, Barbara Steele was immediately cast in AIP's second Poe adaptation, *Pit and the Pendulum*, opposite Vincent Price. She would go on to appear in dozens of European fright movies in the '60s, most of them pushing gore elements to the max.

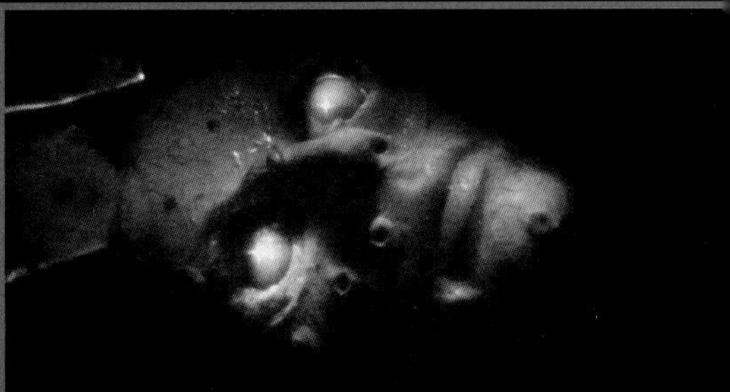

RIGHT: Arguably the most memorable sequences in a film filled with awesome horror scenes... The dead eyes of Asa the witch are a-crawl with living scorpions after the ancient Mask of Satan is removed. Not long after, maggots and worms fester in the sickening mucus of her glowing, reconstituting eyeballs.

Arturo Dominici, who played the villain in Galatea's *Hercules*, is even more frightening as Asa's servant Javuto (her brother in the Italian version), a living dead man who rises from the grave (ABOVE) in a standout sequence.

Director Mario Bava tussles with a fully-made-up Arturo Dominici is this funny publicity still snapped on set.

24 MASQUE OF THE RED DEATH 1964

89 2.35

LOOK INTO THIS FACE
SHUDDER... at the blood-stained dance of the Red Death!
TREMBLE...to the hideous tortures of the catacombs of Kali!
GASP...at the sacrifice of the innocent virgin to the vengeance of Baal!
AMERICAN INTERNATIONAL presents
VINCENT PRICE STARRING IN
EDGAR ALLAN POE'S IMMORTAL MASTERPIECE OF THE MACABRE
THE MASQUE OF THE RED DEATH
in PATHÉCOLOR
Also Starring HAZEL COURT · JANE ASHER
Screenplay by CHARLES BEAUMONT and R. WRIGHT CAMPBELL · From a Story by EDGAR ALLAN POE · Produced and Directed by ROGER CORMAN

WHO MADE IT:

Anglo-Amalgamated (U.K.)/American International Pictures (U.S.) Director: Roger Corman. Producers: Roger Corman, George Willoughby. Writers: Charles Beaumont and R. Wright Campbell, based on a short story by Edgar Allan Poe. Cinematography (Pathecolor) Nicolas Roeg. Music: David Lee. Starring Vincent Price (Prince Prospero), Hazel Court (Juliana), Jane Asher (Francesca), David Weston (Gino), Nigel Green (Ludovico, Francesca's father), Patrick Magee (Alfredo), Paul Whitsun-Jones (Scarlatti), Robert Brown (Guard), Skip Martin (Hop Toad), Verina Greenlaw (Esmeralda).

WHAT IT'S ABOUT:

In medieval Italy, the Red Death ravages the countryside, threatening a local population of peasants. Only in the nearby castle of Prince Prospero is there safety...but the prince is a smug, sadistic, profoundly evil man who scoffs at a prophecy suggesting his undoing and burns the village from which it sprang to the ground. He kidnaps a few locals for his amusement, including a feisty young lady named Juliana, her brave young lover Bruno, and her father. Prospero hosts a gathering of equally corrupt and wealthy visitors, introducing the young girl to his eerie devil-worshipping ways. One vicious guest is tricked into wearing a gorilla costume to Prospero's Masque, only to be burned alive by a vengeful dwarf. Ultimately, the prince and his followers are consumed by the Red Death, which appears to Prospero with his own face at the moment of his gruesome death. Juliana and her lover are spared, and on a cliff overlooking the village Prospero had burned, the various Deaths converge and discuss how many lives they have taken. Then they resume their fatal march throughout the world.

WHY IT'S IMPORTANT:

Shot in England, *Masque of the Red Death* is Roger Corman's next-to-last Poe classic from the '60s (*The Tomb of Ligeia* would follow). Many fans consider it his finest hour as a director; the film seems to be about something more than the juicy but throwaway horrors of *The Raven* and *Tales of Terror*, which immediately preceded it. "I had seen Ingmar Bergman's *The Seventh Seal*, and thought there might be a horror movie application for it," Corman explained in a 1970s interview.

Set in medieval Italy, this tale of an arrogant prince and his "pact with the devil" is not only a showcase for Price (as usual), but a nice opportunity for colorful co-stars Jane Asher, Hazel Court, Patrick Magee and Nigel Green. Aiding the superior cast are superior sets, left over from *Becket* and lushly re-worked by Daniel Haller.

It's scripters Charles Beaumont and R. Wright Campbell this time around, pulling together odds and ends from various Poe stories (*The Gold Bug* gets a nice face-lift) and building a brand-new story concerning the Red Death's ravaging of the countryside, and the fascinating good vs. evil battle of philosophies between a God-fearing peasant girl (Asher) and despotic, devil-worshipping royalty. Price gives welcome psychological dimension to the seemingly heinous Prince Prospero...we almost suspect he may have been a good man gone bad (female victim Asher actually kisses him by tale's end).

Best scenes: Juliana's ordeal after "marrying" the Devil; Hop Toad's fiery revenge against gorilla-costumed Alfredo; the Dance of Death, all of the various, differently colored diseases and plagues in humanoid form, commiserating together.

Inspired by Bergman's *The Seventh Seal*, Corman offers up a different kind of chess game for Death to play.

The battle of moral philosophies between Prince Prospero and Francesca fuels *Red Death*.

Cinematic highpoint: Juliana (Hazel Court) makes a pact with the Devil in a bizarre, ultimately fatal ritual.

Prince Prospero discovers that Death has his own face, and that his deal with Satan won't save him from a grotesque, well-deserved demise.

Roger Corman (center) directs Jane Asher and Vincent Price at the start of the Masque ball sequence.

An opulent Asian tapestry of fear, surreal beauty and dreamlike spirits...

23 KWAIDAN 1964

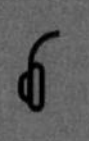

WHO MADE IT:

Toho Company Ltd. (Japan). Director: Masaki Kobayashi. Producer: Shigeru Wakatsuki. Writer: Yoko Mizuki, based on folk stories by Lafcadio Hearn. Cinematography (Eastmancolor): Yoshio Miyajima. Music: Toru Takemitsu. Starring Rentaro Mikuni (Husband "Black Hair"), Michiyo Aratama (First wife "Black Hair"), Misako Watanabe (Second wife "Black Hair"), Tatsuya Nakadai (Minokichi "Woman in the Snow"), Keiko Kishi (Yuki "Woman in the Snow"), Katsuo Nakamura (Hoichi "Hoichi the Earless"), Tetsuro Tamba (Warrior "Hoichi the Earless"), Takashi Shimura (Head Priest "Hoichi the Earless"), Kanemon Nakamura (Kannai "In a Cup of Tea'), Osamu Takizawa (Author/Narrator "In a Cup of Tea").

WHAT IT'S ABOUT:

Four separate tales of the supernatural: In "Black Hair," a poor samurai divorces his beloved wife and marries for money, a union that proves disastrous. Years later, the repentant man returns to his true love...only to find shock and horror awaiting him. In "Woman in the Snow," two woodsmen take refuge from a sudden snowstorm, and the younger of the two witnesses a beautiful ice spirit taking his friend's life with a blast of her freezing breath. Charmed by his innocence, she spares the young woodsman, provided that he never reveals what he has experienced. But years later, he breaks this promise, confessing the details to his wife...which prompts the snow spirit's angry return. In "Hoichi the Earless," a blind musician sings so well that a ghostly imperial court commands him to perform the epic ballad of their death battle, draining away the musician's life in the process. Finally, in "In a Cup of Tea," a veteran samurai drinks water from his cup, glimpses a smiling spirit within the liquid, then must bravely confront the challenging ghost and his supernatural minions.

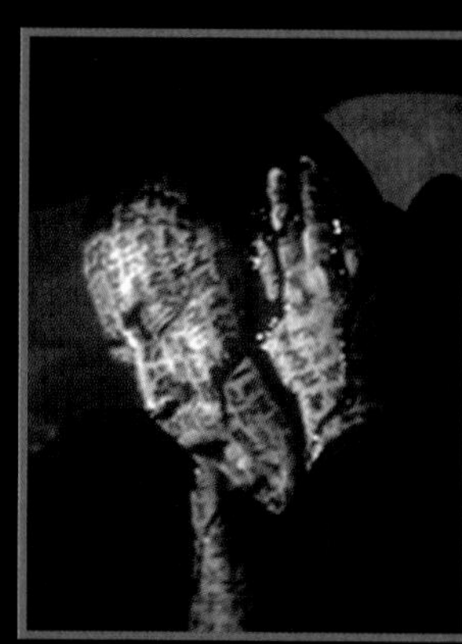

WHY IT'S IMPORTANT:

An answer to fright films as we Western audiences understood them, *Kwaidan* is a must-see horror/fantasy masterpiece, an epic in every sense (including screen shape and running time). Designed with consummate artistry on an Eastmancolor palette that rivals the Technicolor finish of Fellini and Bava, Kobayashi's classic embraces the beauty and poetry of supernatural terror while exploring human ambiguity, often placing mortals and immortals on the same spiritual plane for fascinating moral contests.

All of the stories in this mega-anthology are worthy, although the sad siren of "Woman in the Snow" seems to hold a special place in the heart. The surreal visual universe conceived for this particular entry is perhaps the film's most compelling. For sheer audacity of concept, however, nothing beats "Hoichi the Earless." And just when the viewer begins to feel a tinge of sore-rump exhaustion, "In a Cup of Tea" provides just the right psychological/spiritual tonic to end a well-spent evening at the cinema.

Germany's man-made monster, the forerunner of all Frankensteins...

22 THE GOLEM 1920

 1.33

Poster/photos: © 1920 UFA

WHO MADE IT:

UFA (Germany). Directors: Paul Wegener, Carl Boese. Producer: Paul Davidson. Writers: Henrik Galeen, Gustav Meyrink, Paul Wegener. Cinematography (b/w): Karl Freund. Starring Paul Wegener (The Golem), Albert Steinruck (Rabbi Loew), Lyda Salmonova (Miriam), Ernst Deutsch (Rabbi Famulus), Max Kronert (Temple Servant), Loni Nest (Little girl).

WHAT IT'S ABOUT:

In the 16th Century, the Jews of Prague face persecution from heartless rulers and an unsympathetic population. To protect his people, Rabbi Loew enlists the aid of nether-world demon Astaroth to bestow life into a clay figure known as the Golem, using a forbidden magic word placed into his chest amulet. This humanoid avenger smites Jewish tormentors at the King's prestigious Rose Festival, but eventually becomes a threat to everyone, wreaking havoc and even setting fire to the ghetto. The Golem is finally stopped in his monstrous tracks by an unsuspecting child, who innocently removes the life-giving amulet from his chest and renders him comatose.

WHY IT'S IMPORTANT:

Based on a Jewish fable and granddaddy of all Frankenstein-themed horror tales, *The Golem* was filmed a number of times in Germany during the silent era. It's this ambitious 1920 adaptation that became an iconic classic, establishing some significant horror movie conventions- cinematographer Karl Freund would shoot *Dracula* and *The Mummy* at Universal a decade later -- while delivering an effective social parable -- that is still relevant.

Director/co-writer Paul Wegener plays the title role with primal relish and an elemental grasp of the clay-creature's hollow soul. Persecuted and denied their rights by oblivious aristocrats, the Jews are morally justified in conjuring this fearsome, nonhuman avenger, an all-powerful force of dark justice who evens the score by toppling buildings and terrorizing the ruling elite. But it isn't long before humanity's moral shortcomings corrupt this undertaking, transforming Rabbi Loew's perplexed automaton into a demonic engine of mass destruction. *Golem*'s "death" at the tiny hands of an inquisitive toddler is a poetic finale to his brief, tragic reign of terror.

Horror-fantasy elements aside, Wegener's film also scores as a bold historical epic, offering extravagant sets and raucous crowd scenes that boast hundreds of extras. The fiery destruction of the ghetto rivals some of Hollywood's most ambitious spectacles. As for director of photography Freund, his evocative lighting techniques and atmospheric compositions are impressive throughout, particularly during the "trip to Hell" sequence (Rabbi Loew's audience with floating, stone-faced Astaroth still has the power to creep-out viewers).

In the mid-1980s, Golan-Globus announced a modern version of *The Golem*, supposedly starring Charles Bronson. Although this movie never materialized, a 21s-Century, CG-driven take on the venerable tale seems inevitable.

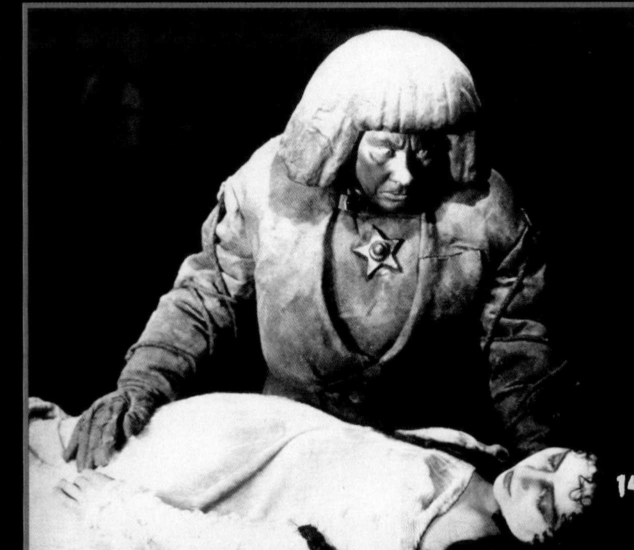

Wells' seminal terror tale inspires landmark fx and a superb performance...

21 THE INVISIBLE MAN 1933

71  1.37

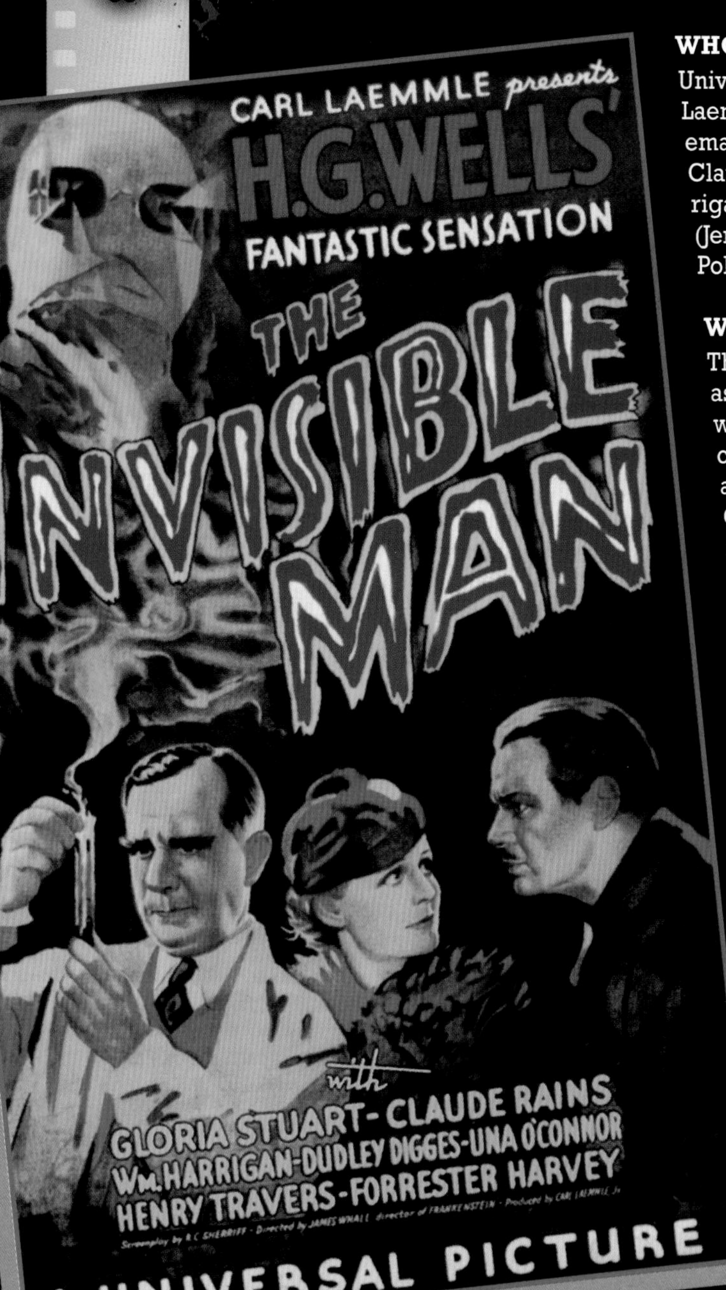

WHO MADE IT:

Universal Pictures (U.S.). Director: James Whale. Producer: Carl Laemmle Jr. Writer: R.C. Sherriff, based on the novel by H.G. Wells. Cinematography (b/w): Arthur Edeon. Music: Heinz Roemheld. Starring Claude Rains (Jack Griffin), Gloria Stuart (Flora Cranley), William Harrigan (Dr. Arthur Kemp), Henry Travers (Dr. Cranley), Una O'Connor (Jenny Hall), Forrester Harvey (Herbert Hall), Holmes Herbert (Chief of Police), E.E. Clive (Constable Jaffers), Dudley Digges (Chief detective).

WHAT IT'S ABOUT:

The mysterious disappearance of chemist Jack Griffin, young associate of Dr. Cranley, greatly worries Cranley's daughter Flora, who loves the missing scientist. Griffin had been working with a chemical called monocane, which is known to bleach and render animals insane. Now a transparent figure swathed in bandages, Griffin takes refuge in an isolated inn, striving desperately to reverse the effects of his experiments. When the locals become too inquisitive, he shocks them by unraveling his bandages to reveal…nothing. Driven mad by the monocane, Griffin, half-serious about conquering the world, enlists the aid of a terrified Dr. Kemp, his former colleague and rival for the affections of Flora. When Kemp betrays him to the police, Griffin vows revenge, and eventually sends the cowardly scientist hurtling to his doom over a cliff. Exhausted at last by his ongoing reign of terror, the Invisible Man is forced out of a burning barn by surrounding policemen. Tracks of his running feet then appear in the snow. A pistol barks twice, and seconds later an imprint of Jack Griffin's fallen body can be seen on the ground. Later, he returns to visibility as he dies in a hospital bed, beloved Flora by his side.

WHY IT'S IMPORTANT:

If 1935's *Bride of Frankenstein* is the greatest horror movie Universal ever made, then *The Invisible Man*, filmed two years earlier, must be classified as the studio's most respectable chiller. Starting with an H.G. Wells pedigree, the story's a canny blend of primitive science fiction and serial-killer suspense on a grandiose scale, ideally suited to director James Whale's eccentric gifts as a filmmaker.

Whale originally wanted Colin (Dr. Frankenstein) Clive to play ill-fated chemist Frank Griffin; he was given Claude Rains instead. With a commanding, throaty, richly-toned voice that eventually became his trademark, Rains throws himself into the showcase role, reciting juicy dialogue with unrestrained relish ("Even the moon is frightened of me!"). Ironically, the actor's small physical stature actually adds to his performance, lending a certain Napoleonic flavoring to the world-threatening Griffin. Other cast members, including Henry Travers and Gloria (*Titanic*) Stuart, provide Rains with competent support. William Harrigan is especially memorable as the tale's sniveling, Judas-like betrayer, Dr. Kemp.

Of course, an exotic concept like invisibility calls for innovative special effects, both physically and optically generated. Universal was truly fortunate to have specialist John P. Fulton on their payroll. Working closely with Whale, he supervised all of the film's challenging visual "gags," which ranged from matted figures/disembodied clothing to life-size bandaged head props.

With a solid story, spotlight lead performance, remarkable fx and a first-rate director, *The Invisible Man* is the rare horror movie that transcends its genre, ultimately earning a reputation as one of the great Hollywood films, period.

John Fulton's amazing fx distinguish *The Invisible Man*. Although the picture was enormously successful, Universal didn't produce their first sequel until seven years later. For *The Invisible Man Returns*, U cast a young Vincent Price as the title threat, although his character was actually more hero than villain. Twice the size of Rains, bandaged Price certainly cut a physically imposing figure, and the actor's voice had it's own unique, disquieting and sinister quality that served the movie well. Two additional sequels were eventually produced (star Jon Hall in both cases) before Abbott and Costello had their inevitable chance to "meet" the man who wasn't

Griffin is smoked out of a burning barn by a small army of policemen in the film's exciting finale.

Desperate scientist Jack Griffin gets mad as hell and turns his insane fury (along with his bizarre sense of wicked humor) against anyone and everyone, especially the irksome locals of an isolated inn.

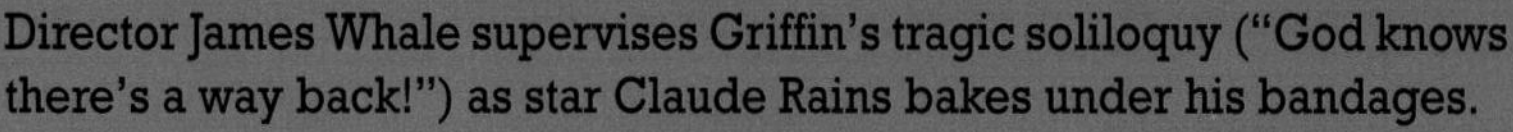

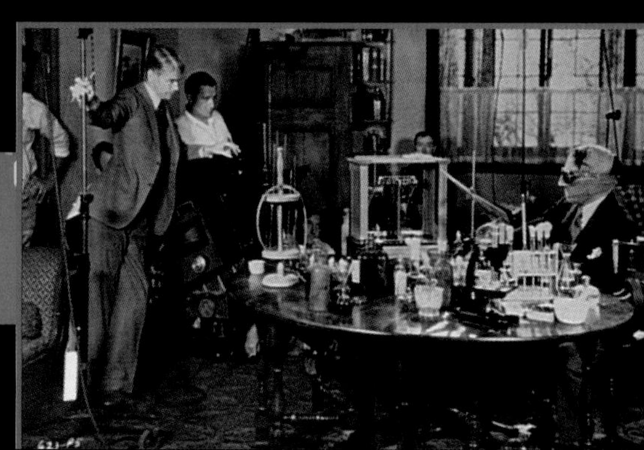

Director James Whale supervises Griffin's tragic soliloquy ("God knows there's a way back!") as star Claude Rains bakes under his bandages.

The first and classiest horror anthology, boasting haunted mirrors and diabolical dummies...

20

1946

1.37

Poster/photos: © 1946 Ealing Studios

WHO MADE IT:

Ealing Studios (U.K.)/Universal Pictures (U.S.). Directors: Charles Crichton, Alberto Cavacanti, Basil Dearden, Robert Hamer. Producer: Michael Balcon. Writers: John V. Baines, Angus Macphail. Cinematographers: Jack Parker, Stanley Pavey, Douglas Slocombe. Music: Georges Auric. Starring Michael Redgrave (Maxwell Frere "Ventriloquist's Dummy"), Mervyn Johns (Walter Craig), Googie Withers (Joan Cortland "Haunted Mirror"), Ralph Michael (Peter Cortland "Haunted Mirror"), Basil Radford (George Parratt "Golfing Story"), Nauton Wayne (Larry Potter "Golfing Story"), Sally Ann Howes (Sally O'Hara "Christmas Party"), Frederick Walk (Dr. van Straaten "Ventriloquist's Dummy"), Robert Wyndham (Dr. Albury "Hearst Driver"), Miles Malleson (Hearse Driver/Bus Conductor "Hearst Driver").

WHAT IT'S ABOUT:

A man joins a group of gathered people and has a disturbing feeling that everything he is currently experiencing has already occurred. This inspires a spate of bizarre stories from the various guests. In one, a man has a startling premonition that saves him from certain death in a traffic accident. Another tale involves the ghost of a lonely little boy who is comforted by a young female partygoer. Especially gripping is a story about a haunted mirror that reflects an old murder, and may inspire a new one. A funny yarn about two competitive golfers follows, along with a nightmarish tale about a ventriloquist threatened by his own malevolent dummy. Ultimately, the man with déjà vu who inspired all the storytelling is swept into a kaleidoscope of madness, mayhem and murder, reliving scenes from the various stories until the living dummy attacks him. Then the man emerges from a deep sleep...it was all a dream. But when he drives to his morning's destination, it turns out to be that same house with that same group of people. And the cycle of terror continues.

WHY IT'S IMPORTANT:

Anthology-style movies have had an uneven history at the box office. Audiences tend to prefer a single plot, theme and set of characters into which they can invest their emotions for ninety some-odd minutes. But of all the popular film genres, horror seems best suited to the fractured, multi-tale format, with or without a unifying "host." And undoubtedly the best of these episodic fright films is one of the first ever made, *Dead of Night*.

Released in the U.S. by horror specialists Universal, this Ealing Studios groundbreaker offers a deft assortment of weird tales, each served by a different director. These episodes range from playfully humorous to deadly terrifying, and are framed by an ultimately even more disturbing mini-story. The final scenes, where elements of all five tales join forces for a nightmarish assault on "dreaming" Mervyn Johns, are unnerving and hallucinatory in the extreme. And the reality of Johns' unique personal horror repeating itself indefinitely is eerily conveyed with footage shown under the end credits, an exact replay of *Night*'s opening shots.

The yarns themselves are odd little supernatural mysteries culminating in bizarre, ironic twist endings. Best among them: "Room for One More?" (Miles Malleson's well-remembered screen moment/line); the haunted mirror (that "other room with the fireplace" still resonates); the ventriloquist dominated by his dummy (Michael Redgrave establishes this chilling prototype); the complex framing device.

In many ways, *Dead of Night* is the horrific story of an unassuming man named Walter Craig (Mervyn Johns)...the victim of his own recurring, multi-leveled nightmare.

The "haunted mirror" reveals a mysterious room where a murder had been committed years earlier. It now compels its current owner (Ralph Michael)to re-enact the crime.

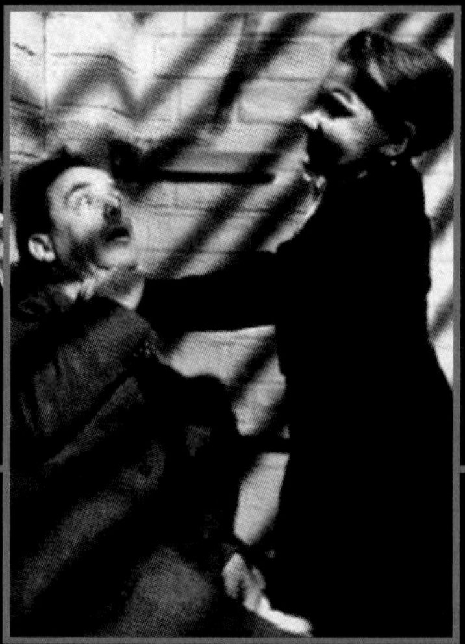

ABOVE, LEFT: The film's framing device erupts into a nightmarish montage, culminating in a murderous attack from walking, strangling Hugo the dummy. RIGHT: Hugo's actual story, last of the group, concerns his diabolical "takeover" of ventriloquist Maxwell Frere (Michael Redgrave). This struggle for control is a plotline revisited in countless short stories and TV episodes.

Universal released a similar horror anthology, *Flesh and Fantasy*, five years earlier. The A-list ensemble includes Charles Winninger and Betty Field.

The Silence of the Lambs 1991

118 1.85

WHO MADE IT:

Orion Pictures (U.S.). Director: Jonathan Demme. Producers: Kenneth Utt Edward Saxon, Ron Bozman. Writer: Ted Tally, based on the novel by Thomas Harris. Cinematography (color): Tak Fujimoto. Music: Howarc Shore. Starring Jodie Foster (Clarice Starling), Anthony Hopkins (Dr. Hannibal Lecter), Scott Glenn (Jack Crawford), Ted Levine (James Gumb, "Buffalo Bill"), Anthony Heald (Frederick Chilton), Brooke Smith (Catherine Martin), Diane Baker (Sen. Ruth Martin), Roger Corman (FB Director), Chris Isaak (SWAT Commander).

WHAT IT'S ABOUT:

The Midwest is being terrorized by "Buffalo Bill," a vicious serial kille who skins his female victims and shoves rare moth cocoons down thei throats. In an unusual scheme, FBI agent-in-training Clarice Starling is selected to interview another psychotic mass murderer, Dr. Hanniba (the Cannibal) Lecter, hoping that this former psychiatrist's insights might shed some light on the current killer's motives and identity But in some ways Lecter is an even greater menace, using his advancec manipulative skills to probe Starling's psyche and bring her owr personal demons to the fore. When a new female victim is kidnappec and imprisoned by Bill, it's a race against time for the novice agent especially since an unwise transfer of Lecter results in his escape…and more cannibalistic slayings. Eventually Clarice mus confront her fears and take on Bill in his own diseased, moth-infestec lair. She prevails, and receives a congratulatory phone call from the still-at-large Lecter…ironically, someone who truly understands anc respects her.

WHY IT'S IMPORTANT:

Like Hitchcock's *Psycho*, *Silence of the Lambs* pushes a crime thrille into the weirder world of extreme horror, providing not one, but twc Norman Bates characters to confound and disturb viewers. As is frequently the case with reality-oriented shockers, a hyper level o both physical and psychological terror stands in for the literally supernatural. These enigmatic, flesh-savoring bogeymen are so freaky they don't require Freddy Krueger-like powers to creep us out…just one protracted stare gets the job done.

But there's more on director Jonathan Demme's mind than simply eliciting gasps from his audience. *Lambs* amounts to a perverse love story between two unique individuals and an exploration of human passion in general. Hannibal the Cannibal is indeed a "monster," but the film is careful to demonstrate the "monstrous" behavior of supposedly normal males who covet what they see just as he does, pursuing self-interests that may be offensive to those who aren't receptive to them. It's here where the casting of attractive but sexually ambiguous Jodie Foster pays off. And if any criticism can be leveled at *Lambs*, it's that Lecter doesn't go far enough in his dissection of agent Starling's psyche during the course of their risky mental duel. Instead, the direct threat is shifted to serial killer #2, with Demme's breathless climax allowing Starling to conquer primal fears and exorcize childhood traumas at the same time.

If nothing else, *Silence of the Lambs* is a reminder that the potential for horrific behavior resides in all of us, as every person is driven by unique and unquenchable passions. With perceptive casting and a psychiatrist's-eye-view of human behavior at its darkest, this

First and greatest of Lewton's horror-noirs; what we can't see can really hurt us...

18 CAT PEOPLE 1942

 1.85 

WHO MADE IT:

RKO Radio Pictures (U.S.). Director: Jacques Tourneur. Producer: Val Lewton. Writer: DeWitt Bodeen. Cinematography (b/w): Nicholas Musuraca. Music: Roy Webb. Starring Simone Simon (Irena Dubrovna Reed), Kent Smith (Oliver Reed), Tom Conway (Dr. Louis Judd), Jane Randolph (Alice Moore), Jack Holt (The Commodore), Elizabeth Russell (The Cat Woman).

WHAT IT'S ABOUT:

Architect Oliver Reed meets an alluring young artist named Irena at a New York zoo, almost instantly falls in love and marries her. But Irena has extreme psychological problems that threaten both her marriage and her very sanity. Believing she was descended from people who had fallen into witchcraft, she is convinced that opening up physically and emotionally will release a great evil. Profoundly unhappy but still in love with his wife, Oliver turns to a female co-worker for sympathy and later, a psychiatrist for help. But soon these two are menaced by what appears to be a phantom panther, which stalks an indoor swimming pool and eventually attacks the disbelieving doctor. Horrified at what she is and what has happened to her once hopeful marriage, Irena returns to the zoo and allows herself to be fatally mauled by the panther she has been rendering.

WHY IT'S IMPORTANT:

It's impossible to explain the effect this movie had on the generation that originally experienced it. "Civilian" filmgoers with no particular fondness for weird subjects couldn't stop talking about "that swimming pool scene," certainly *Cat People*'s cinematic highpoint and a textbook example of what producer Val Lewton was trying to do with the horror-noir genre. And what that was, very specifically, was to turn an unfortunate negative (zero budget) into an ingenious positive (what we don't see is far more terrifying than what we do see). Lewton scoffed at Universal chillers of the day like *The Wolf Man*; to him, showcasing a bogeyman was an immature and bungling way to convey true psychological horror. In many ways, *Cat People* is his very direct answer to that particular film.

Building on reality, Irena's sexual repression provides a fabulous springboard for myriad monsters of one sort or another. The legends of her people simply add texture to this "id" demon unleashed by mounting frustration, and triggered by the disturbed young woman's ill-advised marriage. For a low-budget horror picture, this is all pretty heady stuff. But the public and critics bought it big-time back in 1942, vindicating producer Lewton's faith in the intelligence of his audience. At the heart of the story is bedeviled Irena, played by newcomer Simone Simon. Innocent, irresistible, yet deadly-dangerous, this doomed heroine/villainess is psychologically complex, with vaguely "foreign" Simone uniquely suited to the part. She called upon these same alluring, disquieting qualities for her role as Belle in RKO's *The Devil and Daniel Webster* the year before.

Ironically, Universal finally made a *Cat People* of their own in the early '80s, pretty much abandoning everything that made Lewton's film distinctive in favor of sex, hip music and grotesque transformation sequences. But the original film continues to fascinate and inform, with contemporary thrillers like *The Blair Witch Project* and *Paranormal Activity* owing much to this remarkable, simple and in many ways sweet horror tragedy.

The perfect creative team transforms Poe's moody classic into a new kind of horror film...

17

HOUSE OF USHER 1960

2.35

aka: The Fall of the House of Usher

WHO MADE IT:

American International Pictures/Alta Vista Productions (U.S.). Director: Roger Corman. Producer: Roger Corman. Writer: Richard Matheson, based on the story by Edgar Allan Poe. Cinematography (color): Floyd Crosby. Music: Les Baxter. Starring Vincent Price (Roderick Usher), Mark Damon (Philip Winthrop), Myrna Fahey (Madeline Usher), Harry Ellerbe (Bristol), Eleanor LeFaber (Ghost), Ruth Oklander (Ghost), Geraldine Paulette (Ghost).

WHAT IT'S ABOUT:

Philip Winthrop arrives at the isolated, fog-shrouded Usher mansion, hoping to claim his bride-to-be, Madeline Usher, and return with her to England. But the girl's austere, hyper-sensitive, distantly menacing older brother Roderick insists that she can never leave. He eventually explains that the Usher line is tainted; all of the vile-looking ancestors depicted in family portraits were wicked, depraved and evil characters. If Madeline were to marry and have children, this unspeakable legacy would continue, something that must be prevented at all costs. Torn emotionally by her belief in Roderick's words, and her love for Philip, heart-weakened Madeline appears to die and is promptly laid to rest by her loved ones. But Winthrop soon discovers that his beloved fiancée is subject to cataleptic fits and was deliberately entombed alive by her desperate, half-mad brother. Driven insane herself from the horrendous experience, Madeline escapes confinement and seeks revenge against Roderick. The mansion catches fire in the midst of their violent confrontation, and Winthrop barely escapes with his life as the raging holocaust consumes all. Its inhabitants crushed by falling debris, the remains of the House of Usher gradually sink into the bottomless tarn, ending the family curse forever.

WHY IT'S IMPORTANT:

At the end of the 1950s, poverty row monster movies were on the way out, so producer Roger Corman and American International Pictures took a chance on upgrading their product. *House of Usher* would be a relatively lavish production, shot in anamorphic widescreen and color, boasting a semi-star of some stature, along with the Edgar Allan Poe pedigree. If Hammer could make tasty-enough period horror flicks with next to no money, why couldn't enterprising Americans? Thus, the great Corman/Poe series from AIP was born.

House probably wasn't designed to be part of a series, just a well-crafted style piece that would hopefully please the target demographic. It did a great deal more than that. Psychology student Corman happened to have a special affinity for his subject, and the great artistic collaborators on this project (cinematographer Floyd Crosby, art director Daniel Haller, composer Les Baxter) were also amazingly in sync. To keep a limited tale with limited players in a limited location interesting, the resourceful director uses every cine-trick in the book, giving the movie "special effects-like values" just through the application of a particular lens, or with an imaginative set-up or camera move. Perhaps more so than any of the Poe films that followed, *Usher* is rich with creative directorial flourishes of this kind.

Price, beginning the decade on a high note, cuts an austere and thoroughly convincing figure as Roderick Usher, and he's all the more interesting without his trademark moustache. Young lovers Mark Damon and Myrna Fahey are reasonably competent. But the movie clearly belongs to Price and ace storyteller Corman's visual imagination, which is on colorful display throughout.

ABOVE: an evocative widescreen matte painting of the Usher mansion. RIGHT: *House*'s three major dramatic players, Damon, Price and Fahey.

BELOW: Winthrop's escape from the burning house, accomplished with matte rendering and superimposed flames.

The eerie, color-filtered dream sequence became an AIP Corman-Poe tradition.

Bloody-fingered and furious, Myrna Fahey's rise from her chained coffin is carefully prepared by the Corman crew.

FALL OF THE USHERS

Vincent Price stars as Roderick Usher in Roger Corman's classic Poe adaptation *House of Usher*, which also features Myrna Fahey (right) as Roderick's young, insane, prematurely buried sister Madeline. Last of their ill-fated line, both die spectacularly in the film's fiery finale.

16 JAWS 1975

124 

Poster/photos: © 1975 Universal Studios

The terrifying motion picture
from the terrifying No.1 best seller.
JAWS
ROY SCHEIDER
ROBERT SHAW
RICHARD DREYFUSS
JAWS
Co-starring LORRAINE GARY · MURRAY HAMILTON · A ZANUCK/BROWN PRODUCTION
Screenplay by PETER BENCHLEY and CARL GOTTLIEB · Based on the novel by PETER BENCHLEY · Music by JOHN WILLIAMS
Directed by STEVEN SPIELBERG · Produced by RICHARD D. ZANUCK and DAVID BROWN · A UNIVERSAL PICTURE ·
TECHNICOLOR® PANAVISION®
PG PARENTAL GUIDANCE SUGGESTED
...MAY BE TOO INTENSE FOR YOUNGER CHILDREN

WHO MADE IT:

Universal Pictures (U.S.). Director: Steven Spielberg. Producers: David Brown, Richard D. Zanuck. Writers: Peter Benchley, Carl Gottlieb, Howard Sackler (uncredited), based on a novel by Peter Benchley. Cinematography (Technicolor): Bill Butler. Music: John Williams. Starring Roy Scheider (Police Chief Martin Brody), Robert Shaw (Quint), Richard Dreyfuss (Matt Hooper), Lorraine Gary (Ellen Brody), Murray Hamilton (Mayor Larry Vaughn), Cart Gottlieb (Ben Meadows), Jeffrey C. Kramer (Deputy Hendricks), Susan Backlinie (Chrissie Watkins).

WHAT IT'S ABOUT:

After the gruesome death of a young female swimmer, the residents of Amity, Long Island, begin to realize that an enormous Great White shark is feeding in local waters. Amity's fair-minded police chief Martin Brody tries to deal with the potentially devastating problem, calling in shark expert Matt Hooper and requesting that the beaches be temporarily closed. But the Chief encounters unexpected resistance from island mayor Larry Vaughn, and several other local merchants, who are concerned about what a shark scare might do to their summer business. Working with almost legendary Amity fisherman Quint, an old salt full of dark stories, Brody and Hooper track down the Great White and engage in a dramatic encounter that ultimately sinks their boat and puts their lives in jeopardy. Hooper survives a harrowing shark cage assault and Quint is devoured alive, leaving Brody to fire the fatal shot that ignites a pressurized air tank the creature had lodged in its jaws. Instantly the monster shark is blown to bits, and the threat to Amity is ended. Winded but grateful to be alive, survivors Brody and Hooper find each other and swim back safely to shore.

WHY IT'S IMPORTANT:

Steven Spielberg's *Jaws* has to be classified as a horror film, certainly as a monster movie, even though there's nothing science fictional or supernatural going on (just like Spielberg's "monster truck" from *Duel* was merely a guy driving a diesel when viewed literally). But the larger-than- life qualities of this bloodthirsty, ever-hunting Great White ("Bruce") make him a movie beastie of Kong-like proportions, as if the swordfish from Hemingway's *The Old Man and the Sea* were suddenly on steroids. John Williams' unforgettable musical score, with a distinctive, ultra-heavy, ever-escalating two-note theme, added immeasurably to this first true "summer movie" experience.

Apart from Spielberg's genius as an intuitive filmmaker, the film benefits from first-rate production values and an A-cast, who were wisely encouraged to improvise in order to give this somewhat hard-to-swallow fish story added credibility. The narrative is neatly (too neatly) divided in half, like an especially elaborate ABC two-part *Movie of the Week*, with Part One being a transparent remake of Ibsen's famous morality play *Enemy of the People*, and Part Two a reworking of *The Sharkfighters* and similar films, this time with three, distinctively different personalities forced to work with each other and (ultimately) learn from each other. The chosen actors represent letter-perfect casting: Roy Schneider, the urban cop completely adrift at sea; Richard Dreyfuss, aging hippie/shark professor; and Robert Shaw, a kitschy but entertaining variation of weathered, wise but obsessed mariner Ahab.

Best scenes: the opening attack; nervous Brody at the beach; that head popping up from under the wreck; Quint's evocative speech; the high-powered finale.

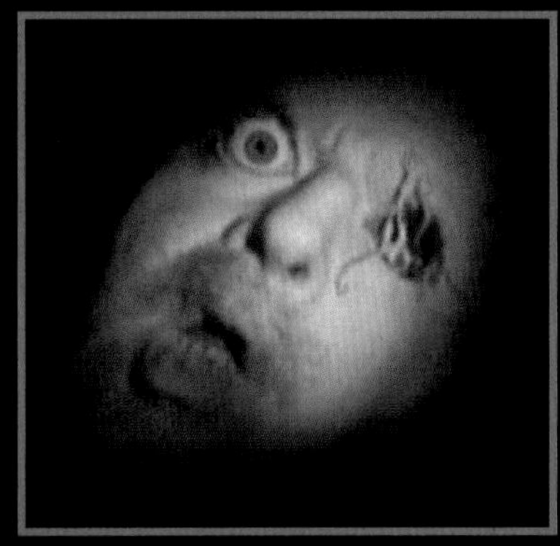

The ultimate moment of horror from *Jaws* doesn't showcase the shark monster itself or even a bloody attack, but the remains of one of its mutilated victims...a shocking surprise for investigating diver Hooper (and the viewing audience).

Universal produced three sequels to the original *Jaws*, all of them unnecessary. The one in 3D is especially offensive, since it was put in production to replace Jack Arnold's slated remake of *Creature from the Black Lagoon* in the mid-'80s.

Quick editing and compelling camerawork helped to disguise the rubbery unreality of "Bruce the shark."

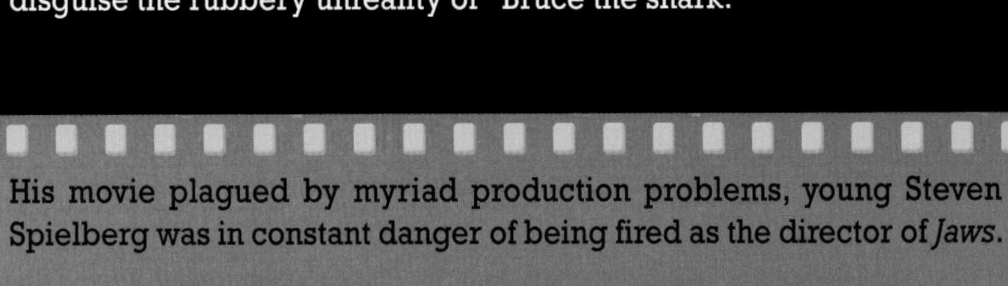

His movie plagued by myriad production problems, young Steven Spielberg was in constant danger of being fired as the director of *Jaws*.

15 DRACULA 1931

WHO MADE IT:

Universal Pictures (U.S.). Director: Tod Browning. Producers: Carl Laemmle Jr., Tod Browning. Writer: Garrett Fort, based on the stage play by Hamilton Deane & John L. Balderston and the novel by Bram Stoker. Cinematography (b/w): Karl Freund. Starring Bela Lugosi (Count Dracula), Helen Chandler (Mina), David Manners (John Harker), Dwight Frye (Renfield), Edward Van Sloan (Van Helsing), Herbert Bunston (Jack Seward), Frances Dade (Lucy Western), Joan Standing (Briggs), Charles K. Gerrard (Martin), Carla Laemmle (Coach passenger), Geraldine Dvorak, Cornelia Thaw, Dorothy Tree (Dracula's wives).

WHAT IT'S ABOUT:

Count Dracula is a vampire who rises from the grave each night to seek victims from whom he can draw the blood he requires. He enlists the aid of an unsuspecting man named Renfield, who visits the Count in his Transylvanian castle in order to make travel arrangements. A stricken Renfield loses his sanity after their initial encounter, and soon becomes Dracula's all-purpose servant as the vampire moves from his native land to England. There, in upper-class society, the Count meets Mina and fiancée Jonathan Harker, along with Dr. Van Helsing, who discovers the monstrous truth about Dracula. After Mina's friend Lucy is bitten by the vampire and transformed into one herself, Van Helsing fears that Mina may be next on Dracula's new list of victims. Working with Harker and ally Dr. Seward, he tracks down the blood-drinker and finally plunges a stake through his centuries-old heart. Mina's trance-like state, induced by the Count, is broken.

WHY IT'S IMPORTANT:

Universal's oft-screened adaptation of *Dracula* is a landmark film for at least three reasons: it was the first significant horror movie of the sound era; it had the guts not to apologize for its supernatural content; and it showed 1930s movie-goers exactly what a "real" vampire looks, acts and sounds like. Although this major role was designed for Lon Chaney Sr. and Conrad (*Man Who Laughs*) Veight seemed the logical casting choice following Chaney's death, it was Hungarian-born Bela Lugosi, veteran of various *Dracula* stage productions, who finally donned the flowing black cape for Hollywood. His extraordinary performance dominates *Dracula*, forever identifying the actor with this particular part (a mixed blessing) and creating a distinctive and iconic fantasy presence that resonates to this day.

In recent years, many have criticized director Tod Browning for "walking through" his creative chores on *Dracula*, comparing the film unfavorably with the Spanish-language version produced simultaneously by Universal. Although there are certainly more inventive camera moves in the alternate incarnation, in many ways it lacks the dreamlike poetry of Browning's "quiet" approach, particularly in the moody Transylvanian sequences. Best scenes (Browning version): everything leading up to Dracula's arrival in England, Renfield's tour-de-force confession ("All these will I give you...if you will obey me!"), and the Count's dramatic confrontation with Dr. Van Helsing in Seward's living room.

Although a tad slow-moving for some current viewers, *Dracula* remains a celebrated horror classic and a showcase for its irreplaceable star. *Twilight* and today's endless stream of teen-themed vampire flicks can trace their genre lineage to this always watchable, always atmospheric "ground zero" original.

Dracula's castle at sunset, courtesy of a glass painting. BELOW: Renfield's cut finger attracts some unwanted attention.

Bela Lugosi wouldn't officially play Count Dracula again until *Abbott and Costello Meet Frankenstein* in 1948, although similar characterizations (*Mark of the Vampire*, *Return of the Vampire*) kept him professionally busy until his death in the late '50s. Despite formidable challenges from Christopher Lee, Klaus Kinski, Frank Langella, and Danny Oldman, his peculiar take remains the character's most iconic screen incarnation.

Lugosi's unique aura has proven timeless and irresistible. Here, he relaxes on set beside a studio arc lamp that simulates sunlight (!).

...Shyamalan redefines the twist ending in this compelling life-after-death mystery...

14 THE SIXTH SENSE 1999

1.85

BRUCE WILLIS

1 SIGHT

2 SOUND

3 SMELL

4 TASTE

5 TOUCH

THE SIXTH SENSE

NOT EVERY GIFT IS A BLESSING.

WHO MADE IT:

Buena Vista Pictures (U.S.). Director: M. Night Shyamalan. Producers: Kathleen Kennedy, Frank Marshall, Barry Mendel. Writer: M. Night Shyamalan. Cinematography (Technicolor): Tak Fujimoto. Music: James Newton Howard. Starring Bruce Willis (Dr. Malcolm Crowe), Haley Joel Osment (Cole Sear), Toni Collette (Lynn Sear), Olivia Williams (Anna Crowe), Donnie Wahlberg (Vincent Grey), Glenn Fitzgerald (Sean), Mischa Barton (Kyra).

WHAT IT'S ABOUT:

Accomplished child psychologist Dr. Malcolm Crowe is shot by a former patient, a tragic defeat for him personally and professionally. Seeking redemption, he dedicates himself to helping other children with similar personality disorders, although this preoccupation has alienated him from his formerly loving wife, Anna. Crowe tries to help Cole Sear, a young boy with a most disturbing secret: he sees dead people, and their frequent visitations terrify him. At the doctor's suggestion, Cole begins to listen to his ghostly guests, who seem to require his help to right past wrongs. The boy finally accepts his curious, oddly-beneficial fate, even confiding in his stunned but loving mother. As for Malcolm, he comes to realize that he's been dead all along, killed by that former patient's bullet, just another ghost Cole was able to connect with. Now that the boy's been set on the right path, he bids his adored Anna farewell in her sleep, and is able to move on.

WHY IT'S IMPORTANT:

Forget the relatively trite title: *The Sixth Sense* is an almost perfect blend of supernatural chiller, psychological character study, buddy movie, and, ultimately, love story. Director M. Night Shyamalan's peculiar creative devices and stylistic ticks are now familiar to most movie viewers, but in '99 his brand of melancholy twist-driven melodrama was as fresh as Haley Joel Osment's unexpected performance. Not since Jennifer Jones beheld the Lady of Lourdes has a young performer so convincingly conveyed a rapport with the spectral unknown. When all-seeing Cole Sear finally comes clean to his sharp and loving mother (the equally wonderful Toni Collette), we not only buy the kid's ghost stories, we believe his no-nonsense mom buys them, too. Meanwhile, Bruce Willis as subdued, humble, redemption-seeking Malcolm Crowe effortlessly conveys the required father-figure warmth and transcendent guilt.

Totally disregarding horror movie conventions, Shyamalan's careful and compelling scenario never loses its audience, in spite of long stretches of character contemplation. When first-rate ghostly shocks do arrive, they are either jolting throwaways (turned heads revealing mutilated faces) or unceremoniously naturalistic (Cole's frothing tent visitor), in keeping with the carefully established mood. The final, celebrated twist compels awestruck viewers to re-visit earlier scenes, and even some undeniable illogic can't reduce this reveal's emotional impact. Add composer James Newton Howard's mournful yet transcendent music and polished production values from Kennedy/Marshall (*Sense* owes something to *Poltergeist*), and we're blessed with one of the finest, most inspired and heartfelt ghostly chillers ever conceived.

13 THE CABINET OF DR. CALIGARI 1919

1.33

WHO MADE IT:

Decla-Bioscop (Germany)/Goldwyn Distributing Company (U.S.). Director: Robert Wiene. Producers: Rudolf Meinert, Erich Pommer. Writers: Hans Janowitz, Carl Mayer. Cinematography (b/w and tints): Willy Hameister. Music: Giuseppe Becce. Starring Werner Krauss (Dr. Caligari), Conrad Veidt (Cesare), Fredrich Feher (Francis), Lil Dagover (Jane Olsen), Hans Heinrich von Twardowski (Alan).

WHAT IT'S ABOUT:

At a carnival in a little German village, a man named Francis is captivated by the performance of Dr. Caligari and his main attraction, the somnambulist Cesare, who can apparently foretell the future. An investigation into the pair's history provokes Cesare to kidnap Francis' girlfriend Jane. When Caligari orders that she be killed, the hypnotized sleepwalker cannot bring himself to commit this vile act. He carries her away and leads the townfolk on a lengthy chase before falling to his death. Ultimately, the entire experience is revealed to be the product of Francis' warped imagination: he, Jane and Cesare are in truth inmates of an insane asylum, while Caligari is their attentive doctor.

WHY IT'S IMPORTANT:

More an experience than a movie (although it does have a fast-paced plot and a twist ending), *The Cabinet of Dr. Caligari* is a masterwork of German silent cinema. Ostensibly a horror film, it explores areas of psychological imbalance so poetically that the film's place as an early, penetrating overview of this subject seems assured. Interestingly, the decision to design *Caligari* as an expressionistic fantasy accounts for its most significant creative feature, although that choice was based on economics rather than artistic preference. Clearly, it's much cheaper to paint shadows on backdrops than constructing and lighting elaborate sets. And the bizarre inner landscape of *Dr. Caligari* called for some pretty detailed environments.

Writers Hans Janowitz and Carl Mayer were fans of Paul Wegener's moody horror films, and it's not surprising that Germany's "master of darkness," Fritz Lang, was originally approached to direct. Instead, that task went to Robert Wiene, who was anxious to work with the offbeat "flat painted sets" technique and pulled out all the creative stops to make this iffy illusion work. Meanwhile, it was the film's cautious producers who ultimately insisted on making the entire story a dream, negating the larger-than-life realities of its two primary "monsters" (Caligari and Cesare). Although this kind of twist is generally considered a cop-out, it actually happens to serve the groundbreaking *Caligari*, transforming Wiene's fanciful thriller into an important early study of dream-state.

Just as Karloff would ultimately dominate *Frankenstein*, so does Conrad Veidt command the screen as Cesare, a sleepwalking murderer under the fiendish control of carnival hypnotist Dr. Caligari. This role would catapult Veidt to international stardom; he'd soon be regarded as Germany's answer to Lon Chaney, and a possible candidate for the coveted part of Count Dracula at Universal Pictures in the 1930s. Truth to tell, there is nothing literally fantastic going on in the plotline of *Caligari* (Cesare is not a ghost or reanimated corpse), but the look of these key characters is decidedly unreal and nightmarish, matching the celebrated sets. Anticipating the horror classics of both Val Lewton and James Whale, the film continues to intrigue and even baffle viewers, who are forced to become dream analysts on the spot. Evaluating the disturbed psyche of artistic German idealists in between wars may not have been the original intent of Caligari's makers, but that angle adds a final element of worth to a thoroughly captivating cinematic experience.

Greatest of all screen monsters, Karloff's creation mixes terror and pathos...

12

FRANKENSTEIN 1931

 71 | 1.37

Poster/photos: © 1931 Universal Studios

WHO MADE IT:

Universal Pictures (U.S.). Director: James Whale. Writers: Francis Edward Faragoh, Garrett Ford; adapted by John L. Balderston from the novel by Mary Shelley. Cinematography (b/w): Arthur Edeson. Music: Bernhard Kaun. Starring Colin Clive (Dr. Henry Frankenstein), Mae Clarke (Elizabeth), John Boles (Victor Moritz), Boris Karloff (The Monster), Edward Van Sloan (Dr. Waldman), Frederick Kerr (Baron Frankenstein), Dwight Frye (Fritz), Lionel Belmore (Vogel), Marilyn Harris (Maria).

WHAT IT'S ABOUT:

Henry Frankenstein, a young scientist, has fashioned a human body and is conducting experiments to bring it to life. His greatly-concerned fiancée, Elizabeth, seeks to stop him and enlists the aid of a friend, Victor, and Frankenstein's professor/mentor, Dr. Waldman. They arrive at Frankenstein's mountain laboratory during a violent thunderstorm just as the final test is completed. Made from human body parts and bombarded by cosmic rays via electricity, the Creature is indeed brought to life. But because it possesses a criminal brain and can do only harm, it must be destroyed for everyone's benefit, a grim task left to Waldman. Recovering from his manic experiments, Henry Frankenstein prepares to marry Elizabeth, even as the Monster murders Dr. Waldman and escapes into the countryside. Quite by accident, it drowns a little girl, and is finally pursued by scores of torch-wielding villagers to an old windmill. Both Doctor and vengeful creation finally confront one another, a violent encounter that results in Henry being throttled, then thrown from a high tower. He somehow recovers, and the townsfolk set the windmill on fire. Frankenstein's man-made monster seems to burn to death as the flames consume him.

WHY IT'S IMPORTANT:

Inspired by silent German horror films like *The Golem*, James Whale's *Frankenstein* is arguably the world's most famous monster movie, establishing Boris Karloff as "king" of the genre and putting Universal Pictures on the map as Hollywood's foremost fear factory. Originally designed as a project for Robert Florey (who wound up directing *Murders in the Rue Morgue* for Universal a year later), the film benefits tremendously from Whale's unique touch and creative instincts.

Karloff is indeed brilliant in his signature role, endowing the fearsome Monster with a sympathetic, childlike quality entirely in keeping with his "newborn" status. Just about as memorable is Colin Clive portraying the tormented, partially-crazed Dr. Frankenstein ("It's alive!"), ably supported by *Dracula* co-star Edward Van Sloan as resident sage/voice of reason Dr. Waldman ("You have created a monster and it will destroy you!"), Dwight Frye as hunchback assistant Fritz and young semi-romantic leads Mae Clarke and John Boles.

A key selling point of the film was Karloff's imaginative make-up, created by legendary monster maker Jack Pierce. This square-headed, neck-bolted image became so iconic that Universal giddily threatened imitators with lawsuits, even though the *Frankenstein* novel itself was in the public domain. Karloff himself suggested the heavy eyelids, which created a corpse-like look, and the removal of his mouth bridge, which enabled his right cheek to appear sunken and skull-like.

A lot has happened in the horror movie genre since 1931. But for sheer originality (the Monster's distinctive look) and pathos (how often do we feel sorry for a movie villain who drowns an innocent child?), nothing can touch the original *Frankenstein*.

"Quite a good scene, isn't it?" Dr. Frankenstein snaps at his unwanted guests before bringing the Monster to life. Helping to make it so are actors Dwight Frye, Edward Van Sloan, John Boles, Mae Clarke and Colin Clive. Karloff's under the sheet.

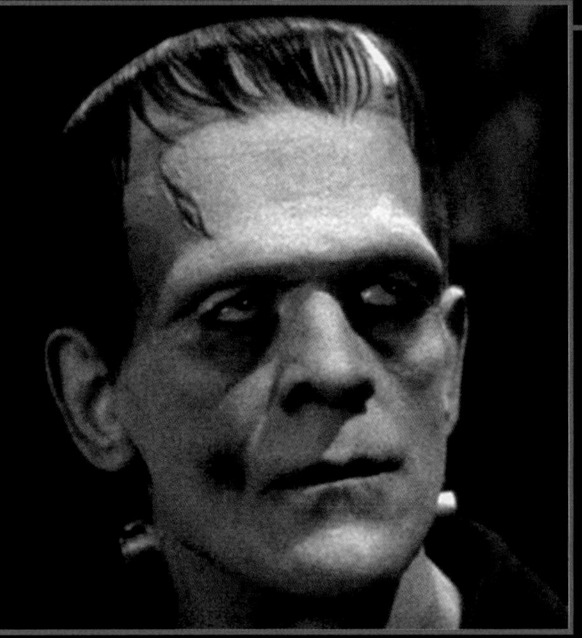

Boris Karloff was 44 when he played the Frankenstein Monster for the first time in 1931.

The Monster's tragic moment with little Maria, one of the film's highlights, was severely edited for many years.

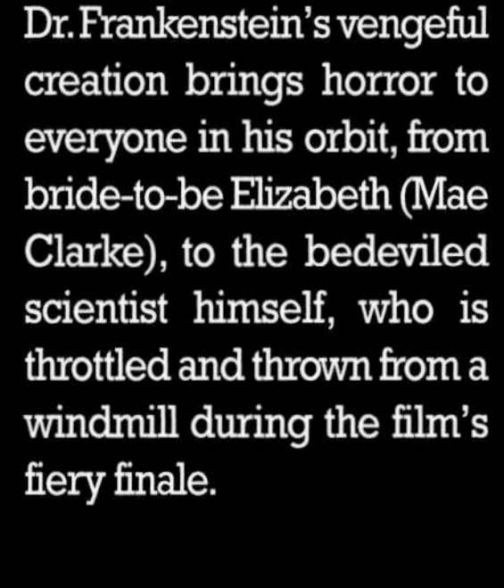

Dr. Frankenstein's vengeful creation brings horror to everyone in his orbit, from bride-to-be Elizabeth (Mae Clarke), to the bedeviled scientist himself, who is throttled and thrown from a windmill during the film's fiery finale.

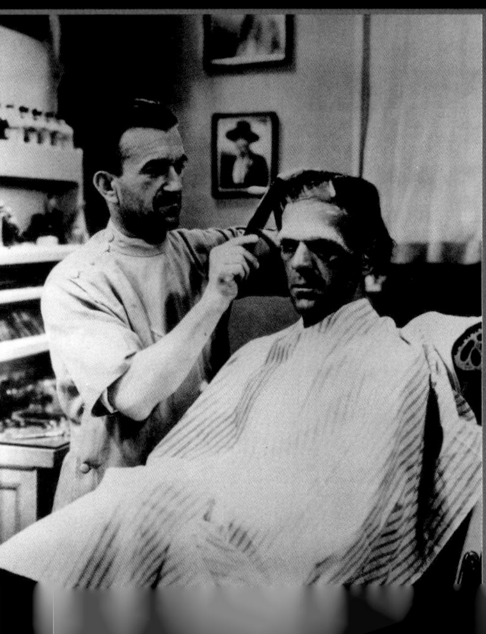

Universal's resident make-up wizard Jack Pierce designed Frankenstein's Monster, although star Karloff had some significant creative suggestions of his own.

11 THE CURSE OF THE WEREWOLF 1961

91  1.85

WHO MADE IT:

Hammer Films (England)/Universal Pictures. Director: Terence Fisher. Producers: Michael Carreras, Anthony Hinds. Writer: Anthony Hinds (John Elder). Cinematography (Technicolor): Arthur Grant. Music: Benjamin Frankel. Starring Clifford Evans (Don Alfredo Corledo), Oliver Reed (Leon), Yvonne Romain (Servant girl), Catherine Feller (Cristina Fernando), Peter Sallis (Don Enrique), Hira Talfrey (Teresa), John Gabriel (The priest), Anthony Dawson (Marques Siniestro), Richard Wordsworth (Beggar), Josephine Llewellyn (Marquesa), Warren Mitchell (Pepe Valiente), Dominique (George Woodbridge), Michael Ripper (Old Soak), Justin Walters (Young Leon).

WHAT IT'S ABOUT:

When a young woman is raped by a man who has been reduced to bestiality, she eventually gives birth to a lycanthrope. Adopted by kindly nobleman Don Alfredo Corledo following the mother's death, this boy, named Leon, shows signs of his unholy affliction at an early age. He must be secured in his room when a terrible bloodlust overtakes him at night, causing his canine teeth to enlarge. With the love of family and the help of a sympathetic local priest, Leon seems to conquer his '"curse," growing to handsome maturity without further incident. But when the young man's primal tendencies are brought to the fore unexpectedly during a visit to a brothel, he transforms into something inhuman and commits several murders. Only the pure love of a girl named Cristina has the power to cure him; Leon is instead captured and imprisoned by disbelieving authorities. As the moon rises, he again transforms into his monstrous other self, breaking free and killing everyone in his path. Cornered in a bell tower, the fearsome werewolf is finally killed by a silver bullet fired by his loving foster father.

WHY IT'S IMPORTANT:

Having revolutionized movies in the late 1950s with mature and stylish takes on classic horror tales, Hammer Films was at the peak of its creative powers as the new decade rolled in. Iconic monsters Frankenstein, Count Dracula, and the Mummy had already received shiny upgrades, so a revised werewolf story was inevitable. Still partnered with Universal, H's producers could have easily dusted off *The Wolf Man* and re-imagined poor Larry Talbot for current audiences (1959's *The Mummy* was a direct remake of Universal's properties). Wisely, they opted for the formula that made Hammer immortal: aggressive originality and a highly sophisticated treatment enlivened by polished color cinematography, meticulous set decoration and gory, unflinching violence. The inevitable project was titled *The Curse of the Werewolf* and it wound up becoming the most definitive example of man-into-beast ever put on the screen.

Not content with telling a solid dramatic story focusing on one key character, Hammer upped the ante by providing a brilliant overview of lycanthropy, elevating this fantasy affliction to semi-reality status with a thorough, generation-spanning structure. Indeed, by establishing the werewolf's mother and father credibly in the lengthy opening sequences, we believe just about everything that follows.

Little Leon's attack of lycanthropy as a child was a startling and unprecedented *Exorcist*-like moment in 1961, and his adult life is equally compelling. Newcomer Oliver Reed was apparently born for this title role, adding a primal, more violently sexual "bad boy" to Hammer's star roster. With a different cinematographer and musical composer as well, a real effort was made to distinguish *Werewolf* from its immediate Hammer predecessors. Indeed, next to their letter-perfect *Horror of Dracula*, it's the British company's most revered contribution to fright cinema, a picture so earnest it even works for anti-horror "civilians."

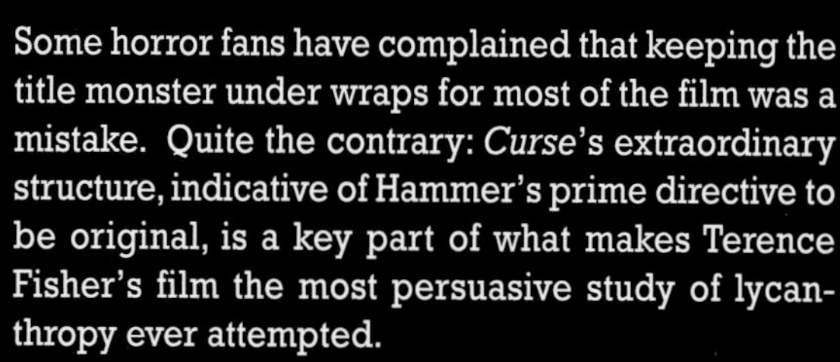

Some horror fans have complained that keeping the title monster under wraps for most of the film was a mistake. Quite the contrary: *Curse*'s extraordinary structure, indicative of Hammer's prime directive to be original, is a key part of what makes Terence Fisher's film the most persuasive study of lycanthropy ever attempted.

The fate of an unfortunate beggar (Richard Wordsworth), Leon the werewolf's beast-like father, is explored methodically at the outset of the film.

Young Leon (Justin Walters) endures an attack of lycanthropy.

ABOVE: Inspired by timber wolves, the Roy Ashton make-up for Oliver Reed was a dramatic, full color departure from Universal's previous wolf-men.

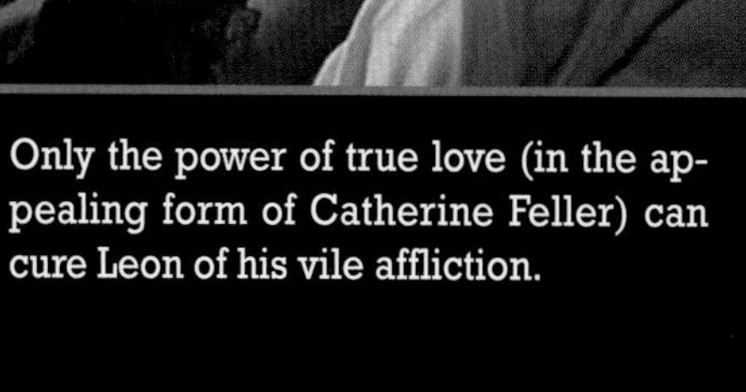

Only the power of true love (in the appealing form of Catherine Feller) can cure Leon of his vile affliction.

The film's busy climax has echoes of Universal's horror classics, with an imprisoned werewolf and torch-brandishing villagers out for blood figuring into the choreography. Although shot in blazing three-strip Technicolor, *Curse* was released stateside in the cheaper and less vivid Eastmancolor process.

Roy Ashton received high marks for his *Werewolf* makeup design, which seems to be channeling elements from both Cocteau's *Beauty and the Beast* and *Curse of the Demon*.

10 NOSFERATU, A SYMPHONY OF TERROR 1922

94 1.33

WHO MADE IT:

Jofa-Atelier Berlin-Johannisthal/Prana-Film Gmbh/Film Arts Guild (Germany). Director: F.W. Murnau. Producers: Enrico Dieckmann, Albin Grau. Writer: Henrik Galeen, based on Bram Stoker's novel *Dracula* (uncredited). Cinematography (b/w): F.A. Wagner. Starring Max Schreck (Graf Orlok), Gustav von Wangenheim (Hutter), Greta Schroeder (Ellen Hutter), Alexander Granach (Knock), Georg H. Schnell (Harding).

WHAT IT'S ABOUT:

Ordered by his employer, real estate agent Thomas Hutter must make the long journey from Wisborg to Transylvania to finalize the selling of a house. Staying at a mountain inn near the castle, he finds the locals to be extremely superstitious, and a book about vampires does little to calm the traveler's nerves. Late the following day, Hutter arrives at his destination and meets Count Orlock himself, a grotesque-looking man with claw-like hands, who is in truth a blood-lusting vampire. Soon Hutter is a prisoner in the Count's castle, powerless as Orlock transports himself out of the country on a ship that he attacks from within, preying on terrified crew members one by one. Now arrived in Wisborg, Count Orlock brings the plague with him, and soon the city is overrun with rats. Somehow, Hutter manages to return to his beloved fiancé Ellen, bringing the book about vampires with him. Understanding what is at stake, Ellen sacrifices her life to destroy Nosferatu, keeping the vampire so preoccupied with the drinking of her blood, that he forgets daylight is upon him. He vanishes in a cloud of smoke.

WHY IT'S IMPORTANT:

An intentional variation on Bram Stoker's *Dracula, Nosferatu, a Symphony of Terror* produced an original screen bloodsucker ultimately as iconic as Bela Lugosi's caped sophisticate. Germany, of course, gave birth to horror cinema in the silent era. And just as *The Golem* showcased the very first Frankenstein-like automaton, *Nosferatu* introduces a genuine vampire to movie audiences, in this case a non-human ratlike creature with strange ears, pointy fangs and enormous talons.

Director Murnau, like Tod Browning after him, makes the most of the atmosphere-rich castle scenes. He's even up to trying some daring stop-motion tricks, as the titular vampire seals himself up in a coffin before his long sea voyage. In keeping with the essence of German expressionism, odd angles abound and ominous shadows creep in and out of carefully-composed shots.

As for Max Schreck, he is Count Orlok, embodying the role simply because there's never been anything quite like him. The character's semi-demonic appearance fits in perfectly with the simple, fable-like ambitions of Murnau's scenario. This is the kind of story where the "power of true love" vanquishes a pointy-eared phantasm, magically reducing him to smoke in the rays of the morning sun. By comparison, later versions of *Dracula* add dimension and some credibility to a vampire's lifestyle, following the Count around as he mingles among mortals in public places. This noxious, stylized entity seems more of an abstraction, a metaphor for the plague. In recent times, Orlok has even been accepted as the "true" appearance of a vampire, with Lugosi's take now viewed as the flamboyant Hollywood interpretation.

Fantasy becomes dark reality in this striking psychological thriller, à la Polanski...

9 REPULSION 1965

105 | 1.85

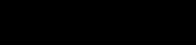

WHO MADE IT:

Tekli-Film Productions Ltd./Compton Films/Royal Films International (U.K.). Director: Roman Polanski. Producer: Gene Gutowski. Writers: Roman Polanski, Gerard Brach, David Stone. Cinematography (b/w): Gilbert Taylor. Music: Chicho Hamilton. Starring Catherine Deneuve (Carole Ledoux), Ian Hendry (Michael), John Fraser (Colin), Yvonne Furneaux (Helene Ledoux), Patrick Wymark (Landlord), Renee Houston (Miss Balch), Valerie Taylor (Madame Denise), James Villiers (John), Helen Fraser (Bridget).

WHAT IT'S ABOUT:

A beautiful but timid manicurist named Carole must face some time alone in the gloomy apartment she shares with her older sister, Helene, who has left for a brief holiday with her boyfriend. Unbalanced and fearful of sex, the young woman descends into total madness, imagining cracks in the wall and nightly visitations from men, who viciously rape her. An unfortunate would-be suitor, Colin, breaks into the apartment, fearing for the seemingly fragile Carole's safety. She bludgeons him to death when his back is turned. A similar fate awaits the arrogant, rent-seeking, sex-hungry landlord, only he is fatally slashed with a straight razor belonging to Helene's suitor. When the couple return at the end of their vacation, they are horrified to find the apartment in shambles and littered with corpses. Still-alive Carole is also discovered, shoved under her bed and numbed to reality.

WHY IT'S IMPORTANT:

Just as Hitchcock's *Psycho* shook up audiences with its blunt violence in 1960, *Repulsion* raises the bar five years later with an even bolder scenario. The film provides no clever twists or unusual structural surprises to distract viewers, just an uncompromising look at total madness and resulting murder, all the more disturbing with chaste, perfectly beautiful Catherine Deneuve at the heart of the bloodbath. Left alone for a stretch in her sister's bleak, nether-world apartment (both *Eraserhead* and *The Shining* owe something to *Repulsion*), Carole's festering demons come to the fore in a variety of horrendous ways. Her nocturnal rape fantasies are shocking and unexpected, but it's their subtle set-up that leaves the creepiest impression. Polanski is a master of eliciting primal fear with the simple devices of a darkened room and the monotonous ticking of an alarm clock. Visceral thrills aside, there is nothing more frightening than hearing an interloper walking about your apartment in the dead of night, just outside your unlocked bedroom. A quick glimpse of Carole's stoic rapist in a suddenly-turned mirror never fails to elicit screams. Still, it's the killings themselves – jolting and abrupt, without ritualistic fanfare - that mostly unnerve audiences. Polanski allows the fawn-like Carole to lose all sense of grace and femininity; she becomes a feral animal, incapable of rational human thought, savagely stabbing or clubbing clueless victims with unrestrained fury. It is a terrifying portrait of a lost soul and the hopeless, pointless nightmare world she has come to inhabit.

Repulsion made 1960s audiences cringe in a way very new to them, opening doors of derangement we always knew existed, but were always too terrified to acknowledge. Not surprisingly, bedeviled genius Roman Polanski leads us right through them.

8 PHANTOM OF THE OPERA 1925

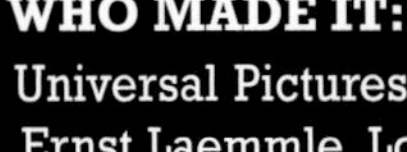

WHO MADE IT:

Universal Pictures (U.S.). Directors: Rupert Julian, Edward Sedgwick Ernst Laemmle, Lon Chaney. Producer: Carl Laemmle. Writers: Ellio Clawson, Raymond Schrock, Bernard McConville, Jasper Spearing Richard Wallace, Walter Anthony, Tom Reed, Frank M. McCormack, fron the composition by Gaston Leroux. Cinematography (b/w with two-strip Technicolor inserts and tints): Milton Bridenbecker, Virgil Miller Charles Van Enger. Starring Lon Chaney (Erik, the Phantom), Mary Philbin (Christine Daae), Norman Kerry (Vicomte Raoul de Chagny) Arthur Edmund Carewe (The Persian), Gibson Gowland (Buquet).

WHAT IT'S ABOUT:

Is the Paris Opera House haunted? That's what the new owners wonder as a strange creature known as the Phantom seems to lurk menacingly in the shadows, sometimes even appearing like an apparition in a box seat. Shockingly, the owners receive orders from the Phantom, demanding that a young performer, Christine Daae appear on stage in a new production. When they refuse, he sends the main chandelier crashing down in the middle of the performance, and several patrons are crushed beneath it. Soon after, the Phantom, masked and mysterious, abducts Christine, and brings her into his weird world beneath the Paris Opera House He claims to be a master musician with grand plans for her voice But ultimately, Christine cannot resist unmasking this tragic figure as he plays on the organ. Much to her horror, the Phantom is revealed as a hideously deformed creature with a monstrous skull-like face that chills the blood. It isn't long before Christine allowed to return to her friends, confesses all to suitor Raoul de Chagny, and a serious hunt for the Phantom of the Opera is underway. After several harrowing perils, Chagny and ally The Persian survive to corner their resourceful quarry, who, because of Christine's pleas, shows them unexpected mercy. A vengeful mob also closes in, and Erik escapes the Opera House to lead them all on a wild coach chase through the city streets. After one final, mocking threat, he is overtaken, beaten to death, and tossed into the river.

WHY IT'S IMPORTANT:

Most people nowadays tend to think of *The Phantom of the Opera* as a hip musical about a tragic artist wearing a half-shattered theatre mask. But for generations, the Phantom and Hollywood's Man of a Thousand Faces, Lon Chaney Sr., were one and the same showcases for a grotesque death's head visage that became iconic for all horror movies. The original silen movie was a phenomenal early success for Universal, cementing the studio's relationship with "horror" subjects following Chaney's first vehicle for them, *The Hunchback of Notre Dame*. *Phantom* plays as a curious mix of classical horror tale, love story, "the show mus go on" theater melodrama, and ultimately, action-packed cliffhanger. Lon Chaney's Erik make-up and histrionics are so impressive tha some of the film's more questionable twists are easily forgiven. The most celebrated scene, of course, is Erik's climactic unmasking Compelling acting, multiple angles, perfect editing and the startling reveal of the Phantom's face add up to an unforgettable high poin in horror movie history.

Universal would revisit its prize property a number of times over the decades, with versions ranging from 1943's Technicolor pseudo-musical starring Claude Rains, to partner Hammer's grisly 1962 reboot (with *Pink Panther*'s Herbert Lom taking over for the film's

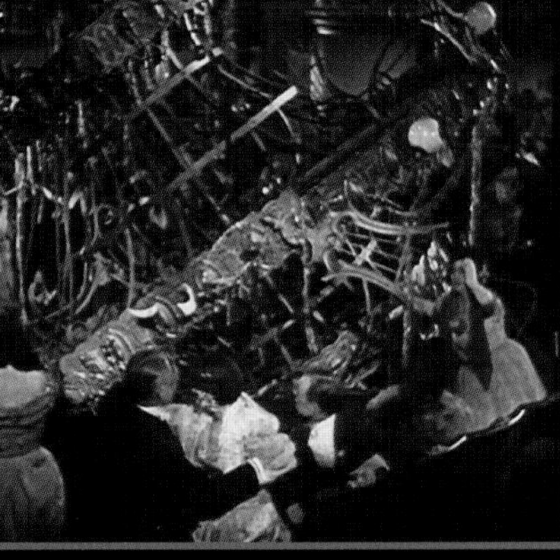

ABOVE: Opera patrons flee in terror after the chandelier crash.

BELOW: Erik's iconic unmasking, courtesy of Mary Philbin. The brilliant, gradually out-of-focus shot of Chaney drawing closer was added for the 1928 edition of the film. All three of these images are presented in their original tints.

The two-strip Technicolor ball sequence, featuring Erik's "Red Death," is one of the film's memorable highlights.

Phantom went through many structural changes from '25-'28; in the original climax, Erik dies at his beloved organ.

Starlet Mary Philbin, "the bravest girl in the world," poses for a publicity photo used to promote her most famous film.

Two of the screen's most memorable shock inducers: Lon Chaney's *Phantom of the Opera* (ABOVE) and the animated wonder *King Kong* (RIGHT, taking on a stegosaurus in a fight scene that was never filmed; notice the club in Kong's hand). INSERT, ABOVE: James Cagney re-enacts the Phantom's unmasking scene in Universal's 1957 Chaney biopic *Man of a Thousand Faces*. INSERT, RIGHT: The King (a full-size prop) certainly has a mouthful in a close-up that was cut from all prints of the movie for close to three decades.

7

King Kong 1933

105 1.37

Poster/photos: © 1933 RKO Pictures

WHO MADE IT:

(RKO) Radio Pictures (U.S.). Directors/Producers: Merian C. Cooper Ernest B. Schoedsack. Executive Producer: David O. Selznick. Writers James Ashmore Creelman, and Ruth Rose, based on a story by Merian C. Cooper and Edgar Wallace. Cinematography (b/w): Eddie Linden J.O. Taylor, Vernon Walker. Music: Max Steiner. Starring Fay Wray (Ann Darrow), Robert Armstrong (Carl Denham), Bruce Cabot (John Driscoll), Frank Reicher (Captain Englehorn), Sam Hardy (Charles Weston), Noble Johnson (Native Chief), James Flavin (Briggs)

WHAT IT'S ABOUT:

Motion Picture producer Carl Denham launches a desperate search for a leading lady to star in his new movie, which is set on a distant uncharted island. He finds down-on-her-luck Ann Darrow, and soon they're off on a mysterious voyage to the South Seas. On a fog shrouded atoll known as Skull Island, Denham and his camera crew promptly run afoul of the local natives, who are so taken with blonde Darrow that they soon kidnap her for sacrifice to their island God This entity turns out to be an outsized gorilla, Kong, who dominates a prehistoric jungle just beyond the great wall that protects the native population. Kong rescues hysterical Darrow from one primeval peril after another, but finally loses this unexpected object of his affection when she is rescued by courageous First Mate John Driscoll. Captured by a resourceful Denham after an attack on the native village, Kong is transported to civilization and garishly put on display in a Manhattan theater, only to escape and wreck havoc with a re-claimed Ann Darrow in his hairy paw Climbing to the top of the Empire State Building with his terrified prize, the giant gorilla is assaulted and shot repeatedly by dive-bombing biplanes. He finally plummets countless stories to his death. Ann survives the fantastic ordeal and is re-united with Jack, while a repentant Carl Denham tragically observes that it was "Beauty killed the Beast."

WHY IT'S IMPORTANT:

Combining several related genres (horror, adventure, sci-fi fantasy) into one unforgettable movie experience, *King Kong* seems to inspire fans of every generation. It's more than just an extraordinary special effects showcase; *Kong* is as heartfelt as it is thrilling, a tribute to spectacular storytelling and wildly imaginative production design.

Basing the lead character of Carl Denham on himself, real-life adventurer Merian C. Cooper envisioned a sweeping jungle cliffhanger involving gorillas, damsels, and monster-like lizards locked in savage combat. After seeing the stop-motion work of Willis O'Brien in *The Lost World*, he realized that this painstaking special effects technique was the only way to correctly realize his totally unprecedented over-the-top vision. And he was right. *Kong* was a smash success with Depression-era audiences during its initial release, forcing MGM to upgrade the *Tarzan* movie series with superior action sequences and production values. It made even more money when it was re-released in 1952, triggering the sci-fi "monster" boom of that era.

In a way, none of this is surprising. A gigantic gorilla on the rampage is certainly an audience grabber to begin with, but pitting him against ferocious dinosaurs on Skull Island amounts to icing on an already spectacular cake. Finally, the jaw-dropping finale in New York City, with Kong battling biplanes atop the largest building in the world, certified Cooper's brainchild as an unparalleled classic.

Unlike both high-profile remakes, the original *Kong* is not a literal dramatization of the *Beauty and the Beast* theme. It's actually a fanciful tale of unrequited love, with Ann Darrow (Fay Wray) quite rightfully scared to death by the monstrous, primordial creature pursuing her.

Willis O'Brien's stop-motion special effects astonished Depression-era moviegoers, with spectacular sequences like Kong pushing his way through the giant doors (LEFT) leaving an indelible impression. Among those inspired by O'Brien's work was young Ray Harryhausen, who became a giant in the animation field himself years later with classics like *7th Voyage of Sinbad* and *Jason and the Argonauts*.

RIGHT: "Run for your lives, Kong's coming!" Stars Bruce Cabot, Fay Wray and Robert Armstrong look extremely convincing in this posed publicity still.

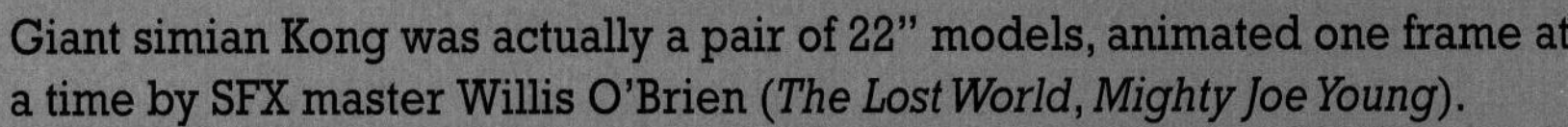

Giant simian Kong was actually a pair of 22" models, animated one frame at a time by SFX master Willis O'Brien (*The Lost World*, *Mighty Joe Young*).

6 NIGHT OF THE LIVING DEAD 1969

96 1.33 

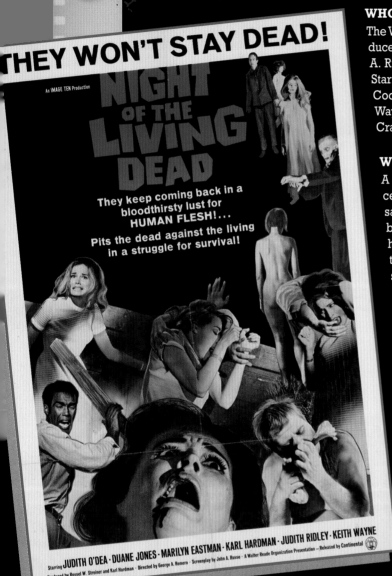

THEY WON'T STAY DEAD!

An IMAGE TEN Production

NIGHT OF THE LIVING DEAD

They keep coming back in a bloodthirsty lust for HUMAN FLESH!...

Pits the dead against the living in a struggle for survival!

Starring JUDITH O'DEA · DUANE JONES · MARILYN EASTMAN · KARL HARDMAN · JUDITH RIDLEY · KEITH WAYNE

Produced by Russel W. Streiner and Karl Hardman · Directed by George A. Romero · Screenplay by John A. Russo · A Walter Reade Organization Presentation — Released by Continental

WHO MADE IT:

The Walter Reade Organization (U.S.). Director: George A. Romero. Producers: Karl Hardman, Russell Streiner. Writers: George A. Romero, John A. Russo. Cinematography (b/w): George A. Romero. Music: Stock. Starring Duane Jones (Ben), Judith O'Dea (Barbra), Karl Hardman (Harry Cooper), Marilyn Eastman (Helen Cooper/Bug-eating Zombie), Keith Wayne (Tom), Judith Ridley (Judy), Kyra Schon Karen Cooper), Charles Craig (Newscaster/Zombie), S. William Hinzman (Cemetery Zombie)

WHAT IT'S ABOUT:

A young woman named Barbra and her brother drive to a remote cemetery to honor a deceased relative. Before long they are savagely attacked by what appears to be a deranged man. Barbra barely manages to escape and finds her way to an abandoned old house, where a resourceful stranger named Ben manages to protect them both not only from the mad attacker, but from a swarm of similarly crazed murderers. It's soon established that, due to a NASA space mishap, dead bodies on Earth have been coming back to life, and these zombie-like mutations appear to have a taste for the living. Joined by a handful of other frenzied survivors, Ben holds off the flesh-eating monsters for as long as he can, but soon their superior numbers prevail and nearly everyone – including Barbra – is killed and devoured. Fighting his way into a barred cellar, Ben somehow survives the harrowing night. But the following day, he is mistaken for one of the living dead and shot through the skull by rescuers. Thrown onto a pyre, his remains are burned with the other mutated bodies.

WHY IT'S IMPORTANT:

Sneaking up on fans like an unexpected firecracker, *Night of the Living Dead* changed the face of uncensored horror cinema for all time. It had the tacky pleasures (and even some of the stock music) of low-budget independent scare flicks, but its unique style of filmmaking (German expressionism meets Vietnam news footage) matched with groundbreaking gore brought things to a whole new level. In short, visionary helmer George Romero redefined the modern horror movie just as surely as Roman Polanski had a year earlier with *Rosemary's Baby*, coming at the genre from an entirely different creative direction.

Part sci-fi thriller, part social commentary, but mostly a "handful of trapped characters under siege" movie, *Living Dead* instills a disturbing sensibility into viewers that's unlike anything Romero has put on screen since. Maybe it's the elegant black-and-white photography, the dreamlike atmosphere, or the sheer psychic assault of the boxed-in situation in general. Proving himself a master of all horror techniques, Romero gets just as much mileage out of darkened hallways and kitchens as he does from close-ups of flesh-eating zombie grandmothers. The choice of African-American actor Duane Jones as the film's hero was inspired and works perfectly for its bleak Vietnam-era "twist" ending; Judith O'Dea is also quite good as the rattled female lead Barbra, and their early and final scenes together resonate. Best moments: the opening cemetery attack; hands pouring through an unguarded window; news reports the hungry little girl; the return of Barbra's brother; the "day after" round-up; end credit still montage.

Like so many horror film franchises from the '70s and '80s, *Night of the Living Dead* was eventually remade in color, some twenty years after its original release. Director Tom Savini's new incarnation provided a few entertaining jolts, but lacked the raw, elemental power

Romero's unflinching classic used its low budget and black-and-white photography to create a new kind of horror movie in 1969. Flesh-eating ghouls were depicted graphically for the very first time.

ABOVE: Star Duane Jones was a daring choice for the film's ill-fated hero, pitted against zombies, panic-stricken housemates, and ultimately trigger-happy rednecks.

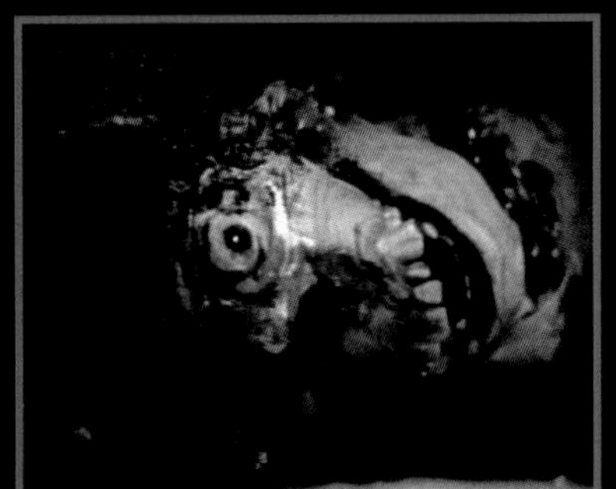

On location in Pittsburg, zombie actors are rigged for some juicy blood kills by *Night* special effects technicians.

5 BRIDE OF FRANKENSTEIN 1935

WHO MADE IT:

Universal Pictures (U.S.). Director: James Whale. Producer: Carl Laemmle Jr. Writers: William Hurlbut, John L. Balderston. Cinematography (b/w): John J. Mescall. Music: Franz Waxman. Starring Boris Karloff (the Monster), Colin Clive (Dr. Henry Frankenstein), Ernest Thesiger (Dr. Pretorius), Valerie Hobson (Elizabeth), Elsa Lanchester (Mary Shelley/The Monster's Mate), Dwight Frye (Karl), Gavin Gordon (Lord Byron), Una O'Connor (Minnie), Douglas Watson (Percy Shelley) O.P. Heggie (Hermit).

WHAT IT'S ABOUT:

Author Mary Shelley continues her infamous fright tale of "Frankenstein," explaining how the man-made Monster survived being burned to death in a windmill besieged by torch-brandishing villagers. Another survivor is Dr. Henry Frankenstein himself, who is soon approached by an eccentric, vaguely sinister colleague named Dr. Pretorius with a most starting project: creating a bride for his living dead man. Meanwhile, the at-large Monster is tormented and re-captured by locals, befriended by a kindly blind hermit who teaches him to speak, and finally approached by Pretorious, who slyly uses him to blackmail Henry into moving forward with their unholy project. But when the artificial female is indeed created, she responds to the hopeful, needy Monster with abject revulsion. Enraged, he throws a lever that blows up the entire laboratory, killing himself, the Bride, and Dr. Pretorius in the process.

WHY IT'S IMPORTANT:

Following the enormous success of 1931's *Frankenstein*, Universal gave director James Whale carte blanche to fashion an even more ambitious sequel. Karloff as the Monster and Colin Clive as his maker would reprise their famous roles, this time supported by eccentric character actor Ernest Thesiger as Frankenstein's sinister colleague, Dr. Pretorius. Several extraordinary sets, a longer shooting schedule and Franz Waxman's pop-operatic music score clearly upgraded this eagerly awaited follow-up, eventually titled *Bride of Frankenstein*. The result was one of the greatest and most beloved horror-fantasies of all time, nothing less than Universal's crown jewel in their celebrated collection of cinematic scarefests.

With a clever set-up by Mary Shelley herself (played by Elsa Lanchester, also starring as the unbilled Bride), the tale unfolds like a dark-edged fairy tale enlivened by a peculiar sense of humor. Even more than in the first movie, Karloff's Monster is a sinned-against, Christlike figure in search of a workable morality. Meanwhile, Ernest Thesiger's Dr. Pretorius threatens to steal the movie throughout, pretty much replacing Henry Frankenstein as the maddest of all mad doctors; he seems to be obsessed with creating life for the pure perverse pleasure of it. It's not surprising, then, that Henry's life is spared at the climax (he was, after all, literally blackmailed into creating the Bride by his wily, kidnapping co-conspirator). Eagle-eyed fans can spot Colin Clive clinging to a wall when the laboratory blows up in a shot representing the film's original, less charitable ending.

Sadly, *Bride* represents James Whale's final association with Universal's Frankenstein series. Rowland V. Lee would direct the next entry,

Boy-meets-girl, monster movie style. Although Karloff was initially against the idea of his famous character talking, it's a welcome new aspect of the mythology that gives Shelley's child-brute added dimension, rendering him even more sympathetic and relatable. Significantly, this angle would be dropped in Universal's later sequels, which seemed content with reducing the venerable Monster to a one-dimensional, henchman-like zombie.

BELOW: captured and imprisoned by the Burgomaster's minions. The Monster is clearly more victim than villain in *Bride of Frankenstein*, although he does commit his share of brutal killings along the way.

Several unusual scenes distinguish *Bride*, from the canny Mary Shelley introduction, to the Monster's memorable encounter with a blind hermit (O.P. Heggie).

Director James Whale discusses a key scene with "queer old gentleman" Dr. Pretorius (Ernest Thesiger).

4 Psycho 1960

109 1.85

WHO MADE IT:

Paramount Pictures (original release/early reissues)/Universal, since 1966 (U.S). Director: Alfred Hitchcock. Producer: Alfred Hitchcock (uncredited). Writer: Joseph Stefano, based on the story by Robert Bloch. Cinematography (b/w): John L. Russell. Music: Bernard Herrmann. Starring Anthony Perkins (Norman Bates), Janet Leigh (Marion Crane), Vera Miles (Lila Crane), John Gavin (Sam Loomis), Martin Balsam (Detective Milton Arbogast), Simon Oakland (Dr. Fred Richmond), John McIntire (Deputy Sheriff Al Chambers), Vaughn Taylor (George Lowery), Frank Albertson (Tom Cassidy), Lurene Tuttle (Mrs. Chambers), Virginia Gregg (Voice of Mother).

WHAT IT'S ABOUT:

Frustrated, attractive secretary Marion Crane steals $40,000 from her employer and drives out of town. Stopping off at a reclusive motel to reconsider her actions, Marion is brutally murdered while showering by what appears to be a maniacal old woman. The killer's soft-spoken son Norman dutifully covers up all evidence of his mother's bloody crime, then must do the same for the body of the private detective she stabs to death a short while later. Eventually Marion's sister Lila and fiancée Sam Loomis descend upon the hotel to get at the truth. After some harrowing encounters, it is Norman himself who is ultimately revealed as the psychotic killer, the son of clinging, possessive but deceased Norma Bates. With the aid of a wig and women's clothing, he "became" his jealous mother to murder the unsuspecting young women he was attracted to. Now apprehended and shut off from reality completely, Norman/Norma sits silently in a white-walled cell, unwilling to even swat a pesky fly.

WHY IT'S IMPORTANT:

Impressed by the big bucks earned by lurid, cheaply-made horror movies of the late '50s, Alfred Hitchcock took a still-amazing 360-degree stylistic turn from the Technicolor pleasures of *North By Northwest* with the grim, gray *Psycho*, arguably his most accomplished movie. A startling melding of the horror and suspense genres, this perverse adaptation of Robert Bloch's sick-to-begin-with story became the yardstick for all such thrillers to come. Hitchcock and screenwriter Stefano seem to revel in misleading their audience, playing with built-in expectations only to gleefully dismember them. Indeed, the shocking death of Janet Leigh mid-way into the movie blew everyone away in 1960…movie stars last through a whole movie, or so we thought. And the shower scene itself, a virtuoso display of direction, editing and musical scoring, remains the most impressive sequence of its kind ever filmed.

Before the role became a caricature, Norman Bates captivated audiences with his instantly likeable but slightly "off" personality. Star Anthony Perkins had already impressed audiences in *Fear Strikes Out*, proving himself more than just the latest male ingénue, and *Psycho* certified his reputation as a better kind of actor. Leigh, Vera Miles, newcomer John Gavin are all fine, and Martin Balsam as detective Arbogast is a definite scene-stealer. But it's Perkins' movie, and Mr. Hitchcock clearly knows it.

Shot swiftly by Hitch's TV series crew and scored by the legendary Bernard Herrmann, *Psycho* is that rare treasure in Hollywood – a totally self-assured, offbeat masterpiece that goes completely against the established grain. In spite of endless sequels and re-imaginings, it endures as a consummate work of cinema art, in addition to one hell of a great horror movie.

LEFT: *Psycho*'s infamous house of horrors, standing grimly on the Universal Studios lot. This iconic structure has been rebuilt several times since 1959 and it turns up continually in Universal movies and TV productions. RIGHT: Mother's corpse, in all its skeletal splendor. Supervised by legendary make-up artist Jack Barron, this grotesque mannequin-like figure provided *Psycho* with a resident "monster." Unlike the film's equally memorable murder house, "Mother" never re-appeared as a prop in other films.

Anthony Perkins was perfectly cast as boy-next-door psychotic Norman Bates, which ultimately became his signature role.

The notorious "shower sequence," a shocking set-piece of groundbreaking violence that was carefully storyboarded, became *Psycho*'s most talked-about scene and one of the most celebrated sequences in movie history.

Detective Arbogast (Martin Balsam) feels Mother's sudden rage.

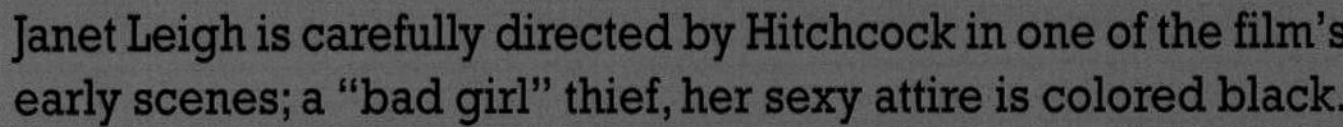

Janet Leigh is carefully directed by Hitchcock in one of the film's early scenes; a "bad girl" thief, her sexy attire is colored black.

3

ROSEMARY'S BABY 1968

 1.85

Poster/photos: © 1968 Paramount Pictures

Mia Farrow

Rosemary's Baby

John Cassavetes

Ruth Gordon / Sidney Blackmer / Maurice Evans / and Ralph Bellamy

WHO MADE IT:

Paramount Pictures (U.S.). Director: Roman Polanski. Producer: Willian Castle. Writer: Roman Polanski, based on the novel by Ira Levin Cinematography (Technicolor): William Fraker. Music: Krzyszto Komeda. Starring Mia Farrow (Rosemary Woodhouse), John Cassavetes (Guy Woodhouse), Ruth Gordon (Minnie Castevet), Sidney Blackme (Roman Castevet), Maurice Evans (Edward "Hutch" Hutchins), Ralph Bellamy (Dr. Abraham Sapirstein), Angela Dorian aka Victoria Vetr (Terry Gionoffrio), Patsy Kelly (Laura-Louise McBirney), Elisha Cook Jr. (Mr. Nicklas), Charles Grodin (Dr. Hill).

WHAT IT'S ABOUT:

Struggling young New York actor Guy Woodhouse and his wife Rosemary move into an exclusive apartment building and befrienc an elderly couple who live next door, the Castevets. Before long Rosemary experiences some bizarre hallucinations and has dreams of demonical rape that appear to be terrifyingly real. A good frienc named Hutch alerts her to the mysterious history of the building and the questionable profile of neighbor Roman Castevet, and soor turns up dead for his trouble. Increasingly paranoid and now pregnant, Rosemary begins to suspect that she and her unborr child are the victims of a vile conspiracy instigated by modern-day witches. Ultimately it's revealed that husband Guy made ar arrangement with the Castevets to allow Rosemary to be impregnated by Satan himself, in exchange for benefits to Guy's acting career. Horrified at this discovery, Rosemary spits ir Guy's face and defies the devil-worshipers, but nevertheless resolves to be a loving mother to her unnatural child.

WHY IT'S IMPORTANT:

Like all great movies, Roman Polanski's *Rosemary's Baby* is a one-of-a-kind experience. Yes, there have been other movies about devil-worshippers (Val Lewton's *The Seventh Victim* ever placed them in New York's Greenwich Village). We need to travel uptown for this harrowing nail-biter, as one o Manhattan's oldest and most mysterious buildings, the Dakota, becomes the basis of Ira Levin's hugely popular novel and ultimately this ultra-hip and stylish, oh-so-'60s film adaptation.

Although William Castle of all people is the producer of *Rosemary's Baby*, he wisely turned over all creative aspects of the project to offbeat, celebrated Euro-filmmaker Polanski. Fragile Mia Farrow was at the height of her '60s popularity (she had jus married Frank Sinatra and was being pursued by all the major studios). An ideal choice for the beset mother of all monsters, young Mia is matched by slimy John Cassavetes as her ambitious actor husband, and a supporting cast that just doesn't quit: neighbors Ruth Gordon and Sidney Blackmer, doctor Ralph Bellamy, best friend Maurice Evans...all do letter-perfect work.

Combining East Coast dialectic comedy and a chic modern romance (Farrow's infamous boyish haircut occurs during the course of the story), Polanski fashions a terror tale set entirely (for the most part) within one building, its secret passageways and hidden rooms al providing decidedly modern spins on *The Old Dark House* motif. Satan's worshippers are a cheeky international bunch, and Levin's central premise (a mocking imitation of the Christ birth) remains a powerful, blasphemous idea. Polanski fully understands a plethora of social and philosophical implications instigated by it, yet never fails to remember that *Rosemary's Baby* is, at its core, a scarifying

Best scenes: Guy's off-camera "deal"; the rape ("This isn't a dream, this is really happeing!"); the telephone booth plea; Rosemary's final entrance. Actually, the whole brilliantly-executed movie could be described as a "best scene" experience.

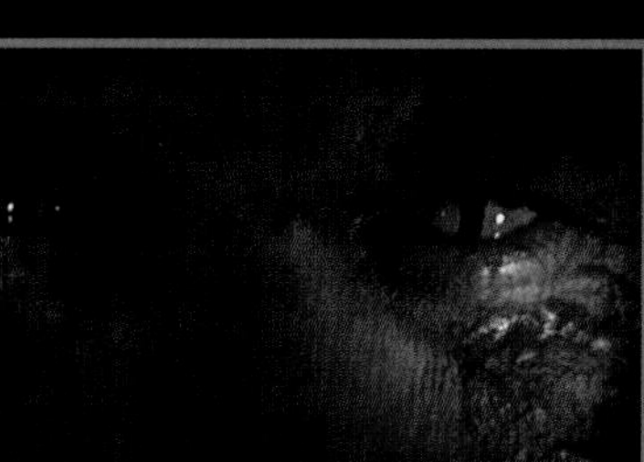

ABOVE: Hutch checks out Rosemary's new bauble, much to the dismay of a grim Roman Castevet. LEFT: Satan's catlike eyes, glimpsed briefly, are visited upon the accursed infant.

Roman Polanski (center, orange shirt) supervises the filming of a fateful dinner scene with the Castevets and Woodhouses.

unparalleled possession drama, devout as it is unflinchingly graphic...

2 THE EXORCIST 1973

 122 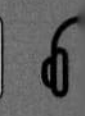 1.85

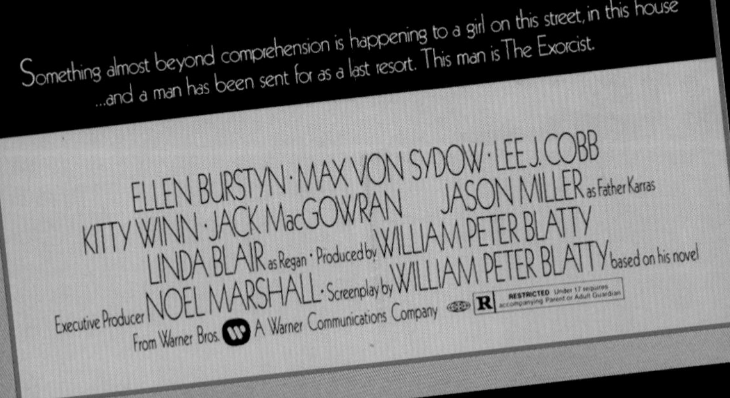

WHO MADE IT:

Warner Brothers/Hoya Productions (U.S.). Director: William Friedkin. Producers: William Peter Blatty, Noel Marshall. Writer: William Peter Blatty, based on his novel. Cinematography (Metrocolor): Owen Roizman. Music: Steve Boedeker. Starring Ellen Burstyn (Chris MacNeil), Jason Miller (Father Karras), Linda Blair (Regan MacNeil), Max Von Sydow (Father Merrin), Lee J. Cobb (Lt. Kinderman), Kitty Wynn (Sharon), Jack MacGowran (Burke Dennings), Reverend William O'Malley (Father Dyer), Barton Heyman (Dr. Klein), Titos Vandis (Karras' uncle), Mercedes McCambridge (Demon voice).

WHAT IT'S ABOUT:

In Iraq during an excavation, elderly priest Lancaster Merrin uncovers some curious artifacts with seemingly supernatural significance. Shortly after, in Georgetown, Washington, a twelve-year-old girl named Regan MacNeil begins behaving in a startling inexplicably deranged manner, confounded medical experts and pushing mother Chris MacNeil to emotional extremes. When science and medicine fail to find an answer, the distraught woman finally appeals to local priest Father Karras for an exorcism. He is a man on the verge of losing his spiritual faith, but after observing the possessed child, he agrees to help. Working with Merrin, the Vatican's most reliable exorcism expert, both holy men confront their supernatural enemy head-on, risking all to drive the vicious demon from young Regan's body. Neither priest survives the excruciating ordeal, but Karras regains his personal faith with a courageous, final act of self-sacrifice, and the stricken child returns to normal.

WHY IT'S IMPORTANT:

Just four years after *Rosemary's Baby*, William Friedkin's *The Exorcist* propelled horror cinema to new heights, pushing the envelope in ways that had the entire nation talking. In short, pea soup will never be thought of the same way again.

Unlike the chic stylish excesses of Polanski's film, *Exorcist* is set in stark reality, a gritty, gray-blue place that often looks like grainy news footage (Friedkin filmed *The French Connection* in very much the same, pseudo-documentary style). After setting this proper atmosphere, he immerses the viewer in a gradual descent into darkness, exploring both the loss/regaining of spiritual faith and the transcendent power of motherhood along the way. Like Janet Leigh in *Psycho*, we the audience are inside Ellen Burstyn's tortured head, taking this grotesque-but-very-real journey along with her through Friedkin's deceptively objective lens. We are also inside Father Karras (Jason Miller) feeling his emotional struggle and need to be "whole" again spiritually by saving a threatened child, even if that means the end of his days.

As for the possessed one, Linda Blair's distorted gnome became an instant icon, although no publicity stills of Dick Smith's brilliant make-up were released to the public. Perhaps even more disturbing than Regan's cracked-face appearance were the foul lines of dialogue she spits at every opportunity (she spits other things, too, directly in the face of stunned Father Karras). It all adds up to an ingenious tale of modern-day possession, made convincing by a perceptive screenplay, completely credible players and a "cold" or detached style of cinematography.

Best scenes: the Iraq prologue; Regan's crucifix masturbation; "Help me" on her stomach; the spider-walk (re-inserted for the Special

In recent years, director Friedkin has gone back to his original film masterpieces and committed some ill-advised tampering. Although Regan's spider-walk (removed from the original release) is indeed worth seeing, the "director's cut/special edition" of *The Exorcist* suffers from pointless extended footage and out-of-place CG effects. For the most accurate and satisfying rendering of this horror mega-classic, make sure you're looking at the 1972 original.

In Georgetown, Washington, possessed child Regan (Linda Blair) is levitated during the course of her grueling exorcism.

Two courageous, dedicated priests risk their lives combating demonic evil.

Regan's "head twist," accomplished with an articulated dummy, was a shocking bit of business back in 1973.

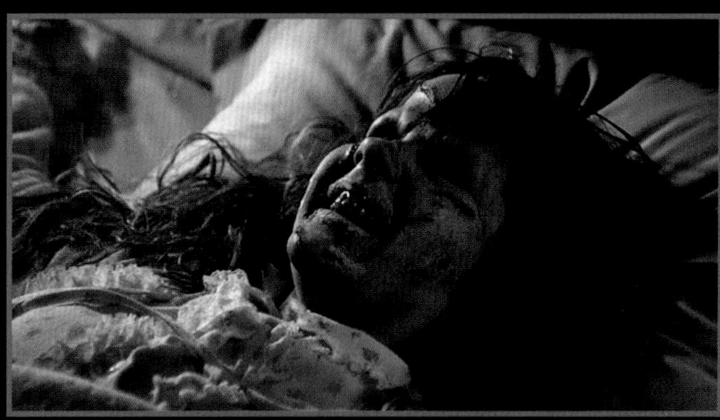

Dick Smith's remarkable possession make-up for Regan won a well-deserved Oscar.

William Friedkin gives youthful star Linda Blair some pertinent direction during the film's earlier scenes.

1

HORROR OF DRACULA 1958

aka: Dracula

WHO MADE IT:

Hammer Films/Rank (U.K.)/Universal International/Warner Bros. cur rent distributor (U.S.). Director: Terence Fisher. Producer: Anthon Hinds. Writer: Jimmy Sangster, based on the novel by Bram Stoker Cinematography (Technicolor): Jack Asher. Music: James Bernard Starring Peter Cushing (Dr. Van Helsing), Christopher Lee (Count Drac ula), Melissa Stribling (Mina Holmwood), Michael Gough (Arthu Holmwood), John Van Eyssen (Jonathan Harker), Carol Marsh (Lucy) Valerie Gaunt (Vampire Woman), Charles Lloyd Pack (Dr. Seward), Jan ina Faye (Tania), Olga Dickie (Gerda), Miles Malleson (Undertaker)

WHAT IT'S ABOUT:

Posing as a librarian, vampire-hunter Jonathan Harker ventures tc the remote castle of Count Dracula to destroy the fountainhead o this vile affliction. Although Harker is himself attacked anc transformed into one of the blood-drinkers, his partner, Dr. Var Helsing, releases him from everlasting torment and retrieves his invaluable diary. Seeking revenge, Dracula leaves his castle to prey on Harker's young fiancée, Mina Holmwood, until she, too, is exorcized by the doctor's driven stake. With the help of Mina's brother Arthur Holmwood, a determined Van Helsing takes steps to protect his ally's endangered wife, ultimately pursuing the vampire king back to his castle for a showdown. There, the twc combatants engage in a spectacular struggle. Fighting for his life, Van Helsing seizes two candlesticks and crosses them together to form a makeshift crucifix, trapping his quarry even as daylight's first rays reduce a writhing Count Dracula to ashes Only the vampire's distinctive ring remains.

WHY IT'S IMPORTANT:

Why is this the best? Easy answer: Vampires are the greates fantasy characters in horror cinema; Count Dracula is the greatest vampire; *Horror of Dracula* is generally regarded as the most satisfying adaptation of Bram Stoker's novel. Ergc Number One.

The somewhat deeper explanation… Although other chillers may be more stylish and artful, *Horror of Dracula* remains the most "perfect" horror movie ever made, not a single one o its Technicolored frames wasted. The legitimate father of al modern fright films, it instantly influenced everything from Hitchcock's *Psycho* ("protagonist" John Van Eysen dies shockingly at the end of the third act, two years before Janet Leigh does the same thing with far fewer clothes on) to *The Exorcist* (there's foreshadowing of Billy Friedkin-style violence in *Horror*'s acclaimed library scene). Christopher Lee's "dark Romeo" Dracula is a fascinating post WWII creation, part fallen aristocrat from another age, part self-loathing drug addict, a man of few words and limitless back-story possibilities. Indeed, Shakespeare couldn't have created a more tragically interesting anti-hero. Matching him shot-for-shot is the equally iconic (and top billed) Peter Cushing, modernizing Dr. Var Helsing into the screen's first cerebral action figure.

Amazingly, *Horror*'s opening titles alone tell you everything you need to know about the main character, moving from an up-angle view of the once-proud falcon, down to a shameful and foul personal crypt, stained with blood. Like all brilliant works of cinema, the more

ABOVE: Count Dracula's dramatic entrance. BELOW: Van Helsing (Cushing) helps Holmwood (Michael Gough) face the reality of vampirism.

Director Terence Fisher encouraged Lee and Cushing to leap atop tables a la Flynn and Rathbone for some unforgettably dynamic set-pieces, including the grisly climax.

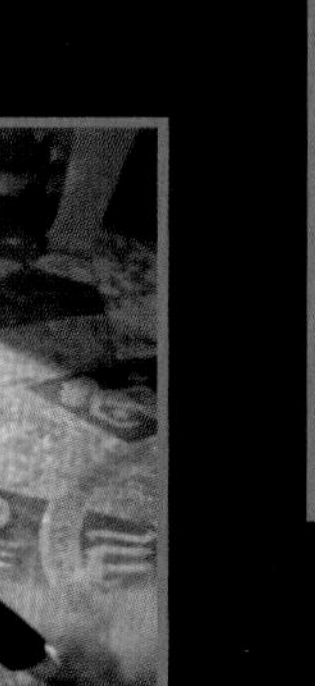

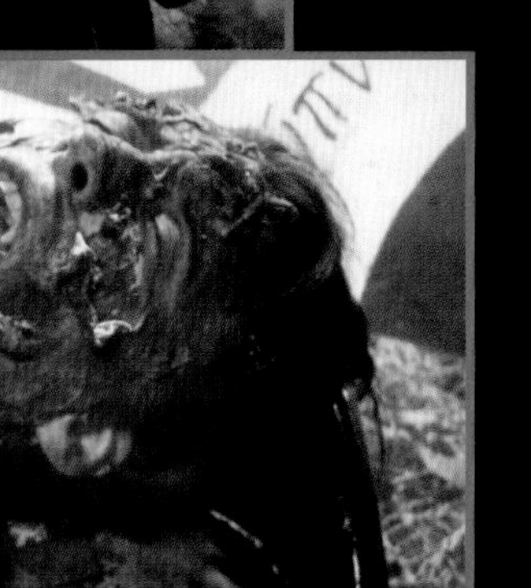

Sadly, Lee's remarkable Dracula characterization would degenerate into a one-dimensional bore in later Hammer "sequels."

ABOVE: Mina Holmwood (Melissa Stribling) in the vampire's embrace. Loaded with nuance and subtext, Fisher's self-assured horror classic impresses from fade-in to finish.

Carol Marsh (Lucy) enjoys a tea break while on set. Notice the crucifix imprint (and how she got it!).

THE LIBRARY SCENE

Shocking, dynamic horror filmmaking at its finest, second only to *Psycho*'s shower sequence

Horror of Dracula's first high-intensity set-piece, the library scene stunned unsuspecting audiences back in 1958, exploding with stark, savage energy unlike anything previously offered in a mainstream horror film. Director Terence Fisher begins the sequence portentously in Jonathan Harker's bedroom, as the librarian/undercover slayer senses someone stirring in the hallway. Investigating, he makes his way downstairs and enters Dracula's library, where the same desperate young woman who approached him earlier appears from behind the door. Once again she implores him for help and this time Harker relents, kindly promising her protection. But the distressed female turns out to be a vampire herself, and her predatory advances toward Jonathan quickly find their mark in a *shocking close-up bite* that generally elicits gasps from the viewing audience.

Next, a full view of the library (ABOVE, EXTREME LEFT) has an agonized Harker recoiling from this unexpected assault, his repelled attacker pushed to the left of the frame. But before we, the startled audience, can get our bearings, the Vampire Woman is distracted by an enraged figure now standing in the distant doorway – Count Dracula, viewed in long shot.

It is with Fisher's cut to a devastating close-up of Dracula (ABOVE, MIDDLE) that this scene erupts into a harrowing, shot-by-shot visceral showcase. No longer the bored aristocrat with tomes to be indexed, Dracula is dramatically revealed as a full-fledged monster, bloody fangs bared like some hate-crazed demon from Hell. More gasps and screams from the movie audience greet this striking, iconic close-up.

But director Fisher doesn't allow viewers to catch their breath. Within seconds, Dracula launches himself upon the table before him, leaps to the other side, grabs his vicious quarry and violently throws her to the floor (ABOVE, EXTREME RIGHT). It all happens in a single camera set-up, with Lee impressively managing his own ambitious stuntwork.

As the shocked and bleeding Harker looks on, the two furious vampires go at each other, centuries-old Dracula swiftly overpowering his current "bride." Jonathan's efforts to stop the violence result in his own one-sided struggle with the Count. Throttled and hurled to the floor, Harker manages to look up long enough to see his adversary carrying the Vampire Woman away in his arms as if she were a lifeless doll. Pausing for a moment in the library doorway, Dracula stares back at his downed houseguest (in long shot, Harker's point-of-view), before abruptly exiting the room. Wounded, physically and emotionally spent by the ordeal, Jonathan collapses into unconsciousness. Fade Out.

The colorful library set has been used in various Hammer horror films.

Superb in its planning and execution, this pivotal *Horror of Dracula* sequence continues to impress cinema scholars half a century after it was made. The "wham!" of Dracula's sudden appearance, the perfectly-composed shots, the sheer audacity of Lee's acrobatic performance...it's nothing less than lightening in a bottle, providing England's Hammer Films with its most enduring creative moment. For fans of the genre, it signaled a whole new era of less suggestive, more adult and graphically violent horror movies.

THE TWO FACES OF DRACULA

Proud and aristocratic, Count Dracula as portrayed by Christopher Lee is a decent man cursed by a vile obsession, "similar to addiction to drugs." The striking contrast between these demeanors fuels *Horror of Dracula*, which forsakes traditional clichés of the vampire genre for a less fanciful, more realistic interpretation of Bram Stoker's immortal character.

AFTERVIEW

Summing up the rest of the best...

BUBBLING UNDER THE TOP 100: *Dawn of the Dead* (George Romero, 1978), *Phantasm* (Don Coscarelli, 1977), *Don't Look Now* (Nicolas Roeg, 1973), *Shadow of the Vampire* (E. Elias Merhige, 2000), *Whatever Happened to Baby Jane?* (Robert Aldrich, 1962), *Evil Dead 2* (Sam Raimi, 1987), *The Leopard Man* (Jacques Tourneur, 1943), *Hostel* (Eli Roth, 2005), *Tales of Terror* (Roger Corman, 1963), *Son of Frankenstein* (Rowland V. Lee, 1939), *The Ring* (Gore Verbinski, 2002), *Blood and Black Lace* (Mario Bava, 1964), *Hangover Square* (John Brahm, 1945), *Onibaba* (Kaneto Shindo, 1964), *The Legend of Hell House* (John Hough, 1973), *The Tingler* (William Castle, 1959), *Viy* (Konstantin Yershocv and Georgi Kropachyov, 1967), *The Orphanage* (Juan Antonio Bayona, 2007), *Son of Dracula* (Robert Siodmak, 1943), *Nosferatu the Vampyre* (Werner Herzog, 1979), *Near Dark* (Kathryn Bigelow, 1987), *Ju-On: The Grudge* (Takashi Shimizu, 2003), *Incubus* (Leslie Stevens, 1964), *Friday the 13th* (Sean S. Cunningham, 1980), *The House That Dripped Blood* (Peter Duffell, 1970).

THE TOP TEN HORROR COMEDIES: *Abbott and Costello Meet Frankenstein* (Charles Barton, 1948), *Young Frankenstein* (Mel Brooks, 1976), *The Fearless Vampire Killers* (Roman Polanski, 1970), *Bubba Ho-Tep* (Don Coscarelli, 2002), *Phantom of the Paradise* (Brian De Palma, 1974), *Ghostbusters* (Ivan Reitman, 1984), *Shaun of the Dead* (Edgar Wright, 2004), *Return of the Living Dead* (Dan O'Bannon, 1985), *Beetlejuice* (Tim Burton, 1988) , *Theater of Blood* (Douglas Hickox, 1973).

UNJUSTLY OVERLOOKED SILENT CLASSICS: *The Student of Prague* (Stellan Rye, 1913), *Homunculus* (Otto Rippert, 1916), *The Avenging Conscience* (D.W. Griffith, 1914), *Seven Footprints to Satan* (Benjamin Christianson, 1929), *London After Midnight* (Tod Browning, 1927), *A Blind Bargain* (Wallace Worsley, 1922), *The Conquering Power* (Rex Ingram, 1922), *The Last Warning* (Paul Leni, 1929), *The Hunchback of Notre Dame* (Wallace Worsley, 1923), *Haxan* (Benjamin Christianson, 1920), *Faust* (F.W. Murnau, 1926), *The Cat and the Canary* (Paul Leni, 1927).

THE TOP FIVE HORROR SHORT SUBJECTS: *Frankenstein* (Edison, 1910), *Un Chien Andalou* (Luis Bunuel, 1929), *The Tell Tale Heart* (Jules Dassin for MGM, 1941), *An Occurence at Owl Creek Bridge* (Robert Enrico, 1963), *Michael Jackson's Thriller* (John Landis, 1985).

MOST STARTLING MOMENT IN A HORROR MOVIE: Sissy Spacek's hand thrusting up from her grave to grab Amy Irving in the final dream sequence from *Carrie* (see page 83). Runner-up: that head with the missing eyeball emerging from under the ship to freak out Richard Dreyfuss in *Jaws* (see page 157).

LEFT: devilish *Haxen*. BELOW: *The Tell-Tale Heart.*

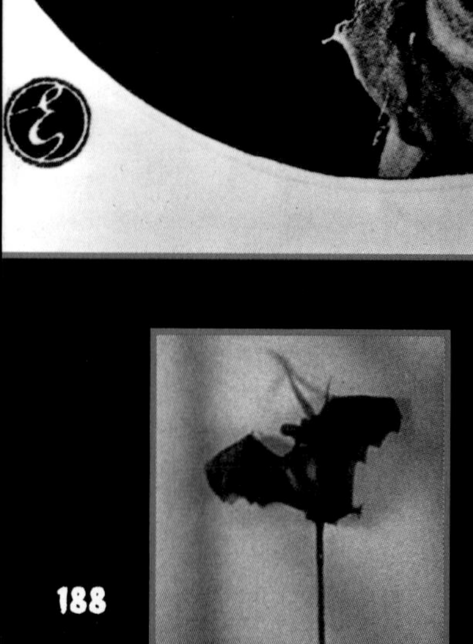

MOST HORRIFIC SEQUENCE IN A NON-HORROR MOVIE: Ray Milland's "bat attack" D.T. hallucination from *The Lost Weekend*. Runner-up: the elaborate Hell sequences from *Dante's Inferno* (1935).

LON CHANEY SR. The celebrated "Man of a Thousand Faces" is unique in horror movie history. Not only is he the first American A-list actor known primarily for macabre roles, but he also conceived, designed and applied his own groundbreaking make-ups. Some of Lon Chaney's best-known horror characters from the mid-to-late '20s include the corpse-like *Phantom of the Opera*, the misshapen *Hunchback of Notre Dame*, and the top-hated, shark-toothed grinning vampire from *London After Midnight*. He was slated to play *Dracula* in 1931, but he passed on before production began.

BORIS KARLOFF. *Famous Monsters* editor Forry Ackerman once crowned Boris Karloff (aka William Henry Pratt) "the King," and the great British gentleman's appeal as an iconic horror star certainly hasn't diminished over the years. His inherent sense of menace is matched by a remarkable, inspiring face (especially to creative make-up artists), resulting in such iconic monster personas as Frankenstein's Monster, the Ghoul and the Mummy. But Karloff was an unforgettable presence in horror films even without elaborate make-up or costuming, captivating audiences with his unique, always compelling blend of villainy and pathos

BELA LUGOSI. Melodramatic and "out there" even by 1931 standards, Hungarian-born Bela Lugosi is without a doubt the most idiosyncratic of horror film actors...foreign, smoothly Satanic, evil in a bizarre way that seemed to defy traditional categorization. Perhaps for that reason, Lugosi instantly embodied what audiences came to accept as a prototypical screen vampire, from dapper appearance to thick, vaguely menacing accent. Though instantly typed, the resourceful performer proved he could play "normal" in Edgar Ulmer's *The Black Cat,* and was brilliantly juicy in an anti-suave role as hunchbacked Igor in *Son* and *Ghost of Frankenstein.*

CHRISTOPHER LEE. Tall, self-assured and austere, Christopher Lee provides a commanding presence in horror films that suits him well as a villain (the various Dracula films) and occasionally as a darker-than-usual hero (*The Devil's Bride*). Along with fellow Brit Peter Cushing, Lee helped put Hammer Films on the pop cultural map back in the late '50s, revitalizing gothic horror movies with realism and often bloody violence. Also like Cushing, Lee's work in fantasy thrillers eventually led to significant roles in later, far more ambitious productions (*Star Wars*, *Sleepy Hollow*, *Lord of the Rings*) helmed by childhood fans-turned-major league filmmakers.

VINCENT PRICE. The only star to successfully navigate both key periods of Hollywood horror (late '30s/early '40s, and the '60s/'70s), Vincent Price is a curious combination of smooth-but-hulking villainy and sinister, fey menace. Generally over-the-top but also distinctive and theatrical in the best sense of the term, he brings dignity to the genre, bridging the stylistic gap between classical and modern movies. In later years, Price found a constant admirer in director Tim Burton, who cast him in several of his scary-themed fantasy films (including VP's final screen effort, *Edward Scissorhands*).

PETER CUSHING. Probably the most trustworthy and comforting voice in horror cinema, Peter Cushing is ironically best remembered for his turn as the nefarious Baron Frankenstein in Hammer's seminal horror flicks of the '50s, '60s and '70s. An accomplished actor with enormous personal empathy, Cushing made a splash, along with colleague Christopher Lee, when Hammer re-invented spooky cinema post-WWII, appearing almost non-stop in screen fantasies ever since. One of his most memorable twilight roles was the heartless bureaucrat Grand Moff Tarkin in 1977's *Star Wars*.

PETER LORRE. Peter Lorre's bug-eyed, generally unsavory screen persona was dramatically introduced in the classic German morality play *M*. He soon brought this peculiar brand of movie villainy to pre-war Hollywood, establishing himself as both an A-list character actor in major productions (*The Maltese Falcon*, *Casablanca*), and a dependable star in lower-budget horror films (*Mad Love*, *Face Behind the Mask*, *The Beast with Five Fingers*). In the '60s, diminutive Lorre often teamed with super-tall Vincent Price in Roger Corman's Poe adaptations, adding broad but affectionate humor to the series formula.

JOHN CARRADINE. Another successful Hollywood character actor who became a horror movie specialist, the highly-theatrical Carradine shuttled between prestigious, A-level projects (*The Grapes of Wrath*, *The Ten Commandments*) and decidedly lesser films for studios like Monogram and PRC. "I made a lot of great movies in my time," the actor once said, "and a lot of crap." At Universal in the '40s, Carradine replaced Lugosi as the studio's resident Count Dracula, and also impressed genre fans with his 1944 turn as Bluebeard, for Edgar Ulmer. He continued to work well into his old age, eventually passing the family's acting torch to scions Keith, Robert and David.

BARBARA STEELE. The first authentic femme fatale of horror movies, dark, sensuous Barbara Steele haunted many a fanboy's dreams back in the early '60s after her unforgettable turn as Asa the vampire-witch in Mario Bava's *Black Sunday*. Pulling off the not-so-easy trick of appearing lovely and arousing in one shot, utterly disgusting in the next (here's an actress who had no aversion to grotesque horror make-ups that had scorpions and maggots crawling out of her eye sockets!), Steele continued to inspire fans with a plethora of European-produced horror flicks, most of them cheaply made and more than a little sadistic.

LON CHANEY, JR. Would Lon Chaney Jr. have become a horror star if his dad hadn't been Hollywood's Man of a Thousand Faces? Doubtful. But Chaney Jr. did indeed achieve pop cultural immortality as Universal's *The Wolf Man* in 1941, and enjoyed the interesting distinction of playing all of the studio's legendary bogeyman right after that – Dracula, Frankenstein's Monster and The Mummy. Chaney Jr. continued to work until his death in the mid-'60s, alternating between less important horror pictures and significant character roles in prestigious Stanley Kramer movies (*High Noon*, *The Defiant Ones*), recalling his promising 1940 debut as Lennie in *Of Mice and Men*.

THE TOP TEN HORROR MOVIE DIRECTORS (sans Hitchcock and Polanski)

1. JAMES WHALE. Frankenstein, The Old Dark House
2. TERENCE FISHER. Horror of Dracula, The Devil's Bride
3. ROGER CORMAN. House of Usher, Pit and the Pendulum
4. WES CRAVEN. Last House on the Left, Scream
6. GEORGE ROMERO. Night of the Living Dead
7. JACQUES TOURNEUR. Cat People, Curse of the Demon
8. JOHN CARPENTER. Halloween, The Thing
9. DARIO ARGENTO. Deep Red, Suspiria

INDEX

MYSTERY SOLVED: The werewolf on page 5 is none other than Universal's Wolf Man. That's Lon Chaney Jr. himself wearing a re-imagined, never-filmed make-up conceived in the early '40s by original creator Jack Pierce (seen here transforming Chaney Jr. into a more traditional-looking version of the character). The studio had planned a Technicolor epic called *The Wolf Man vs. Dracula* in 1943, with Chaney playing both roles, but this ambitious project was nixed in favor of Claude Rains' *Phantom of the Opera*. When lycanthrope Larry Talbot finally met up with Abbott and Costello in 1948, new studio make-up supervisor Bud Westmore was calling the shots…and Hollywood's favorite werewolf was back on model.

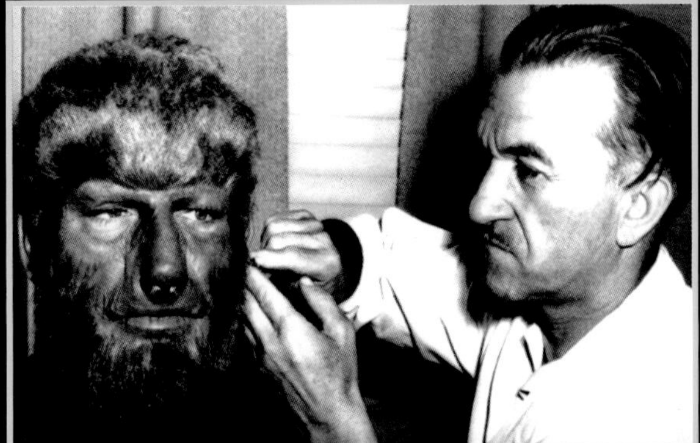